Karen Brown's
ITALY
Charming Bed & Breakfasts

Written by
NICOLE FRANCHINI

Illustrations by Elisabetta Franchini
Cover Painting by Jann Pollard

Karen Brown's Country Inn Series

Karen Brown Titles

Austria: Charming Inns & Itineraries
California: Charming Inns & Itineraries
England: Charming Bed & Breakfasts
England, Wales & Scotland: Charming Hotels & Itineraries
France: Charming Bed & Breakfasts
France: Charming Inns & Itineraries
Germany: Charming Inns & Itineraries
Ireland: Charming Inns & Itineraries
Italy: Charming Bed & Breakfasts
Italy: Charming Inns & Itineraries
Portugal: Charming Inns & Itineraries
Spain: Charming Inns & Itineraries
Switzerland: Charming Inns & Itineraries

To

Luisa, Alan, and Baby Finnbar

With Much Happiness

The painting on the front cover is a scene in the Chianti region of Tuscany

Editors: Nicole Franchini, Karen Brown, June Brown, Clare Brown, Iris Sandilands.

Illustrations: Elisabetta Franchini; Cover painting: Jann Pollard.

Maps: Susanne Lau Alloway—Greenleaf Design & Graphics. Cover photo: Jann Pollard..

Copyright © 1985, 1986, 1988, 1992, 1993, 1995, 1996, 1997, 1998 by Karen Brown's Guides.

This book or parts thereof may not be reproduced in any form without obtaining written permission from the publisher: Karen Brown's Guides, P.O. Box 70, San Mateo, CA 94401, USA, email: karen@karenbrown.com.

Distributed by Fodor's Travel Publications, Inc., 201 East 50th Street, New York, NY 10022, USA.

Distributed in the United Kingdom by Random House UK, 20 Vauxhall Bridge Road, London, SW1V 2SA, phone: 44 171 973 9000, fax: 44 171 840 8408.

Distributed in Australia by Random House Australia, 20 Alfred Street, Milsons Point, Sydney NSW 2061, Australia, phone: 61 2 9954 9966, fax: 61 2 9954 4562.

Distributed in New Zealand by Random House New Zealand, 18 Poland Road, Glenfield, Auckland, New Zealand, phone: 64 9 444 7197, fax: 64 9 444 7524.

Distributed in South Africa by Random House South Africa, Endulani, East Wing, 5A Jubilee Road, Parktown 2193, South Africa, phone: 27 11 484 3538, fax: 27 11 484 6180.

A catalog record for this book is available from the British Library.

Library of Congress Cataloging-in-Publication Data

Franchini, Nicole, 1959–
    Karen Brown's Italy : charming bed & breakfasts / written by
  Nicole Franchini ; illustrations by Elisabetta Franchini ; cover
  painting by Jann Pollard -- [Totally rev. 5th ed.]
      p.   cm. -- (Karen Brown's country inn series)
    Includes index.
    ISBN 0-930328-69-8 (pbk.)
    1. Bed and breakfast accommodations--Italy--Guidebooks. 2. Italy-
  -Guidebooks. I. Brown, Karen, 1956–   . II. Title. III. Series.
  TX907.5.I8F73   1997
  647.9445'03--dc21   97-9466
                                                            CIP

Contents

ITALIAN FARMER'S POEM

Our memories are crouched
in silence within the belly of the earth.
Yet it takes only a day of sunshine,
an impromptu storm in the sky,
the perfume of freshly cut hay,
and immense fields dotted with golden haystacks,
to ignite in us the memories
of certain evenings spent full of gaiety.

It was at sunset when we used to join together
in the barn filled with grain
to celebrate the end of the harvest.
The "gioanassa" musician friend,
pressing the keys of his worn-out accordion,
succeeding in emitting the notes
to a waltz or mazurka, leaving us
drunk with happiness.

One more glass of wine before the night
fades into day.
One more toast to bid farewell
to another summer
that crossed the path of our youth.

Anonymous

Introduction

BED AND BREAKFAST ITALIAN-STYLE—*agriturismo*, as the bed and breakfast activity is called in Italy, has made great strides over the past decade. The bed and breakfast concept is relatively new to Italy, which followed suit after France and England originated the trend. Accommodations vary from simple farmhouses to noble country villas, all promising unique and memorable stays. "*Agritourism*" travel offers visitors to Italy the unique opportunity to observe daily life "up close" as a guest in someone's home. It is a superb way to interact directly with Italians, experiencing their way of life as a participant rather than just an observer. It offers a more intimate contact with the country's traditional ways of life than can ever be experienced during hotel stays. It is the alternative vacation for curious visitors who wish to explore the back roads of this fascinating country and depart with a more in-depth understanding of Italians and their lifestyles than they could possibly get from city stays and sightseeing alone. The individual who will benefit most from agritourism will have an open, inquiring mind and a certain amount of flexibility. In return, agritourism rewards the traveler with a feeling of being "at home" while abroad. The warm welcome and the value you'll receive will tempt you back to the agritourism track year after year.

HISTORY: *Agriturismo*, defined as agricultural tourism, was launched in 1965 as part of the Italian government's national agricultural department's plan to make it possible for farmers to supplement their declining income in two ways: through offering accommodation to tourists and through direct sales of their produce.

After World War II, during reconstruction and the subsequent industrial boom, Italians abandoned the countryside in droves in search of employment in urban centers, reducing the rural population from eight to three million people. Consequently, farmhouses, villas, and castles all across the country were neglected and went to ruin. This phenomenon also disrupted the centuries-old tradition of passing customs and property from one generation to the next.

The agritourism concept, with its government funding, proclaimed tax breaks, and an increasing need to escape congested cities, has lured proprietors back to their land and ancestral homes, providing them with the incentive to restore and preserve these historical buildings (with many treasures among them), without spoiling the natural landscape. An additional consequence is an improved distribution of tourism between Italy's overcrowded cities and the countryside which serves to raise awareness of the many marvelous historical and cultural attractions, from art and architecture to scenery and cuisine, that await tourists off the beaten track.

Each of Italy's 20 regions participates in agritourism, with a full 60% of participants concentrated in Tuscany and Trentino-Alto Adige. This fifth edition of *Italy: Charming Bed & Breakfasts* includes selections from 14 of Italy's regions. Unfortunately, this type of accommodation is still very scarce in Italy's southernmost regions such as Calabria,

Basilicata, and Campania. We are happy to offer a selection of nine bed and breakfasts in Sicily, where a law permitting agritourism activity was passed just a few years ago.

In practical terms, agritourism was developed to stimulate the local economy in rural areas by encouraging the creation of accommodation (rooms, apartments, and campgrounds) in places where they had never before been available. In a more long-term and idealistic sense, it was hoped that the promotion and development of tourism in rural Italy would also bring about greater environmental awareness and rescue traditional folklore and customs, such as regional cuisine and handicrafts, from oblivion.

For Italians, agritourism facilitates an exchange of views between farmers and urbanites who come in search of a peaceful vacation surrounded by natural beauty. In fact, agritourism and the rich culture of the farmer represent for many an affirmation and validation of their heritage. Lamentably, some Italians still have a misconception of agritourism because it was originally organized as an exchange of very basic room and board for work in the fields. A wave of positive press in the past five years and higher quality standards have helped enormously to change this outdated image.

Controversy also surrounds the fact that there are few established regulations governing this type of activity, and they differ greatly from one region to another. Consequently, no clearly defined quality standards exist and those participants with limited economic resources resent wealthier proprietors, whom they accuse of running accommodations resembling hotels more than farm stays. Moreover, it does not simplify matters that agritourism is organized in typical Italian fashion, with responsibility divided among three associations, each with its own regulations, politics, and guidelines. Each association produces a directory (in Italian) and may be contacted by writing to:

AGRITURIST, Corso Vittorio Emanuele 101, Rome 00168, Italy
TERRANOSTRA, Via 14 Maggio 43, Rome 00187, Italy
TURISMO VERDE, Via E. Franceschini 89, Rome 00155, Italy

About Bed & Breakfasts

Our goal in this guide is to recommend outstanding places to stay. All of the bed and breakfasts featured have been visited and selected solely on their merits. Our judgments are made on charm, setting, cleanliness, and, above all, warmth of welcome. However (no matter how careful we are), sometimes we misjudge an establishment's merits, or the ownership changes, or unfortunately sometimes standards are not maintained. If you find a recommended place is not as we have indicated, please let us know, and accept our sincere apologies. The rates given are those quoted to us by the bed and breakfast: please use these figures as a guideline only and be certain to ask at the time of booking what the rates are and what they include.

ACCOMMODATION

The most important thing to remember as you consider an agritourism vacation is that you will be staying in the private homes of families that are obligated to run their bed and breakfasts without hiring additional personnel aside from family and farmhands. Do not forget that, in most cases, the primary responsibility of your hosts is the running of their farm, so, with a few exceptions, do not expect the service of a hotel. Rooms may not necessarily always be cleaned daily (sometimes beds are changed only every three days). Nevertheless, do anticipate a comfortable and enjoyable stay, because the proprietors will do everything possible to assure it. Cost will vary according to the level of service offered. (For the traveler's convenience, some city hotels have been included that are similar to a bed and breakfast in style, but go by the name *Albergo*, *Pensione*, or Hotel.)

ROOMS: Agritourism accommodation should not be thought of strictly in terms of the British definition of bed and breakfasts, as in Italy they vary greatly according to each proprietor's interpretation of the concept. The bed and breakfasts in this guide have been described in terms of the criteria used in their selection—warmth of hospitality, historic character, charm of the home, scenery, proximity to sites of touristic interest, and quality of cuisine. Obviously, all of these attributes are not always found in each one. Most of them have an average of six rooms situated either within the family's home or in a separate guesthouse. We have tried to include only those with en-suite bathrooms, as our readers have requested (although for the budget traveler this may not be a priority). Having another bed or two added to a room at an extra charge for families with small children is usually not a problem. According to newly established laws of the European Community four years ago, all new or renovated establishments must now offer facilities for the handicapped. It is best to enquire about the individual bed and breakfast's facilities when making reservations.

APARTMENTS: Since more and more travelers are learning that it is much more advantageous to stay for longer periods in one place (distances are so short between towns within a specific region), apartment-type accommodations with fully-equipped kitchenettes are flourishing. And, in fact, jumping around from one place to another for one or two nights defeats the purpose of a more intimate contact with host families. Apartment accommodation is offered either within the farmhouse along with other units for two to six persons, or as a full house rental for six to ten persons. They are rented by the week from Saturday to Saturday throughout the country, the exception being during the low season. No meals are included unless the bed and breakfast also has a restaurant or makes special arrangements for breakfast. Rates include use of all facilities, unless otherwise indicated, linens, and utilities. There is usually an extra charge for heating and once-a-week cleaning. Average apartments for four persons run $500 weekly, a rate hotels cannot beat.

FOOD

A highlight of the agritourism experience is without a doubt the food. Most travelers would agree that a bad meal is hard to find in Italy, a country world famous for its culinary skills. In the countryside you'll be sampling the traditional recipes from which Italian cuisine originates. Since, whenever possible, all of the ingredients come directly from the farms where you'll be staying, you'll discover the flavorful difference freshness can make. A peek into the farm kitchen is likely to reveal pasta being rolled and cut the old-fashioned way—by hand. Many country cooks prefer to prepare food using traditional methods, and not rely on machines to speed up the process. Guests are usually welcomed into the kitchen for a look around and actual cooking lessons are becoming very popular.

MEALS OFFERED: Bed and breakfasts often serve a Continental breakfast only, of coffee, tea, fresh breads, and jams. However, many prepare other meals and offer (sometimes require) half- or full-board plans. Half board means that breakfast and dinner are both included in the daily per-person room rate. Full board includes the room and all three meals and is less common, since most guests are out and about during the day, or prefer one lighter meal. Dinner is a hearty three-course meal, often shared at a common table with the host family, and most times includes wine and other beverages. Menus might be set daily, according to the availability of fresh produce, or a limited choice may be given. Some farms have a full-fledged restaurant serving non-guests as well. Travelers who are not necessarily guests at a particular bed and breakfast may take advantage of this opportunity to sample other fare. It is advisable to reserve in advance.

ENGLISH

English spoken at each bed and breakfast has been indicated as follows: fluent, very well, well, some, little, or none. We would like to note, however, that this is just an indication, as the person who speaks English may or may not be there during your stay. In any case, it is helpful (not to mention rewarding) to have a few basic Italian phrases on hand. A phrase book or dictionary is indispensable. And when all else fails, the art of communicating with gestures is still very much alive in Italy!

LENGTH OF STAY

Agritourism is most advantageous for those who have more than the standard one week to travel. Bed-and-breakfast accommodations take longer to reach, for one thing, and **often they are neither set up nor staffed for one-night stays** which increase costs and defeat the purpose. There are numerous exceptions, however, especially in bed and breakfasts near cities, where overnight guests are accepted. It is noted in the description where a minimum stay is required.

WHEN TO VISIT

Since agritourism accommodation is usually in permanent residences, many remain open all year, but most are open only from Easter through November. If you are traveling outside this time, however, it is worth a phone call to find out if the bed and breakfast will accommodate you anyway (at very affordable rates). The best time for agritourism is without a doubt during the spring and fall months, when nature is in its glory. You can enjoy the flowers blossoming in May, the *vendemia*, or grape harvest, at the end of September, the fall foliage in late October, or olive-oil production and truffle hunts in November and December. Southern Italy can be mild and pleasant in the winter, which might be perfect for travelers who like to feel they are the only tourists around. The vast majority of Italians vacation at the same time, during the month of August, Easter weekend, and Christmas, so these time periods are best avoided, if possible.

WHAT TO SEE AND DO

Bed and breakfast proprietors take pride in their farms and great pleasure in answering questions about their agricultural activity. They will often take time to explain and demonstrate procedures such as wine making, olive pressing or cheese production. They are the best source for, and are happy to suggest, restaurants and local itineraries including historic sites, picturesque villages, and cultural activities. Your hosts feel responsible for entertaining their guests and many have added swimming pools or tennis courts if they are not already available in the vicinity. Other activities such as archery, fishing, hiking, and biking are sometimes offered. Horseback riding has made an enormous comeback and farms frequently have their own stables and organize lessons and/or excursions into the countryside. In most circumstances, a charge is made for these extra activities.

PLANNING YOUR TRIP

Italian Government Travel Offices (ENIT) can offer general information on various regions and their cultural attractions. They cannot offer specific information on restaurants and accommodations. Offices are located in:

Chicago: Italian Government Travel Office, 401 N. Michigan Ave., Suite 3030, Chicago, IL 60611 USA; tel: (312) 644-0996, fax: (312) 644-3019. (Open 9 am to 1 pm. Mail, fax, or phone only.)

Los Angeles: Italian Government Travel Office, 12400 Wilshire Blvd., Suite 550, Los Angeles, CA 90025, USA; tel: (310) 820-0098, fax: (310) 820-6357.

New York: Italian Government Travel Office, 630 5th Ave., Suite 1565, New York, NY 10111, USA; tel: (212) 245-4822, fax: (212) 586-9249.

Montreal: Italian Government Travel Office, 1 Place Ville Marie, Suite 1914, Montreal, Quebec H3B 3M9, Canada; tel: (514) 866-7667, fax: (514) 392-1429.

London: Italian State Tourist Office, 1 Princes Street, London WIR 8AY, England; tel: (0171) 408-1254, fax: (0171) 493-6695.

Sydney and Auckland: These areas are covered by the Tokyo office—Italian Government Travel Office, Itaria Seifu Kanko Kyoku (ENIT) Lion's Building -1-1-2, Moto Akasaka Minato-Ku, Tokyo 107 Japan; tel: (3) 3478-2051 or 2052, fax: (3) 3479-9356.

RATES

Room rates vary according to size, location, season, and level of service. Rates range from $50 to $200 for a double room with breakfast (indicated as B&B in the following descriptions) and from $35 to $100 per person for room with half board (dinner also included). The majority of the bed and breakfasts selected for this guide have private bathrooms. **Approximate prices for 1998 are indicated in lire and are by no means fixed**. Rates include tax and breakfast unless otherwise indicated, and are **confirmed at time of reservation**. Because of its cost advantages, agritourism is an ideal choice for a family vacation. Children under eight are offered a discount and hosts will almost always add an extra bed for a small charge. There are some wonderful benefits to traveling in the low season (November to March with the exception of holidays) in Italy. The considerable reduction in bed-and-breakfast rates combined with irresistibly low air fares makes it a super-economical vacation. And then, there's the ultimate advantage of not having to fight for space with crowds of other tourists. Italy is all yours!

CREDIT CARDS

Credit cards are rarely accepted, cash being the preferred method of payment. When "plastic payment" is taken, the type of card accepted will be indicated as follows: AX: American Express; MC: Master card; VS: Visa; or all major.

Introduction–About Bed & Breakfasts

RESERVATIONS

Whether you plan to stay in several bed and breakfasts or decide to remain for an extended period in just one, **advance reservations are preferred.** Not only do many of the bed and breakfasts have only a few bedrooms available, but also they are usually in private homes which are not prepared to take walk-in traffic. There are several ways to make a reservation:

Fax: Many places to stay (especially in or near cities) have fax numbers. Faxing is a quick way to make a reservation (remember to include your fax number for their response). We provide you with a reservation request letter in Italian with an English translation on the following page. Be sure to spell out the month since Europeans reverse the American numbering system with dates—e.g., 6/9 means September 6 to them, not June 9.

Letter: You can write to the bed and breakfast (allow up to six weeks for an answer because mail to and from Italy is very slow). Make photocopies of the sample reservation-request letter. (Again, be sure to spell out the month.) Frequently a deposit is requested in order to confirm the reservation.

Reservation Service: If you want to pay for the convenience of having the reservations made for you, pre-payments made, vouchers issued, and cars rented, any of the bed and breakfasts in this guide can be booked through **Hidden Treasures of Italy,** a booking service run by the author of this guide, Nicole Franchini. Further information on services and charges and the request form are on pages 243–244.

Telephone: You can call the bed and breakfast directly. This is very efficient since you will get an immediate response. (The level of English spoken is given in each bed and breakfast description.) To telephone Italy from the United States, dial 011 (the international code), then 39 (Italy's code), then the city code (dropping the 0 outside Italy), and the telephone number. Italy is six hours ahead of New York.

Travel Agent: Travel agents will charge for their services since it is time consuming to make reservations and most places to stay are too small to pay any commission.

BED & BEAKFAST or HOTEL NAME & ADDRESS—clearly printed or typed

Vi prego di voler confermare la seguente prenotazione al più presto:
Please confirm the following reservation at your earliest convenience:

Numero delle camere o appartamenti _____ con bagno o doccia privata a _____ posti letti
Number of rooms or apartments with private bath or shower for how many persons

Numero di adulti _____   Numero di bambini _____ Età _____
Number of adults   *Number of children and ages*

Numero delle camere o appartamenti _____ senza bagno o doccia privata _____ posti letti
Number of rooms or apartments without private bath or shower for how many persons

Numero di adulti _____   Numero di bambini _____ Età _____
Number of adults   *Number of children and ages*

Data di arrivo _____   Data di partenza _____
Date of arrival   *Date of departure*

Tipo di servizio richesto:
Type of meal plan requested:

_____Pernottamento con prima colazione (*B&B*)

_____Mezza Pensione (*Half Board—breakfast and dinner included*)

_____Pensione Completa (*Full Board—all three meals included*)

Costo giornaliero: B&B (two persons) _____

Daily rate   MP (Half Board—per person) _____

                                       PC (Full Board—per person) _____

Ci sono ulteriori sconti per bambini e quanto? _____
Is there a discount for children and what is it?

E necessario una caparra e quanto? _____
Is a deposit necessary and for how much?

Ringraziando anticipatamente, porgo distinti saluti,
Thanking you in advance, I send my best regards,

YOUR NAME, ADDRESS, TELEPHONE & FAX NUMBER—clearly printed or typed

Reservation Request Letter in Italian

FINDING YOUR BED AND BREAKFAST

At the back of the book is a key map of the whole of Italy plus 13 regional maps showing each recommended bed and breakfast's location. The pertinent regional map number is given at the right on the *top line* of each bed and breakfast's description. To make it easier for you, we have divided the location maps with grids of four parts, a, b, c, and d, as indicated on each map's key. Directions to help you find your destination are given after each bed and breakfast description. However, they are only a small clue, as it would be impossible to find the space to give more details, and to know from which direction the traveler is arriving. The beauty of many of these lodgings is that they are off the beaten track, but that characteristic may also make them very tricky to find. If you get lost, a common occurrence, first keep your sense of humor, then call the proprietors and/or ask locals at bars or gas stations for directions. As previously mentioned, detailed maps for the area in which you will be traveling are essential. It is important to know that addresses in the countryside often have no specific street name. A common address consists of the farm name, sometimes a *localita* (an unincorporated area, or vicinity, frequently not found on a map) and the town name followed by the province abbreviated in parentheses. (The bed and breakfast is not necessarily in that town, but it serves as a post office reference.) The localita can also be the name of the road where the bed and breakfast is located, to make things more confusing. We state the *localita* as the third line of the bed and breakfast information.

TRANSFERS INTO CITIES: Travelers from abroad normally arrive by plane in Milan, Rome, or Venice and pick up their rental car at the airport. However, if your first destination is the city and you plan on picking up your car after your stay, approximate transfer rates are as follows:

MILAN

From Malpensa to city by taxi (70 min)	Lire 125,000
From Malpensa to city by bus	Lire 18,000
From Linate to city by taxi (20 min)	Lire 45,000
From Linate to city by bus	Lire 2,500

ROME

From Da Vinci to city by train (30 min)	Lire 13,000
From Da Vinci to city by taxi (45 min)	Lire 80,000

VENICE

From airport to city by waterbus (1 hour)	Lire 15,000
From station to city by waterbus (15 min)	Lire 4,000
From station to city by private watertaxi	Lire 85,000

REGIONAL FARM NAMES

The following names for farms, seen throughout this guide, vary from area to area.

azienda agricola—a general term meaning farm, not necessarily offering hospitality

borgo—a small stone-walled village, usually of medieval origins

casale, casolare—variations of farmhouse, deriving from "casa"

cascina and ca'—farmhouse in Piedmont, Lombardy, and Veneto

fattoria—typically a farm in Tuscany or Umbria

hof and maso—terms meaning house and farm in the northern mountain areas

locanda—historically a restaurant with rooms for travelers passing through on horseback

masseria—fortified farms in Apulia, Sicily

podere—land surrounding a farmhouse

poggio—literally describes the farm's position on a flat hilltop

tenuta—estate

torre—tower

trattoria—a simple, family-run restaurant in cities and the countryside

villa and castello—usually former home of nobility and more elaborate in services

About Italy

The following pointers are given in alphabetical order, not in order of importance.

BANKS

Banking hours are Monday through Friday from 8:30 am to 1:30 pm and 3 to 4 pm. *Cambio* signs outside and inside a bank indicate that it will exchange traveler's checks or give you cash from certain credit cards. Also privately run exchange offices are available in cities with more convenient hours and comparable rates.

DRIVING

A car is a must for this type of travel—most bed and breakfasts are inaccessible by any other means of transportation. A car gives the traveler a great deal of independence (public transportation is frequently on strike in Italy), while providing the ideal means to explore the countryside thoroughly. It is best to reserve a vehicle and pre-pay by credit card before your departure to ensure the best rates possible.

DRIVER'S LICENSE: An International Driver's Permit is not necessary for renting a car as a tourist: a foreign driver's license is valid for driving throughout Italy, which is not quite the "vehicular-free-for-all" you may have heard about, at least not outside big cities (particularly Rome, Florence, and Milan). When visiting Rome, it's advisable to do so at the beginning or end of your trip, before you pick up or after you drop off your car, and, by all means, avoid driving within the city. Italians have a different relationship with the basic rules of the road: common maneuvers include running stop lights and stop signs, triple-parking, driving at 100 mph on the highways, passing on the right, and backing up at missed highway exits. But once out of the city, you will find it relatively easy to reach your destination. Road directions are quite good in Italy and people are very willing to help.

DISTANCES: Distances are indicated in kilometers (one kilometer equals 0.621 mile), calculated roughly into miles by cutting the kilometer distance in half. Distances between towns are also indicated in orange alongside the roads on the Touring Club Italiano maps. Italy is a compact country and distances are relatively short, yet you will be amazed at how dramatically the scenery can change in an hour's drive.

GASOLINE: Gas prices in Italy are the highest in Europe, and Americans often suspect a mistake when their first fill-up comes to between $45 and $80 (most of it in taxes). Some stations now accept Visa credit cards, and the ERG stations accept American Express. Besides the AGIP stations on the autostrade, which are almost always open, gas stations observe the same hours as merchants, closing in the afternoon from 12:30 to 4 and in the evening at 7:30. Be careful not to get caught running on empty in the afternoon! Many stations have a self-service pump that operates on off-hours and accepts only 10,000-lire bills.

MAPS: An above-average map of Italy is absolutely essential for this type of travel. The Touring Club Italiano maps, in an easy-to-read three-volume format divided into North, Central, and South is a superior selection. Even the smallest town or, better, *localita* is indicated in the extensive index. In addition, places of particular interest are underlined or boxed in green, as are exceptionally scenic roads. Another fine choice are the Rand McNally *Hallwag* maps. Depending upon your itinerary, you need either their *Northern Italy* or *Southern Italy* map, or both (the whole-country map isn't specific enough). Each comes with a small index booklet to help you locate the towns.

ROADS: Names of roads in Italy are as follows:

Autostrada: a large, fast (and most direct) two- or three-lane tollway, marked by green signs bearing an "A" followed by the autostrada number. As you enter you receive a ticket from an automatic machine by pushing a red button. Payment is made at your exit point. If you lose your card, you will have to pay the equivalent amount of the distance from the beginning of the autostrada to your exit.

Superstrada: a one- or two-lane freeway between secondary cities marked by blue signs and given a number. Speed limit: 110 kph.

Strada Statale: a small one-lane road marked with S.S. followed by the road number. Speed limit: 90 kph.

Raccordo or *Tangenziale*: a ring road around main cities, connecting to an autostrada and city centers.

ROAD SIGNS: Yellow signs are for tourists and indicate a site of historical or cultural interest, hotels, and restaurants. Black-and-yellow signs indicate the name and location of private companies and industries.

TOLLS: Tolls on Italian autostrade are quite steep, ranging from $15 to $20 for a three-hour stretch, but offering the fastest and most direct way to travel between cities. Fortunately for the agritourist, tollways are rarely necessary. However, if it suits your needs, a *Viacard*, or magnetic reusable card for tolls, is available in all tollway gas stations for 50,000 or 90,000 lire (the lines for the automatic machines taking these cards are always shortest).

HOLIDAYS

It is very important to know Italian holidays because most museums, shops, and offices are closed. National holidays are listed below:

New Year's Day (January 1)   Assumption Day (August 15)
Epiphany (January 6)   All Saints' Day (November 1)
Easter (and the following Monday)   Christmas (December 25)
Liberation Day (April 25)   Santo Stefano (December 26)
Labor Day (May 1)

In addition to the national holidays, each town also has its own special holiday to honor its patron saint. Some of the major ones are listed below:

Bologna—St. Petronio (October 4)   Palermo—Santa Rosalia (July 15)
Florence—St. John the Baptist (June 24)   Rome—St. Peter (June 29)
Milan—St. Ambrose (December 7)   Venice—St. Mark (April 25)

The Vatican in Rome has its own schedule. The museums are closed every Sunday, except the last Sunday of each month when admission is free.

REGIONS

For reference, the 20 regions of Italy from north to south, with their capital cities in parentheses, are as follows:

NORTH—Valle d'Aosta (Aosta), Liguria (Genova), Piedmont (Torino), Friuli Venezia Giulia (Trieste), Trentino-Alto Adige (Trento & Bolzano), Lombardy (Milan), Veneto (Venice), and Emilia-Romagna (Bologna).

CENTRAL—Tuscany (Florence), Umbria (Perugia), Marches (Ancona), Lazio (Rome), Abruzzo (L'Aquila), and Molise (Campobasso).

SOUTH—Campania (Naples), Apulia (Bari), Calabria (Cantazaro), Basilicata (Potenza), Sicily (Palermo), and Sardinia (Caliari).

SAFETY

If certain precautions are taken, most unfortunate incidents can be avoided. It is extremely helpful to keep copies of passports, tickets, and contents of your wallet in your room in case you need them. Pickpocketing most commonly occurs in cities on buses, train stations, crowded streets, or from passing motorbikes. WARNING: At tollway gas stations and snack bars, **always** lock your car and beware of gypsies and vendors who try to sell you stolen merchandise. This practice is most prevalent south of Rome. In general, **never** leave valuables or even luggage in the car. Also, **never** set down luggage even for a minute in train stations.

Introduction–About Italy

SHOPPING

Italy is a shopper's paradise. Not only are the stores brimming with tempting merchandise, but the displays are works of art, from the tiniest fruit market to the most chic boutique. Each region seems to specialize in something: in Venice hand-blown glass and handmade lace are popular; Milan is famous for its clothing and silk; Florence is a center for leather goods and gold jewelry; Rome is a fashion hub, where you can stroll the pedestrian shopping streets and browse in some of the world's most elegant shops boasting the latest designer creations. Religious items are also plentiful in Rome, particularly near St. Peter's Cathedral. Naples and the surrounding area (Capri, Ravello, and Positano) offer delightful coral jewelry and also a wonderful selection of ceramics. You will be enticed by the variety of products sold at the farms such as wines, virgin olive oil, jams and honeys, cheese, and salami, along with local artisans' handicrafts. NOTE: For reasons of financial control and the tax evasion problems in Italy, the law states that clients **must** leave commercial establishments with an official receipt in hand, in order to avoid fines.

For purchases over 300,000 lire an immediate cash refund of the tax amount is offered by the Italian government to non-residents of the EU. Goods must be purchased at an affiliated retail outlet with the "tax-free for tourists" sign. Ask for the store receipt **plus** the tax-free shopping receipt. At the airport go first to the customs office where they will examine the items purchased and stamp both receipts, and then to the "tax-free cash refund" point after passport control.

US customs allows US residents to bring in $400-worth of foreign goods duty-free, after which a straight 10% of the amount above $400 is levied. Two bottles of liquor are allowed. The import of fresh cheese or meat is strictly restricted unless it is vacuum-packed.

TELEPHONES

The Italian phone company (the infamous SIP, now called TELECOM) has been an object of ridicule, a source of frustration, and a subject of heated conversation since its inception, and rightfully so. Over half of the phone calls initiated are never completed. Although more modern systems are being installed, it remains one of the most archaic, inefficient, and costly communication systems in the developed world, though touch-tone phones are now found in parts of some cities. To make matters at least not any worse, keep the following in mind (and be prepared to "try, try again"): to make a call within Italy, always dial "0" before the area code; from outside Italy, the "0" is eliminated. Telephone numbers can have from four to eight digits so don't be afraid of missing numbers. Cellular phone numbers begin with 0330, 0336, or 0337.

Dial 113 for emergencies of all kinds—24-hour service nationwide.

Dial 116 for Automobile Club for urgent breakdown assistance on the road.

Remember that no warning is given when the time you've paid for is about to expire (the line just goes dead), so put in plenty of change. Unused coins will be refunded. There are several types of phones (in various stages of modernization) in Italy:

Gray phones (slowly being phased out) are best for local calls. These take *gettoni,* or tokens, which are available at bars and tobacco stores for 200 lire.

Regular rotary phones in bars, restaurants, and many bed and breakfasts, which you can use *a scatti,* meaning you can pay the proprietor after the call is completed.

Bright orange pay phones which accept 500-, 200-, and 100-lire coins as well as *gettoni.* Bright orange pay phones as above with attached apparatus permitting insertion of a *scheda telefonica,* or reusable magnetic card worth 5,000 or 10,000 lire.

NOTE: Due to the ongoing modernization process of telephone lines, phone numbers are constantly being changed, making it sometimes very difficult to contact lodgings (many times they are not listed under the lodging's name). A recording (in Italian) plays for only two months indicating the new number. If you are calling from the United States and your Italian is not up to par, we suggest you ask the overseas operator to contact the Italian operator for translation and assistance.

To call the United States from Italy, matters have been eased by the ongoing installation of the Country Direct System, whereby with one 200-lire coin you can reach an American operator by dialing either 172-1011 for AT&T or 172-1022 for MCI. Be patient and wait the one to two minutes before a recording or US operator comes through. Either a collect call or a credit-card call can then be placed. If you discover this system doesn't work from some smaller towns, dial 170 to place a collect call, or, in some cities, try dialing direct (from a *scatti* phone), using the international code 001 + area code + number.

TIPPING

Hotels: a service charge is included in the daily rate. A token tip for the chambermaid for longer stays is common practice. Restaurants: 15% is included in the bill's total. It is customary, however, to leave from 3,000–8,000 lire for the waiter, depending on service. Taxis: 10%.

TRAIN TRAVEL

Although a car is an absolute necessity to reach most bed and breakfasts, it is often convenient and time-saving to leave the car and take a train for day trips into the city. NOTE: A new policy has just been established by the country's national train network— your ticket must be stamped with the time and date **before** you board the train; otherwise, you will be issued a 40,000 lire fine. Tickets are stamped at small and not very obvious yellow machines near the exits to the tracks. Unstamped tickets may be reimbursed with a 30% penalty. It is strongly advised that you purchase your ticket (including seat reservation) in advance through a local travel agency when you arrive in order to avoid long lines at the station. The IC and EC trains to major cities are the most efficient.

We wish you the best in your travels to Italy and always welcome your comments and suggestions. *Buon Viaggio!*

Bed & Breakfast Descriptions

In the heart of the wine valley of Piedmont, just outside and above the town of Alba, is the stately, cream-colored villa belonging to Giuliana Pionzo and her husband—Cascina Reine's gracious hosts. Besides a lovely flower garden and above-ground pool (open only in July and August), the large home has a terra-cotta roof, a lovely arcaded patio, and a fabulous view over Alba's rooftops and the surrounding countryside. Wicker chairs with plump floral cushions invite guests to relax on the patio, where at sunset they may also enjoy a refreshing mint drink with the *simpatico* hosts. Accommodation is offered within the ivy-covered main house, each room finely decorated with antiques, paintings, and the family's personal objects. A suite consisting of two bedrooms, bath, kitchenette, and large terrace is ideal for a family of four. Other newer rooms have been added in the wing adjoining the villa, one with its own terrace and kitchenette. Breakfast is served either outside on the patio overlooking the vineyards and orchards or inside in the pristine dining room with vaulted ceilings. Alba has some of the finest restaurants in Italy and is also famous for its wines and annual truffle festival. *Directions*: From Alba follow signs for Barbaresco and Mango. Halfway up the hill on a large curve, watch for a small yellow sign which indicates a gravel road on the left and then the wrought-iron gates of the property at the end of the road.

CASCINA REINE
Hostess: Giuliana Pionzo
Localita: Altavilla 9
Alba (CN) 12051, Italy
Tel & fax: (0173) 440112
www.karenbrown.com\italy\cascinareine.html
9 rooms, 7 with private bathrooms
Lire 110,000–150,000 double B&B
Breakfast only (dinner upon request)
Open all year
English spoken well, Region: Piedmont

Seven kilometers from historic Bergamo and within easy reach of beautiful Lakes Como, Iseo, and Garda is the home of the region's agritourist president, Gianantonio Ardizzone. On the property, next to the recently constructed residence where he and his family live, is a sprawling 15th-century farmhouse and barn complex of the type known in Lombardy as a *cascina*. Installed within the cascina are five guest apartments, each including one or two bedrooms, bathroom, and kitchen. The apartments are furnished modestly but comfortably, with a decidedly rustic ambiance within and without. Restoration of the cascina is ongoing and it is nestled in pretty surroundings, looking onto the small town of Nese and backing onto the green hills where well-tended riding horses are kept. Gianantonio delights in showing guests his hobbies—a collection of antique farm tools and ostrich breeding—and son Fabio takes care of guests' daily requests. No meals are served here, but a nearby trattoria adequately appeases the appetite, or you may want to do some shopping before you arrive and come ready to prepare your own meals. The Grumello offers self-sufficient, conveniently located accommodation and exceptional value. Your hosts are exceptionally helpful and sincerely warm. *Directions*: Exit from A4 autostrada at Bergamo and follow signs for Valli di Bergamo, Valle Seriana. Exit at Alzano after 6 km and follow hospital signs; go straight on for Nese and turn left on Via Grumello.

CASCINA GRUMELLO
Hosts: Gianantonio Ardizzone family
Localita: Fraz. Nese
Alzano Lombardo (BG) 24022, Italy
Tel: (035) 510060, Fax: (035) 711020
www.karenbrown.com\italy\cascinagrumello.html
5 apartments
Lire 35,000 per person (heating/cleaning extra)
No meals served
Open all year
Credit cards: VS
Some English spoken, Region: Lombardy

For something very different from the more hotel-like ambiance of the Locanda of Ansedonia, the Grazia farm next door is an excellent alternative. Gracious and warm hostess, Signora Maria Grazia, divides her time between Rome and the 300-acre property she inherited from her grandfather. The dramatic cypress-lined driveway takes you away from the busy Aurelia road up to the expansive salmon-hued edifice with its arched loggia. The hosts' home, office, three guest apartments, farmhands' quarters, and horse stables are all housed within the complex which is encased by superb country and sea views in all directions. From here one can enjoy touring Etruscan territory: Tuscania, Tarquinia, Sovana, Sorano, and the nearby ruins of Cosa, or stay seaside on the beaches of Feniglia on the promontory of Argentario. Comfortable accommodations pleasantly decorated with homey touches are offered within any of three apartments for two to six persons including living area and kitchen. Our favorite is the two-bedroom apartment on the second floor capturing the front view to the sea through the trees. Maria Grazia can suggest a number of local restaurants specializing in seafood. Tennis and horseback riding are available. Altogether a delightful combination. *Directions*: Take the coastal Aurelia road from Rome and after the Ansedonia exit turn right into an unmarked driveway immediately after the Pitorsino restaurant.

GRAZIA
Hosts: Maria Grazia Cantore family
Via Aurelia, km 140.1
Orbetello Scalo (GR) 58016, Italy
Tel & fax: (0564) 881182 or (06) 483945
3 apartments for 2 to 4 persons
Lire 100,000–200,000 per apartment daily
3-day minimum stay
No meals served
Open all year
English spoken well, Region: Tuscany

Few visitors to the spiritual city of Assisi are aware that the Subasio mountains flanking it feature some of the most breathtaking scenery in the country. Nestled there is a cluster of stone houses known as Le Silve, a village which served as a haven for 10th-century pilgrims traveling from the Adriatic coast to Rome. Carrying on that tradition of offering home-cooked meals and impeccable hospitality, Signora Taddia has recreated an ambiance of utter tranquillity, while adding her own touch of elegance. The guestrooms are tastefully furnished with simple antiques which blend harmoniously with the preserved medieval architecture. The main house contains 15 bedrooms with private bathrooms, and panoramic views, reception, and a living room with fireplace. The auxiliary house has a beamed dining room, billiard and card rooms. This bed and breakfast features many of the amenities of a luxury hotel, including swimming pool, tennis, and horseback riding and for this reason has become a member of the Romantik Inns group. *Directions*: From Assisi go in the direction of Gualdo Tadino. One passes close to and should not miss the Eremo (site of St. Francis's retreat). Take the winding uphill road at the sign for Armenzano and follow it for 15 km. The hotel is after Armenzano village and is well marked.

LE SILVE DI ARMENZANO
Hostess: Daniela Taddia
Localita: Armenzano
Assisi (PG) 06081, Italy
Tel: (075) 8019000, Fax: (075) 8019005
www.karenbrown.com\italy\lesilvediarmenzano.html
15 rooms with private bathrooms, 4 suites,
* 7 apartments*
Lire 280,000 double B&B
Open March to November
Credit cards: all major
Fluent English spoken, Region: Umbria

The delightful Malvarina farm has all the ingredients for the perfect bed and breakfast: charming country-style accommodations, excellent local cuisine, a warm and congenial host family, and an ideal location. Just outside town, yet immersed in lush green vegetation at the foot of the Subasio mountains, the property is comprised of the 15th-century stone farmhouse where the family lives and four independent cottages (converted barn and stalls) divided into bedrooms and suites with en-suite bathrooms, plus three apartments with kitchenettes for two to four persons. *Casa Angelo* holds several bedrooms plus a sweet breakfast room with a corner fireplace and cupboards filled with colorful *Deruta* ceramics. Great care has obviously been taken in the decor of rooms, using Mamma's family's heirloom furniture. The old wine cellar has been cleverly converted into a cool and spacious taverna dining room with long wooden tables for dining *en famille*. A collection of antique farm tools and brass pots cover walls near the enormous fireplace. Horses are available for trekking into the scenic national park just beyond the house. *Directions*: Exit at Capodacqua from the Perugia-Spello route 75. Turn right then left on Via Massera (Radio Subasio sign) and follow the road up to Malvarina.

MALVARINA
Hosts: Claudio & Luciano Fabrizi
Localita: Malvarina 32
Assisi (PG) 06080, Italy
Tel & fax: (075) 8064280
www.karenbrown.com\italy\malvarina.html
10 rooms with private bathrooms, 3 apartments
Lire 120,000 double B&B (3-day minimum stay)
 100,000 per person half board
Breakfast & dinner served
Open all year
Credit cards: all major
Some English spoken, Region: Umbria

Fabrizio and Bianca, the Milanese hosts originally from this part of Umbria, restored their inherited La Fornace farmhouse, situated in the very desirable touring location of Assisi, with their guests' comfort foremost in mind. With careful attention to detail, four comfortable apartments were fashioned within the three stone houses, each with one or two bedrooms, bathroom, fully equipped kitchenette, and eating area. Interesting decorating touches such as parts of antique iron gates hung over beds, terra-cotta and white ceramic tiles in the immaculate bathrooms, and antique armoires give the accommodations a polished country flavor. *Le Pannocchie*, the largest of the four, includes a corner fireplace, while *Papaveri*, on the second floor, looks out over the flat cornfields up to magnificent Assisi and the Subasio mountains beyond. The Cascioli family takes care of guests' needs when the owners are not in residence and assures that each room is stocked with breakfast fixings each morning. At guests' request guided tours are arranged to Umbria's top sights. Besides a lovely swimming pool for guests, bikes, ping-pong, and games for children are on hand. *Directions*: From Perugia-Spoleto highway 75, exit at Ospedalicchio on route 147, turn left for Tordibetto after the bridge, then right for Assisi and follow signs for La Fornace.

PODERE LA FORNACE
Hosts: Bianca & Fabrizio Feliciani
Via Ombrosa 3
Tordibetto di Assisi (PG) 06081, Italy
Tel & fax: (075) 8019537 or (0330) 282154
www.karenbrown.com\italy\poderelafornace.html
4 apartments
Lire 120,000–260,000 daily per apartment
3-day minimum stay
Breakfast included with weekly stays
Closed February
English spoken well (hosts), Region: Umbria

Situated just a few kilometers from the Gulf of Taranto, and strategically based between the cities of Gallipoli, Taranto, and Lecce, is the villa of retired Alitalia executive Giacinto Mannarini, a sprawling, whitewashed modern inn built on the original site of the Mudonato castle. Signor Mannarini offers warm hospitality in ten guestrooms in the main house, which are reached through separate entrances off an arcaded breezeway. Spotless rooms are furnished with rustic reproductions in dark wood. Triple rooms now have air conditioning installed and an apartment for four people includes a living room but no kitchen facilities. The property covers 100 acres of forest and olive groves and boasts a lovely swimming pool (open from mid-June) with a kitchen serving meals on the poolside patio. The fine cuisine (cited in the Veronelli restaurant guide) is prepared from the freshest available produce and features homemade pastas (the local *orecchiette*, or ear pasta) and desserts. Vegetarian dishes are also available, as is a full American breakfast. Signor Giacinto is a delightful host and is knowledgeable on his native Apulia. *Directions*: From Taranto take route 7 through Manduria and Avetrana. Three km out of town toward Salice turn left at the sign for Mudonato.

BOSCO DI MUDONATO
Host: Giacinto Mannarini
Via per Salice-Casella Postale 2
Avetrana (TA) 74020, Italy
Tel & fax: (099) 9704597
www.karenbrown.com\italy\boscodi mudonato.html
10 rooms with private bathrooms
Lire 170,000 double B&B (3-day minimum)
  120,000 per person half board
3-day minimum stay
Advance reservation required by fax
All meals served
Open all year English spoken well, Region: Apulia

After many years of traveling to Italy at any free opportunity, Jennie and Alan left England to move to Tuscany and fell in love immediately with Villa Mimosa, a rustic 18th-century home with a shady front courtyard. Alan got to work right away with restoring and transforming the upstairs into guest quarters, creating three sweet bedrooms, each with a different scheme. He added small, but very practical bathrooms in each room. A cozy sitting room plus library with grand piano are reserved upstairs for guests and decorated with their own antiques shipped over from England. Jennie and Alan's idea with offering few rooms was to share their passion for this part of the country known as Lunigiana (very near the Cinque Terre coastal area and one hour from both Parma nad Lucca) and give their guests lots of personal attention, while making them feel right at home. Guests are treated to breakfast on the terrace overlooking the vegetable garden and Apennine mountains and delight in Jennie's creative cuisine based on fresh garden vegetables and local recipes. This is the perfect stopover. *Directions*: Exit from the A15 autostrada (Parma-La Spezia) at Pontremoli from the north or Aulla from the south and head north alongside the autostrada toVillafranca, then Bagnone. Enter town through the gateway and turn left at Via N Quartieri. Go uphill for 3 km and Villa Mimosa is on the right-hand side before the church.

VILLA MIMOSA
Hosts: Jennie & Alan Pratt
Localita: Corlaga
Bagnone (MS) 54021, Italy
Tel & fax: (0187) 427022
3 bedrooms with private bathrooms
From lire 120,000 double B&B
Breakfast, dinner upon request
Open all year
English spoken fluently, Region: Tuscany

In the heart of the Veneto region, south of Vicenza, lies the Castello winery and estate, a handsome 15th-century villa watching proudly over the sweet town of Barbarano Vicentino and the home of the Marinoni family for the past century. Signora Elda, along with her two young sons, carries on the tradition. The large walled courtyard with manicured Renaissance garden is bordered by the family's home, the guesthouse (originally farmer's quarters), and converted barn, where concerts and banquets are organized. A lovely courtyard overlooks the family's expansive vineyards from which fine red wines are produced. The independent two-story guesthouse overlooking the garden can be rented out as one house or divided into three apartments. It has just been renovated, with each apartment having one or two bedrooms, bathroom, kitchenette, and one communal living room. It has been decorated very simply but pleasantly with the family's furnishings. An extra charge is made for heating. This is an excellent, economical base from which to visit the Veneto region. It's an easy drive to Padua and Venice where you may opt to leave your car and take the train. *Directions*: Exit from the A4 at Vicenza Est towards Noventa Vicentino, then Barbarano Vicentino. Follow signs to Castello (20 km).

IL CASTELLO
Hosts: Elda Marinoni family
Via Castello 6
Barbarano Vicentino (VI) 36021, Italy
Tel: (0444) 886055, Fax: none
www.karenbrown.com\italy\ilcastello.html
3 apartments
Lire 210,000–245,000 per person weekly
No meals served
1-week minimum stay
Open all year
English spoken well, Region: Veneto

La Casa Sola is just that—an elegant villa standing alone on a hilltop surrounded by bucolic countryside. The gracious proprietors and hosts, a noble Genovese family, are assisted by the local Regoli family who tend to the gorgeous 400-acre vineyard estate. There are six large guest apartments within a rose-covered stone farmhouse just down the road from the main villa. All the apartments are installed on two floors, comprised of a living room, kitchen, bedrooms, and baths, with private entrances and garden. Each apartment is furnished in style with refined country antiques, numbers 3 and 5 being the loveliest. Details such as botanical prints hung with bows, eyelet curtains, fresh flowers, and a bottle of wine are welcome touches. Number 5, for up to eight people, is a favorite, with three bedrooms, fireplace, and magnificent views over the Barberino Valley. "Il Capanno" in the converted barn is a delightful "nest" for honeymooners. An inviting cypress-edged swimming pool overlooks the valley. An ideal touring base in a tranquil, romantic setting. *Directions*: Exit at San Donato off the Firenze-Siena superstrada. One and a half km after San Donato at the church, turn right for Cortine/Casa Sola, and follow it for 2½ km.

FATTORIA CASA SOLA
Hosts: Count Gambaro family
Localita: Cortine
Barberino Val d'Elsa (FI) 50021, Italy
Tel: (055) 8075028, Fax: (055) 8059194
7 apartments
Lire 750,000–2,400,000 weekly (July &
* August)*
Breakfast & dinner served upon request
Open all year
English & French spoken well, Region: Tuscany

Strategically positioned midway between Siena and Florence sits the square stone farmhouse dating to 1700 owned by Gianni and Cristina, a couple from Milan who have dedicated their lives to the equestrian arts. The Paretaio appeals particularly to visitors with a passion for horseback riding, for the de Marchis offer everything from basic riding lessons to dressage training, and day outings through the gorgeous surrounding countryside. In fact, the Paretaio is recognized as one of the top riding "ranches" in Tuscany. On the ground floor is a rustic, warm living room with country antiques, comfy sofas, and piano enhanced by a vaulted brick ceiling and worn terra-cotta floors. Upstairs, the main gathering area is the dining room which features a massive fireplace and a seemingly endless wooden table. Access to the six bedrooms is from this room, and each is stylishly decorated with touches such as dried flowers, white lace curtains, and, of course, equestrian prints. A vast collection of over 300 pieces with an equestrian theme is displayed about the home. The Paretaio also organizes courses in Italian and is an excellent base for touring the heart of Tuscany. The swimming pool gives splendid views over olive groves and vineyards. *Directions*: Head south from Barberino on route 2 and after 2 km take the second right-hand turnoff for San Filippo and continue on 1½ km of dirt road to the house.

IL PARETAIO
Hosts: Cristina & Giovanni de Marchi
Localita: San Filippo
Barberino Val d'Elsa (FI) 50021, Italy
Tel: (055) 8059218, Fax: (055) 8059231
www.karenbrown.com\italy\ilparetaio.html
6 rooms with private bathrooms
Lire 130,000–170,000 double B&B
  100,000–120,000 per person half board
Open all year
English & French spoken well, Region: Tuscany

La Chiara farm, dating back to 1600 and covering 45 hectares of woods, vineyards, and olive groves, is conveniently located between Siena and Florence in the heart of Chianti, yet affords a feeling of escape. Eleven bedrooms, five with private baths, are dispersed throughout the main villa, which also contains a large living room, kitchen, and dining room where the mostly farm-fresh vegetarian meals using produce from the organic gardens are served. The common rooms and high-ceilinged bedrooms are very modestly furnished with worn country furniture, but are spacious and airy, offering scenic views over the serene countryside. Extra beds can easily be added to rooms, making the Chiara an ideal and economical choice for families traveling with children. The lemon greenhouse and another barn structure have recently been restructured into two apartments. Headed by young and extremely personable Gaia and her husband, the farm is abuzz when groups come for special lectures and courses on art and psychology. There is a small swimming pool not far from the house and horses are available for trekking. *Directions*: Exit at San Donato from the Firenze-Siena highway and after passing San Donato, turn right for Cortine/Casa Sola. Continue to Prumiano (approximately 7 km).

LA CHIARA DI PRUMIANO
Hosts: Gaia Mezzadri & Egidio Pastori
Strada di Cortine 12
Localita: Prumiano
Barberino Val d'Elsa (FI) 50021, Italy
Tel: (055) 8075583, Fax: (055) 8075678
www.karenbrown.com\italy\lachiaradiprumiano.html
11 rooms, 5 with private bathrooms
2 apartments
Lire 100,000 double B&B
All meals served
Closed January
English spoken well, Region: Tuscany

When the Caccetta family from Rome, along with two other families, purchased the 250-acre property 20 years ago, they were true pioneers in the agritourism field. After many years of bringing back life to both the land and 16th-century hunting lodge, today they have a self-sufficient farm producing Chianti, white and rosé wines, grappa, and olive oil. Spacious guestrooms are divided between the main house, with two suites and three bedrooms, and an adjacent recently restored house. All are decorated with care and attention to detail using lovely family antiques which blend in perfectly with the overall ambiance. The very cozy common rooms downstairs include a living room with fireplace and stone walls, card room, small bar area, and dining rooms where breakfast and dinner are served. A forest-green tartan carpet covers floors and family photos and paintings adorn walls. During the warmer months, a buffet breakfast and dinner are served outside under the pergola overlooking deep woods. For those who prefer to stay put, a swimming pool, grass tennis courts, hiking trails, and horseback riding are all available. *Directions*: From the Siena-Florence highway, exit at San Donato and follow the road for Tavarnelle, then Barberino and turn right at the sign for La Spinosa. Take the dirt road to the end.

LA SPINOSA
Hosts: Paolo Caccetta & Danila Maneri
Via Le Masse 8
Barberino Val d'Elsa (FI) 50021, Italy
Tel & fax: (055) 8075413
5 rooms, 4 suites with private bathrooms
Lire 220,000–260,000 double B&B
  150,000–170,000 per person half board
3-day minimum stay
Breakfast & dinner served
Open all year
English spoken very well, Region: Tuscany

The Dreikirchen is situated up in the Dolomite foothills with an enchanting view over a lush green valley and distant snowcapped mountain peaks. The young and energetic Wodenegg family works diligently at making guests feel at home in their lovely residence and running the restaurant which serves typical local meals to non-guest patrons as well since it shares the site of a unique historical monument—*Le Tre Chiese*, three curious, attached, miniature medieval churches. This unique inn is reachable only by taxi or Jeep, or on foot. An exhilarating half-hour hike takes you up to the typical mountain-style chalet with wood balconies in front. The most charming rooms are those in the older section, entirely wood-paneled, with fluffy comforters and old-fashioned washbasins. The rambling house has several common areas for guests as well as a swimming pool. This is truly an incredible spot, near Siusi Alps and Val Gardena where some of the best climbing in Europe can be found. *Directions*: Exit from the Bolzano-Brennero autostrada at Klausen and take the road south to Ponte Gardena and through Barbian to Bad Dreikirchen's parking on the right (after 1 km). Call the hotel from the village for a pick-up by Jeep (lire 20,000).

BAD DREIKIRCHEN
Hosts: Wodenegg family
San Giacomo 6
Barbian, (BZ) 39040, Italy
Tel & fax: (0471) 650055
www.karenbrown.com\italy\baddreikirchen.html
30 rooms, 10 with private bathrooms
Lire 60,000–103,000 per person half board
3-day minimum stay
Breakfast & dinner served
Open May 7 to October 18
English spoken well, Region: Trentino-Alto Adige

The expansive Pomurlo farm, home to the congenial Minghelli family, covers 370 acres of hills, woods, and open fields and is an excellent base for touring Umbria. A winding dirt road leads to the typical stone house which contains a restaurant featuring farm-fresh specialties. An antique cupboard and old farm implements on the walls enhance the rustic setting. Three "country suites" are situated beneath the restaurant, each consisting of two bedrooms, bathroom, and kitchenette. Comfortable and cheerful, the suites are decorated with wrought-iron beds, colorful bedspreads, and typical regional country antiques. A nearby converted stall houses two adorable independent rooms looking out over the lake. Other guestrooms and apartments are found in two large hilltop homes commanding a breathtaking view of the entire valley with its grazing herds of longhorn cattle. The main house, a 12th-century tower fortress where the inn's personable hostess Daniela resides, accommodates guests in three additional suites of rooms. Breakfast fixings are provided in rooms. The recent acquisition of the neighboring property has resulted in a new complex (*Le Casette*) of three stone farmhouses containing several other mini-apartments and a restaurant around a large swimming pool. *Directions*: The farm is conveniently located near the Rome-Florence autostrada. Take the Orvieto exit from the A1 autostrada. Follow signs for Todi, **not** for Baschi. On route N448 turn right at the sign for Pomurlo.

POMURLO VECCHIO
Hosts: Lazzaro Minghelli & family
Localita: Lago di Corbara
Baschi (TR) 05023, Italy
Tel: (0744) 950190 or 950475, Fax: (0744) 950500
25 rooms & apartmrnts
Lire 75,000–85,000 per person half board
Trattoria on premises
Open all year
Some English spoken, Region: Umbria

The Locanda, a pale-yellow-and-brick house dating from 1830, sits on the border between Tuscany and Umbria and is an excellent base from which to explore this rich countryside. The villa's dining room features a vaulted ceiling in toast-colored brick, an enormous fireplace, French windows opening out to the flower garden, and antiques including a cupboard adorned with the family's blue-and-white china. The upstairs quarters are reserved primarily for guests, and contain five comfortable rooms and an inviting sitting room and library. The cozy bedrooms have mansard ceilings, armoires, lovely linens, and washbasins. Two additional guestrooms are located on the ground floor of the converted barn between the house and a small garden. They are more spacious and modern in decor. Cordial hostess Palmira assists with local itineraries. Excellent regional cook, Eurica, creates divine vegetarian dishes with local produce and enjoys giving short informal cooking lessons to guests. Siena is only 45 kilometers away, and the quaint medieval and Renaissance villages of Pienza, Montepulciano, and Montalcino are close by. *Directions*: Exit from the Rome-Florence autostrada at Val di Chiana. Head toward Bettolle, then bear right toward Siena. Follow signs for La Bandita.

LOCANDA LA BANDITA
Hostess: Palmira Fiorini
Via Bandita 72
Bettolle-Sinalunga (SI) 53040, Italy
Tel & fax: (0577) 624649
www.karenbrown.com\italy\locandalabandita.html
7 rooms with private bathrooms
Lire 140,000 double B&B
* 95,000 per person half board*
Breakfast & dinner served
Open all year
Credit cards: all major
English spoken well, Region: Tuscany

Le Mezzelune sits contentedly immersed in the countryside at 3 kilometers from the Tuscan coast between Livorno and Piombino (where ferryboats depart for Elba). Luisa and Sergio, looking for a change in lifestyle, left their fashion business in Parma a year ago and came to settle in this peaceful and varied landscape after the extensive restoration work on the stone farmhouse was completed. The stylish and impeccable home clearly reflects the personalities of the warm and reserved hosts who were their own architects in the tasteful designing of both the interiors and exterior. Although the idea of offering hospitality came in a second phase, it was a logical and natural one since the four corner bedrooms upstairs each has its own large private terrace and immaculate floral-tiled bathroom. Each one offers splendid views over fruit orchards and olive groves all the way to the sea. While the hosts occupy the cupola, guests have a separate entrance to the upstairs rooms, giving utmost privacy to all. Common areas include the living room with open kitchen with large arched window and doors which look out to the surrounding garden. Day trips include Volterra and San Gimignano, private beaches, visits to the wine estates of Bolgheri, and biking in the nearby nature park. *Directions*: Exit from Aurelia on route 1 at Bibbona and turn left. Pass through the town of La California and turn left for Bibbona. The podere is before town, well marked to the left.

PODERE LE MEZZELUNE　　　*New*
Hosts: Luisa & Sergio Chiesa
Via Mezzelune 126
Bibbona (LI) 57020, Italy
Tel & fax: (0586) 670266
4 rooms with private bathrooms, 1 apartment
Lire 190,000–220,000 double B&B
Breakfast only
Open all year
No English spoken, Region: Tuscany

This guide includes some small bed-and-breakfast-like urban hotels for the convenience of travelers who would like to do some metropolitan sightseeing. For some reason, the city of Bologna is often bypassed by visitors, despite its rich past, beautiful historic center, arcaded streets, and elegant shops. Cristina and Mauro Orsi, the owners of the splendid Hotel Corona d'Oro, mentioned in another of our guides, *Italy: Charming Inns & Itineraries,* own two other centrally located, smaller hotels: the Orologio and the Commercianti. Just steps away from Bologna's main piazza and basilica you find the recently renovated Orologio, so-called because it looks onto city hall with its clock tower. The hotel has thirty-one rooms, and one apartment, on three floors, and the intimate atmosphere of a family-run establishment. The newly remodeled guestrooms are pleasantly decorated with pretty floral-print wallpaper, photographs of the city from the 1930s, and simple reproduction furniture. A welcome treat is the full breakfast buffet served in the dining room. Bicycles are available free of charge to our readers to visit the city's historical center. The owners also organize personalized cooking classes and private tours of Bologna and surrounding cities. *Directions*: Located in the heart of the old city.

HOTEL OROLOGIO
Hostess: Cristina Orsi
Via IV Novembre 10
Bologna 40123, Italy
Tel: (051) 231253, Fax: (051) 260552
www.karenbrown.com\italy\hotelorlolgio.html
E-mail: hotcorona@iperbole.bologna.it
31 rooms with private bathrooms, 1 apartment
Lire 210,000–300,000 double B&B
Breakfast only
Open all year
Credit cards: all major
English spoken well, Region: Emilia-Romagna

A pocket of absolutely stunning yet unexplored countryside is the Oltrepo Pavese hills, 60 kilometers south of Milan. It is predominantly wine country producing top-quality Cortese, Pinot, Barbera, and Riesling. Less than an hour's drive away is the Alba/Asti wine region of Piedmont and the Italian Riviera. Also not to be missed is historic Pavia and its celebrated Certosa monastery. What better place to set up a home base than the Castello di Stefanago where a variety of accommodation is available. The two Baruffaldi brothers work diligently at producing wines and maintaining their 600-acre property. The 12th-century castle perched atop a hill and taking in spectacular views houses the host families and five lovely apartments for two to five persons. Each has a bathroom, living area, and kitchenette and has been decorated appropriately with the family's period furniture. Below the castle on the road is a restored farmhouse "La Boatta" where a restaurant and six sweet double bedrooms are available. Each room has coordinated Provençal-patterned spreads and curtains with spotless bathrooms. Typical meals are served using fresh produce directly from the farm. *Directions*: Exit at Bereguardo/Pavia on the A7 autostrada from Milan. Follow it to Pavia (skirting the city) and then Casteggio. Drive on to Montebello-Borgo Priolo-Fortunago-Stefanago and up the long drive to the castle.

CASTELLO DI STEFANAGO
Hosts: Patrizia & Giacomo Baruffaldi
Borgo Priolo (PV) 27040, Italy
Tel: (0383) 875227 or 875413, Fax: (0383) 875644
6 rooms with private bathrooms, 5 apartments
Lire 90,000–240,000 double B&B
* 80,000–150,000 per person half board*
All meals served
Open February to November
Credit cards: all major
Some English spoken, Region: Lombardy

Just off the busy road that connects the major towns of Umbria—Perugia, Assisi, Spoleto, and Todi—is the elegant country house Giulia, which has been in the Petrucci family since its 14th-century origins. Later additions were built on to the main stone villa, one of which Signora Caterina has opened up to guests. Time seems to have stood still in the six bedrooms, all but one with en-suite bathroom, and filled with grandmother Giulia's lovely antique iron-wrought beds, armoires, and period paintings. They are divided among three floors, accessed by a steep stone staircase, the largest having a ceiling fresco depicting the local landscape. Breakfast is served either in the chandeliered dining room upstairs, with Oriental carpets, lace curtains, and a large fireplace, or under the oak trees in the front garden during the warmer months. The family's frescoed quarters can be rented out for weddings. Part of the barn has been recently converted into two independent units which include a fully equipped kitchenette for up to four persons. Although the large swimming pool overlooks a rather barren field and the distant main road, it is a welcome respite after a full day of touring, which guests will be doing a lot of from this strategically convenient location. *Directions*: Just off the Perugia-Spoleto route 75 between Trevi and Campello.

CASA GIULIA
Hostess: Caterina Alessandrini Petrucci
Via SS Flaminia km.140.1
Bovara di Trevi (PG) 06039, Italy
Tel: (0742) 78257, Fax: (0742) 381632
www.karenbrown.com\italy\casagiulia.html
6 rooms, 5 with private bathrooms
2 apartments
Lire 160,000 double B&B
* 115,000 per person half board*
Breakfast only, Open all year
Some English spoken, Region: Umbria

The town of Brisighella is a gem. The town comes to life during June and July with its annual Medieval Festival when games of the period are re-enacted, and medieval music, literature, and dance are produced. Locals attire themselves in appropriate costume and the village's narrow streets are illuminated nightly by torches for the occasion. Just out of town, past the thermal hot springs, sits the sweet home of a young Milanese couple, Ettore (a former architect) and Adriana, with its 10 hectares of vineyards and orchards. Guests are treated to the host's excellent Sangiovese and Chardonnay wines. The Matareses have renovated the barn next to their small stone house, creating four guestrooms as well as a rustic dining area with exposed beams and a large fireplace where guests gather for typical Romagna-style meals. Rooms are decorated with simple country furnishings. The atmosphere is casual and the value excellent. While in the vicinity don't miss the mosaics in Ravenna, the historical center of Bologna, and the international ceramic museum in Faenza. *Directions*: Take the Faenza exit from the A14 between Bologna and Rimini. Follow signs for Brisighella or Firenze. At town turn left for Terme/Modigliona. Il Palazzo is the third house on the left after the Hotel Terme.

IL PALAZZO
Hosts: Ettore Matarese family
Via Baccagnano 11
Brisighella (RA) 48013, Italy
Tel & fax: (0546) 80338
4 rooms, 2 with private bathrooms, 1 apartment
Lire 90,000 double B&B
* 70,000 per person half board*
3-day minimum stay or 20% surcharge
All meals served
Open all year
English spoken well, Region: Emilia-Romagna

Yet another new arrival in the fast-growing agritourism sector is the lovely 300-acre countryside property of the Toscano brothers. Giovanni and his bride, Isabelle, transfered from Florence to be permanent residents at his grandfather's vineyards. After years of meticulous restoration work on the group of three stone houses, they opened doors to guests last year offering very comfortable accommodation within seven apartments. The peach house is where the couple resides while the adjacent pale-yellow building holds two large apartments. The third stone structure with the remaining five apartments has an arched loggia on the second floor. Rooms are tastefully decorated with antiques and country fabrics, enhancing the original beams and brick floors. The landscaping with its many cypress trees is as impeccable as the general ambiance. Attention to detail is evident also in the organization of activities and local itinerary suggestions for guests. Beautiful scenery surrounds you throughout, especially by the pool, seemingly part of the natural setting. *Directions*: From A1 autostrada exit at Valdarno, and follow signs for Montevarchi, Bucine (8 km). From town follow signs up to Iesolana, passing over a stone bridge (2 km) to the end of the road.

IESOLANA **New**
Hosts: Giovanni & Isabelle Toscano
Localita: Iesolana
Bucine (AR) 52021, Italy
Tel: (055) 992988, Fax: (055) 992879
Cellphone: (0336) 321674
7 apartments
Lire 150,000–300,000 daily for 2 persons
2-day minimum stay (1 week July & August)
No meals served Open all year
Credit cards: MC, VS
English spoken well, Region: Tuscany

After living in South Africa for 20 years, the Tosi family returned to their homeland in search of a piece of land that in some way resembled their beloved Africa. The Montebelli property, situated in *Maremma*, the wild west of Italy, fit the bill with its 300-plus acres of mountain, hills, and plain, all close to the sea, the essential element, according to Lorenzo, which brings about *allegria* in people. Lorenzo and his *simpatica* wife, Carla, now divide their time and energy between their guests and production of wines and olive oil. At the foot of the hills is the main guest house where most of the rooms are situated. Others, each with separate entrance, are in two one-story wings connecting to an outdoor dining area. The best rooms are in the main house, decorated tastefully with antiques and including all the amenities of a regular hotel. The half-board requirement allows guests to sample the marvelous cuisine of the area within the characteristic dining room featuring the stone wheel from the original press. This is unexplored territory, full of historical treasures and Etruscan remains. And if that's not enough, scenic walks in the surrounding woods, a swimming pool, tennis courts, and horseback riding (at extra cost) are available. *Directions*: From the north, exit at Gavorrano Scalo from Aurelia route 1 for Ravi then Caldana. Two km past Caldana, turn at the sign for Montebelli and follow the dirt road to the end.

MONTEBELLI
Hosts: Carla & Lorenzo Tosi
Localita: Molinetto
Caldana (GR) 58020, Italy
Tel: (0566) 887100, Fax: (0566) 81439
21 rooms with private bathrooms
Lire 100,000–160,000 per person half board
2-night minimum stay, 1 week high season
All meals served
Open all year, Credit cards: all major
English spoken well, Region: Tuscany

The quaint village of Calvi is just on the border between the regions of Lazio and Umbria and conveniently located at 15 kilometers from the autostrada and 70 kilometers from Rome. Sandro and his charming wife, Louise from Sweden, divide their time between Rome and the countryside where their farm's activities include production of wine and olive oil and horse breeding. The fascinating family residence in town is an historic palazzo dating back to the 15th century filled with period furniture, paintings, and frescoed ceilings. From their windows they look onto the bright yellow farmhouse where hospitality is offered within five comfortable apartments. Accommodations on the first and second floors are a combination of one or two bedrooms, living room with fireplace, fully equipped kitchen, and bathroom. The house has recently been restored with new bathrooms and tiled floors while maintaining original beamed ceilings and a country flavor in furnishings. Fresh fixings for breakfast are left for guests in the apartments. Besides wandering around the many villages of the Sabina area, you can conveniently visit Orvieto, Todi, and Spoleto, under an hour away, or relax by the pool overlooking the beautiful hillside. *Directions*: Leave the Rome-Firenze autostrada A1 at Magliano Sabina. After Magliano, follow signs for Calvi. In town ask for Via Roma.

CASALE SAN MARTINO
Hosts: Louise & Sandro Calza Bini
Via Roma 2a
Calvi (TR) 05032, Italy
Tel: (0744) 710644 or (0368) 435100, Fax: none
www.karenbrown.com\italy\casalesanmartino.html
5 apartments for 2 to 6 persons
Lire 80,000–220,000 daily per apartment
Weekly stay required July & August
2-day minimum stay, No meals served
Open March to December
English spoken well, Region: Umbria

For those who have a passion for horseback riding, or with an urge to learn, La Mandria provides the opportunity to do either while on holiday. Host and horseman Davide Felice Aondio's horse farm has been in existence for over 35 years and has been a model for riding resorts. Situated near the foothills of the Alps and between the cities of Turin and Milan, the vast, flat property borders a 5,000-hectare national park, offering spectacular scenery and endless possibilities for horseback excursions. The complex is made up of horse stables, indoor/outdoor ring, haylofts, guestrooms, dining room, and the private homes of the proprietor and his son, Marco's, family. The whole forms a square with riding rings in the center. As a national equestrian training center, lessons of every nature are offered for all ages. Six very basic bedrooms with bath are reserved for guests, and good local fare is served in the rustic dining room. Golf, swimming, and tennis facilities are available nearby. Two side trips that must not be missed are first, to lovely Lake Maggiore, and then to the intriguing medieval town of Ricetto where the houses and streets are made of smooth stones. *Directions*: Take the Carisio exit from the Milan-Turin autostrada. Head toward Biella, but at the town of Candelo turn right for Mottalciata. Mandria is on the right.

LA MANDRIA
Hosts: Marco Aondio family
Candelo (VC) 13062, Italy
Tel & fax: (015) 2536078
www.karenbrown.com\italy\lamandria.html
6 rooms with private bathrooms
Lire 120,000 double B&B
  100,000 per person half board
All meals served
Open all year
English spoken well, Region: Piedmont

Poetically named after a classic Italian tale by Cesare Pavese, a native of this area, the *Luna e i Falo* (meaning the moon and the fire) farmhouse was lovingly restored by Turin couple Ester and Franco Carnero. The ritual described in the story is still performed in August every year when local farmers burn old grapevines under the full moon in hopes of a good crop. On that night, the bonfires dotting hills surrounding the farm create quite a spectacle. The Carneros' brick home has arched windows and an arcaded front terrace, with three double or triple rooms and one apartment for four persons within the villa which they have made available to visitors. For a country home, the spacious living/dining area is elaborately furnished with Renaissance period pieces. The bedrooms reveal a combination of old and new decor and sweeping views of the countryside, known for its wineries. The emphasis at the Luna e i Falo is on the cuisine: the proprietors previously owned a highly regarded restaurant in Turin, and continue to practice their culinary skills, producing delicacies such as excellent handmade pastas. *Directions*: From Asti follow the signs for Canelli and, before town, take a right up the hill to Castello Gancia. The farmhouse is on the right after Aie.

LA LUNA E I FALO
Hosts: Ester & Franco Carnero
Localita Aie 37, Canelli (AT) 14053, Italy
Tel: (0141) 831643, Fax: (0141) 823209
www.karenbrown.com\italy\lalunaifalo.html
3 rooms with private bathrooms
1 apartment for 4 persons
Lire 150,000 double B&B
  120,000 per person half board
2-day minimum stay
Breakfast & dinner served
Open all year
No English spoken (French), Region: Piedmont

North of Florence between Prato and Pistoia is a pocket of little-known, yet entrancing countryside comprising the Calvana mountains and Bisenzio valley. Grazia, Mario, and their three children have lived there all their lives and love sharing their enthusiasm for the area by offering accommodation to visitors. Although access to the rather plain-looking house is by a congested side entrance, the property is beautifully situated overlooking a wooded valley and private lake at the back. What really counts here is the hosts' warmth and their sincere effort to make their guests feel at home. The bedrooms for two to three persons with accompanying immaculate baths are sweet and simple, decorated with comfortable, old-fashioned furniture. Guests convene downstairs for breakfast and dinner in the rustic dining room with exposed beams and fireplace. Off the dining room is the kitchen, where you can watch fresh pasta being rolled out for meals which reflect the influence of the bordering regions of Tuscany and Emilia. A visit to the welcoming Ponte alla Villa offers an opportunity to familiarize yourself with the customs of an area off the beaten track. *Directions*: From Prato, take route 325 north for 25 km to Vernio, then bear left toward Cantagallo. Watch for signs for the bed and breakfast at Luicciana.

PONTE ALLA VILLA
Hosts: Grazia Gori & Mario Michelagnoli
Localita: Luicciana 273-La Villa
Cantagallo (FI) 50040, Italy
Tel: (0574) 956094 or 956244, Fax: none
8 rooms with private bathrooms
Lire 70,000 double B&B (2-day minimum stay)
* 60,000 per person half board*
All meals served
Open all year—weekends only during winter
Very little English spoken, Region: Tuscany

La Minerva is located in a quiet section of Capri, slightly off the beaten track, yet still quite central, permitting easy access to the more bustling areas of town—a walker's paradise with no motorized transportation allowed. The street-level entrance is the hotel's third-floor living room, a vast chamber with stark-white tiled floors and ground-to-ceiling windows overlooking the sea. This captivating view will strike you every time you come and go, or eat breakfast, as the same panorama greets you in the dining room. The rest of the small hotel is beneath, with the reception and breakfast area on the ground floor. Signora Esposito has decorated the 18 rooms sweetly and simply with colorful tiled floors and scattered antiques. Each bedroom has a private balcony overlooking umbrella-pine woods and the sea. All rooms also have their own bath, done in blue and white tile. The family lives in one section of the building, but share with guests their homey living room, with family photos and lace doilies on the tables. This is a peaceful spot to get away, but not too far away. *Directions*: It's best to stop by the tourist office as you get off the ferry and get a map of Capri, showing the Via Occhio Marino.

LA MINERVA
Hosts: Luigi Esposito family
Via Occhio Marino 8
Capri (NA) 80073, Italy
Tel: (081) 8377067, Fax: (081) 8375221
18 rooms with private bathrooms
Lire 180,000–210,000 double B&B
Breakfast only
Open Easter to October
Credit cards: all major
Some English spoken, Region: Campania

The Villa Krupp is a pleasant small hotel whose claim to local fame can be found in its guest book, boasting such illustrious names as Lenin and Gorky. Signor Coppola, the cordial and proud proprietor, took over the property in 1964. The charming hotel contains 12 bedrooms, each with its own bath, in a somewhat modern and boxy building alongside the host's own residence. The Krupp is dramatically situated in one of the most beautiful corners of Capri's Augusto Park, atop a steep, sheer cliff dropping to the sparkling turquoise sea beneath. The site overlooks the Faraglioni rock formation (a symbol of the island) and Marina Piccola, one of Capri's two ports. A thousand steps lead from its top edge down to the seaside. The Villa Krupp has its own set of steps leading up to the best vantage point from which to admire this spectacular panorama. The light-filled guestrooms, each featuring its own terrace and bath, are decorated with simple antiques and tiled with the brightly colored ceramics typical of Capri. Room number 18 is a particular favorite due to its relatively large sea-view terrace. Breakfast is served on the veranda or outside on the flowered terrace. *Directions:* Take the cable car up to Capri, walk through the main square, then down the Via Emanuele to Matteotti (on the right).

VILLA KRUPP
Hosts: Coppola family
Viale Matteotti 12
Capri (NA) 80073, Italy
Tel: (081) 8370362 or 8377473
Fax: (081) 8376489
12 rooms with private bathrooms
Lire 170,000–230,000 double B&B
Breakfast only
Open all year
Some English spoken, Region: Campania

Capri has long had a reputation for being an exclusive island and with prices substantially higher than the rest of the country, only the elite were able to afford to vacation there. However, the cost of tourism across Italy has soared, bringing other destinations more in line with Capri in terms of expense, therefore making it relatively more affordable than it once was. Unfortunately, agritourism does not exist on the island, but there are several small, family-run hotels that provide a bed-and-breakfast "feeling." One such establishment belongs to Antonino Vuotto and his wife, a local couple who have opened up their centrally located, prim white home in the town of Capri, making four bedrooms available to guests. The rooms are very clean and neat, with typically tiled floors, and private baths and balconies in each. Some even have a view of the sea. Breakfast is not served because there are no common rooms for guests. The Villa's convenient location makes it easy to get to any of Capri's fine restaurants for breakfast, lunch and dinner. *Directions*: Take the cable car up to Capri. Go through the main town square to Via Emanuele, past the Quisisana Hotel and continue to the end of the street. Turn left onto Via Certosa, then left again on Cerio. The Villa is on the corner and is not marked with a sign.

VILLA VUOTTO
Hosts: Antonino Vuotto family
Via Campo di Teste 2
Capri (NA) 80073, Italy
Tel: (081) 8370230, Fax: none
4 rooms with private bathrooms
Lire 120,000 double (no breakfast)
No meals served
Open all year
Very little English spoken, Region: Campania

The Ombria farmhouse nestles amidst the foothills just 30 kilometers from both beautifully austere Bergamo and Lecco on Lake Como. Bed-and-breakfast/restaurant activity in this 1613 stone house began after meticulous restoration by owner Luciano Marchesin, who has just retired, leaving the business in the capable hands of the Vergani brothers, part of his staff from the beginning. An arched entryway leads into a stone courtyard with gazebo and open grill, where tables are set for summer meals. The Ombria is well known for its exceptional restaurant where locals enjoy candlelit regional cuisine at long tables in the intimate stone-walled dining room—as long as they make reservations three months in advance! For those retiring to bed early, it would be best to avoid weekends. The spacious doubles, which accommodate up to four persons, are decorated with country antiques and wrought-iron beds. Original fireplace, exposed beams, warm wood floors, and stone walls make them very appealing and cozy. Special attention has been given to bathrooms which are beautifully tiled and rather luxurious. Readers give Ombria a high rating. *Directions*: From autostrada A4, exit at Dalmine and follow signs for Lecco on route 36. After Pontida, turn right at the sign for Celana and continue on to Celana, then Ombria (total 15 km).

OMBRIA
Hosts: Alberto & Giuseppe Vergani
Localita: Celana
Caprino Bergamasco
(BG) 24030, Italy
Tel & fax: (035) 781668
www.karenbrown.com\italy\ombria.html
3 rooms with private bathrooms
Lire 95,000 per person half board
Breakfast & dinner served
Open all year
Some English spoken, Region: Lombardy

After 20 years of managing guided tours throughout Italy, Welsh-born Maureen, along with her architect husband, Roberto, has literally brought her expertise "home" to their newly opened "Torretta." Restoration work on the three-story 15th-century building, tucked away on a narrow cobblestoned street of this charming village, began just last year. The entrance stairway leads to a large open and cozy living room with fireplace off which all seven bedrooms lead. Beamed rooms are individually decorated with a mix of country furnishings and pretty floral bedspreads, and each has an en-suite bathroom and marvelous views over the terra-cotta-tiled rooftops of medieval Casperia. Breakfast and dinner upon request are served upstairs in the family's mansard living room with a set of three enormous beams cutting across the room, open kitchen, and terrace looking up to the wooded Sabine mountain range. This virgin territory is filled with hilltop villages to explore, besides being on the border of Umbria and a 45-minute train ride from Rome. Delightful hostess Maureen and daughter, Kathleen, also a top-rated guide, customize itineraries for their guests, while Roberto specializes in ancient Roman architecture and archaeology. You are in good hands! *Directions*: Coming from Rome, exit at Fiano Romano from autostrada A1 and continue in the direction of Passo Corese, Cantalupo, and Casperia. The village is closed to traffic and accessible by foot only.

A TORRETTA   New
Hosts: Maureen & Roberto Scheda
Via Mazzini 7
Casperia (RI) 02041, Italy
Tel & fax: (0765) 514640
7 rooms with private bathrooms
Lire 130,000 double B&B
2-day minimum stay
Breakfast & occasional dinner served
Open all year
English spoken fluently, Region: Lazio

A stay at the Villa Aureli with Count and Contessa di Serego Alighieri (descendants of Dante) can only be memorable. With its back to the town and looking out over the Italian Renaissance garden and surrounding countryside, the imposing brick villa has been standing for the past 300 years. When it was bought by the di Serego family in the 18th century, it was meticulously restored and embellished with plasterwork, decorative painted ceilings, richly painted fabrics on walls, ornately framed paintings and prints, colorful tiles from Naples, and Umbrian antiques. Left intentionally intact by the Count, who disdains overly restored historical homes, the elegant apartments for guests maintain their original ambiance. They can accommodate from four to six persons and are spacious, having numerous sitting rooms with fireplaces. A small swimming pool set against the villa's stone walls is a refreshing spot for dreaming. The villa serves as an ideal base from which to explore Umbria and parts of Tuscany, as well as special local itineraries prepared by the Count. *Directions*: Exit from the Perugia highway at Madonna Alta and follow route 220 for Citta della Pieve. After 6 km, take the left for Castel del Piano.

VILLA AURELI
Hosts: Leonardo di Serego Alighieri family
Via Cirenei 70
Castel del Piano Umbro (PG) 06071, Italy
Tel & fax: (075) 774141 or Tel: (075) 5736707
2 apartments
Lire 1,400,000–2,150,000 weekly
No meals served
Open all year
English spoken well, Region: Umbria

What a pleasant surprise to discover the Solarola, a sunny yellow villa as its name implies, in the flat countryside around Bologna. It is, in a word "perfect." Gracious hosts Antonella and Valentino (a renowned architect), took over the family farm several years ago, transforming one of its two turn-of-the-century villas into a private home and the other into a guesthouse with five double rooms, a restaurant, living room, billiard room, and outdoor gazebo, and beautiful swimming pool. Ten more rooms with air conditioning were opened after that in the former barn directly in front with downstairs living room and library. Antonella decorated the guest villas to be romantic and refined, yet warm and inviting. Each room is named after a flower and everything from wallpaper, botanical prints, and fluffy comforters to motifs on lampshades and bed frames, bouquets, and even room fragrance conform to the floral theme. Victoriana abounds in details such as cupboards filled with china, lace curtains and doilies, dried-flower bouquets, old family photos, and Tiffany lamps. In addition, Antonella is known for her refined cuisine (Michelin rated), creating inventive combinations with the freshest of ingredients. *Directions*: Exit from autostrada A14 at Castel S. Pietro and turn right towards Medicina for 5 km. Turn right at Via S. Paolo, follow the road to the end then turn left on Via S. Croce to Solarola.

LOCANDA SOLAROLA
Hosts: Antonella Scardovi & Valentino Parmiani
Via San Croce 5
Castel Guelfo (BO) 40023, Italy
Tel: (0542) 670102 or 670089, Fax: (0542) 670222
www.karenbrown.com\italy\locandasolarola.html
15 doubles with private bathrooms
Lire 280,000–300,000 double B&B
All meals served
Open all year, Credit cards: all major
Some English spoken, Region: Emilia-Romagna

The Villa Gaidello farm has been written up on several occasions (in *Bon Appetit, Cuisine, Eating in Italy*), mostly as a result of its superb cuisine. There is nothing extravagant about hostess Paola Bini's recipes, carefully prepared by local women. Rather, the secret to her success seems to lie in the revival of basic traditional dishes using the freshest possible ingredients. Pasta is made daily (a great treat to watch) and features all the local variations on tagliatelle, pappardelle, and stricchettoni. Reservations for dinner must be made several days in advance. Paola is one of the pioneers in agritourism, transforming her grandmother's nearly 200-year-old farmhouse into a guest house and restaurant 20 years ago. One to five guests are accommodated in each of the three suites, which include kitchen and sitting room. The suites are cozy and rustic with exposed-brick walls, country antiques, and lace curtains. The dining room, set with doilies and ceramic, is situated in the converted hayloft and overlooks the vast garden and a small pond. The Gaidello provides a convenient stopover just off the Bologna-Milan autostrada. *Directions*: Exit the A1 autostrada at Modena Nord (or Bologna Nord from the south). Follow Via Emilia/route 9 towards Castelfranco. Turn left on Via Costa (hospital) and follow signs to Gaidello.

VILLA GAIDELLO
Hostess: Paola Bini
Via Gaidello 18
Castelfranco Emilia (MO) 41013, Italy
Tel: (059) 926806, Fax: (059) 926620
www.karenbrown.com\italy\villagaidello.html
3 suites with private bathrooms
Lire 190,000 double B&B
All meals served
Closed August, restaurant closed Sundays
Credit cards: all major
Very little English spoken, Region: Emilia-Romagna

A really unique stay involving an exceptional culinary experience can be found at the Borgo Villa a Sesta, a complete medieval stone village in the middle of the beautiful countryside of Chianti. The estate produces Chianti wines and olive oil, and offers seven lovely apartments of various sizes within the village. They are all well furnished with a mix of antiques and contain one or two bedrooms, new bathroom, living room, and fully equipped kitchen. Four are situated in a three-story brick house overlooking the vineyards and swimming pool. What really makes the stay here so special is a meal at the nearby Bottega del'30, an intimate eight-table restaurant, well known for its superior cuisine—the two establishments work hand in hand. A meal at Bottega del'30, run by energetic and congenial hosts, Franco Camelia and French-born Helene Stoquelet, is sure to be a memorable event. They have spent the past year developing their newly opened Tuscan cooking school, with both an authentic country kitchen and a fully equipped modern kitchen, which is truly impressive. A lovely dining room with long wood table is where everyone joins together for lunch after a lesson (available weekly or daily). Not to be missed! *Directions*: From Siena on route 73 exit at Castelnuovo Berardenga. Pass the town and continue for San Gusme. Villa a Sesta is on the left 2 km after the turnoff for San Gusme.

BORGO VILLA A SESTA
Host: Oskar Sigrist
Localita: Villa a Sesta
Castelnuovo Berardenga (SI) 53019, Italy
Tel: (0577) 734064, Fax: (0577) 734066
7 apartments for 2 to 6 persons
Lire 180,000–320,000 per apartment
3-day minimum stay, 1 week July & August
Lunch with cooking school, dinner at Bottega del'30
Open all year
Some English spoken, Region: Tuscany

While roving our way back to Umbria from the Adriatic coast through picture-perfect landscapes, we came upon the Giardino degli Ulivi bed and breakfast and were immediately intrigued. The absolutely charming accommodation is actually part of a 12th-century stone village and faces out to the rolling hills splashed with bright patches of yellow sunflowers and backed by a mountainside. The scenery per se is enough to leave one in awe, let alone Maria Pia's marvelous cuisine with its Michelin rating. The carefully restored building, left ingeniously intact, thanks to her architect husband, Sante, includes the stone-walled restaurant downstairs with its many intimate nooks, centered around the ancient wine-making press. The five bedrooms upstairs off two sitting rooms with fireplace have wrought-iron beds, antique bedside tables, and beamed ceilings. The favorite corner bedroom (at a higher rate) has a large arched window taking in the breathtaking view. While their son, Francesco, tends to the breeding of horses, daughter Raffaele assists guests with the many interesting itineraries in the area (Camerino, San Severino, Matelica, and Fariano—famous for its paper industry). A real sense of discovery is experienced in this authentic region which has been able to keep traditions and folklore intact. *Directions*: From Castelraimondo follow route 256 towards Matelica, turning at the first left for Castel S. Maria then Castel S. Angelo.

IL GIARDINO DEGLI ULIVI
Hosts: Sante Cioccoloni family
Localita: Castel S. Angelo
Castelraimondo (MC) 62022, Italy
Tel & fax: (0737) 642121 or (0737) 640441
5 rooms with private bathrooms
Lire 110,000–150,000 double B&B
  Reduced rates for stays of 3 or more days
All meals served
Closed 2 weeks November, Credit cards: AX, VS
English spoken well, Region: Marches

To the west of Cortina, the most fashionable ski area in the Dolomites, is Val Gardena, which is almost too storybook perfect to be true. The valley, once part of Austria, still preserves its Germanic heritage in its language, cuisine, and culture. This adorable bed and breakfast is owned and run by a young local couple with four children. The crisp white house with its old stone-and-wood attached barn has been in the same family for over 400 years and was recently renovated, giving the property a fresh new look. The entrance foyer walls are adorned with antique farm tools, harnesses, and cow bells. On the same floor is a dining room with individual tables where guests enjoy breakfast with a view of the velvet green hillside. The five guestrooms, all but one with private bath, are simply and comfortably furnished with pinewood beds and armoires, bright-orange curtains, and fluffy comforters. Stepping out on the balcony reveals a breathtaking panorama of the pine-covered mountains. The Riers are happy to suggest scenic places to explore by car or on foot, and know the best places for rock climbing up into one of the most spectacular ranges in Europe. *Directions*: Exit at Bolzano Nord from the Verona-Brennero autostrada and follow signs for Siusi. Beyond town, before Castelrotto, turn right for Alps, then left for Marmsolerhof.

MARMSOLERHOF
Hosts: August Rier family
San Valentino 35
Castelrotto (BZ) 39040, Italy
Tel: (0471) 706514, Fax: none
5 rooms, 4 with private bathrooms
Lire 60,000 double B&B
Breakfast only
Open all year
Very little English spoken (German)
Region: Trentino-Alto Adige

Tucked away off a winding mountain road in the enchanting Siusi Alps is a typical Tyrolean farmhouse, called *mas* in this northern region of Alto Adige. The Jaider family has resided here ever since the 15th century, traditionally maintaining a dairy farm. Their inviting home is colorfully accented with green shutters and flower-laden boxes at every window. Two wooden barns are connected to the residence via a stone terrace. Signora Jaider runs her home with the hotel efficiency which has come to be expected by visitors to this predominantly German-speaking area, once belonging to Austria. Meals are served out on the terrace in clement weather, or in the original dining room, whose charm is enhanced by the low, wood paneled ceiling (so constructed to retain heat) with its hand-painted edelweiss flowers. Cuisine in this region reflects its Austrian heritage, with *speck* ham, meat and potatoes, and apple strudel winning over pasta dishes. Lovely country antiques are dispersed throughout the house and the eight bedrooms, which are wood-paneled from floor to ceiling and have pretty valley views. Two guestrooms include balconies. *Directions*: Exit at Bolzano Nord from autostrada A22, following signs for Fie and Alpe di Siusi. Pass through Siusi and turn off to the left for Tisana. San Osvaldo is on the left after Tisana.

TSCHOTSCHERHOF
Hosts: Jaider family
San Osvaldo 19
Castelrotto (BZ) 39040, Italy
Tel: (0471) 706013, Fax: none
8 rooms with private bathrooms
Lire 75,000 double B&B
* 55,000 per person half board*
All meals served
Open March to October
Very little English spoken (German)
Region: Trentino-Alto Adige

Liguria is the sliver of a region touching France and boasting the Italian Riviera with its port towns of Portofino, Santa Margherita, San Remo, and Cinque Terre. From the busy coastal town of Sestri Levante, an 8-kilometer rough and winding road leads up a mountain to the rather remote but serene Monte Pu farm, where Aurora and Pino migrated from Milan. The three-story, peach-color brick farmhouse complex, dating from 1400, commands a marvelous sweeping view over wooded mountains and valleys down to the sea. The guestrooms, a combination of triples and quads, are simple and immaculate, with light-pine furniture and wildflower bouquets. Downstairs is the warm and airy dining room where a full country breakfast awaits guests each morning. Dinner, prepared by a local woman, is served outside in the courtyard in warmer months. The culinary emphasis is on vegetarian dishes such as risotto, soups, and salads, prepared with ingredients straight from the garden. Horses are available for riding in the forest preserves surrounding the property. Aurora and Pino take time from their busy schedule of running the farm and looking after a new baby to assist guests with itineraries. *Directions*: Exit from the Genova-Livorno autostrada at Sestri Levante and follow signs for Casarza Ligure. After town turn right for Campegli Massaco and then onward to Monte Pu.

MONTE PU
Hostess: Aurora Giani
Castiglione Chiavarese (GE) 16030, Italy
Tel & fax: (0185) 408027
www.karenbrown.com\italy\montepu.html
9 rooms, 5 with private bathrooms
1 apartment
Lire 120,000 double B&B
* 85,000 per person half board*
All meals served
Open Easter to December
English spoken well, Region: Liguria

Five years ago Michela and Paolo, an enterprising host of American descent, bought and restored a small roadside hotel and transformed it into a pleasant bed and breakfast. A part of the pale-yellow house with brick trim is reserved for themselves, leaving 11 rooms for guests. With floral bedspreads and matching beds and armoires, each bedroom has its own bathroom. Downstairs to the left of the reception area is a large restaurant specializing in typical Tuscan fare. Divided by a brick archway, it has a bar and is adorned with colorful ceramic plates from Deruta. Paolo gets very involved with his guests, helping to plan individualized itineraries between Tuscany and Umbria. In the evening guests and many locals come back to either a wine-tasting or cocktail hour before settling down to a meal. Although on the road just before town, without any outdoor space for lounging, this is an excellently located stopover with easy access to the autostrada. *Directions*: Exit at Chianciano and follow signs to Chiusi. La Querce comes up quickly on the left-hand side.

LA QUERCE   New
Hosts: Michela & Paolo Bartolozzi
Localita: Querce al Pino 41
Chiusi (SI) 53043, Italy
Tel: (0578) 274308, Fax: (0578) 274449
E-mail: la querce@krenet.it
11 rooms with private bathrooms
Lire 96,000–126,000 double B&B
All meals served
Restaurant closed Wednesdays
Open all year
Credit cards: all major
English spoken fluently, Region: Tuscany

We were delighted to hear that one of our favorite bed-and-breakfast hostesses, the delightful Stella Casolaro, has started another bed and breakfast in her new home after having sold the Scuderia in Badia di Passignano. If you were ever one of her fortunate guests, you would understand why travelers come back and stay with her year after year. Her new location, 35 kilometers west of Siena, is in the lesser-known, more rugged part of the Tuscan countryside. In fact, much to the delight of husband, Carlo, who has a passion for hunting for porcini mushrooms, dense woods cover the entire area. Not to be missed are the mystic ruins of San Galgamo cathedral. The white 60-year-old house with encircling garden is right on the edge of the quaint village of Ciciano. Three sweet bedrooms, each with its own bathroom (two just outside the room), and a living room have been reserved for guests on the couple's second floor, while they reside on the third floor. All rooms have a double wrought-iron bed with a variety of country antiques in keeping with the simple yet homey ambiance. At just 2 kilometers from the home is Stella's miniature restaurant, Il Minestraio, where she shows off her talent for pasta and soup dishes. It's like "coming home." *Directions*: From Siena, take route 73 towards Grosseto. After Frosini, turn off to the right for Chiusdino, then Ciciano. Ciciano is 45 km from the seaside.

CASA ITALIA
Hosts: Stella & Carlo Casolaro
Via Massetana 5
Ciciano-Chiusdino (SI) 53010, Italy
Tel: (0577) 750656, Fax: none
3 rooms with private bathrooms
Lire 90,000 double (no breakfast)
Lunch & dinner served in restaurant
Open all year
No English spoken, Region: Tuscany

In the hills of western Umbria bordering Tuscany and overlooking the Tiber and Chiana valleys, is the typical farm property of the Nannotti family. Renato and Maria Teresa used to run a restaurant nearby and seven years ago decided to open a bed and breakfast and serve delicious Tuscan-Umbrian recipes directly at home. The two adjacent red-stone houses include seven guestrooms, one apartment, and the family's private quarters. Two of the ground-floor rooms take in the splendid view, another has an upstairs terrace, and all are decorated in a simple and pleasant country style with antique armoires and wrought-iron beds. Renato specializes in organic produce and makes his own wine and oil, which are brought directly to the dining room table or served out under the porch. Maria Teresa makes sure her guests feel right at home by creating an easy, informal ambiance. Young daughter, Aureliana, along with her two brothers, all help out. Being just a kilometer from the charming village and having easy access to the autostrada dividing the two regions make this a winner touring location. There are also bikes, a park for children, many farm animals, and horses to ride. *Directions*: Exit at Chiusi from the north or Fabro from the south and follow signs for Citta della Pieve. In town follow signs for Ponticelli—the bed and breakfast is well marked before this town.

MADONNA DELLE GRAZIE   **New**
Hosts: Nannotti family
Via Madonna delle Grazie 6
Citta della Pieve (PG) 06062, Italy
Tel & fax: (0578) 299822
7 rooms with private bathrooms
1 apartment
Lire 75,000–85,000 per person half board
Breakfast & dinner served
Open all year
Some English spoken, Region: Umbria

British expatriate Dawne Alstrom finally found the farmhouse property of her dreams five years ago and immediately set about organizing major restoration work on the crumbling stone house—last year the ground floor was completed in record time and the final results are indeed splendid. Dawne's organizing skills learned in film production enabled her to coordinate the various artisans quite naturally, and her years of stylist experience were put to use in ingenious decorating, incorporating fireplaces and antique pieces she bought to create an authentic Italian country home. Two lovely luminous bedrooms with large bathrooms are located on the ground floor off the cozy living room with its music and reading library. The remaining three upstairs are also decorated with fine antiques and are all corner rooms with another sitting room, allowing privacy and total silence. The atmosphere is that of a continual house party and guests convene in the delightful country kitchen around an enormous table for delectable meals. The vineyards out back creep right up to the pool. From here Tuscany, Umbria, and unusual "backroad" local attractions are all at your fingertips. Truly special. *Directions*: From Rome leave the A1 autostrada at Attigliano and head towards Bomarzo, turning right on a road parallel to the autostrada for Civitella and Castiglione. Take a left turn towards Civitella and before town take Via Ombricolo on the left. The house's gate is second on the left.

L'OMBRICOLO
Hostess: Dawne Alstrom-Viotti
Via Ombricolo
Civitella d'Agliano (VT) 01020, Italy
Tel & fax: (0761) 914735
www.karenbrown.com\italy\lombricolo.html
5 rooms with private bathrooms
Lire 180,000 double B&B Lire 150,000 per person half board
Breakfast & dinner served
Open all year, Credit cards: MC, VS
Fluent English spoken, Region: Lazio

Ten years ago Rosemarie and Filippo bought and restored the elegant 16th-century Villa Montesolare (sun colored as its name implies), opening its doors to guests. Crowning a summit in unspoiled countryside (on one side—the approach side has unfortunately been invaded with new construction, invisible from the villa) between Umbria and Tuscany, just south of lovely Lake Trasimeno, the villa overlooks its surrounding estate of olive trees and vineyards. A wide gray-stone staircase leads up to the eight guestrooms and two suites, all with private bath and furnished in appropriate period style with carefully selected antiques. Five more romantic suites and five double bedrooms are located within two 17th-century farmhouses on the property. Across from the cozy bar at the entrance, where guests enjoy a cocktail before dinner, is the intimate and elegant frescoed dining room, where varied Tuscan cuisine is presented under Rosemarie's supervision. Guests are made to feel at home, whether relaxing in the impressive powder-blue upstairs salon with glass chandelier and massive stone fireplace, or wandering through the Italian Renaissance lemon-tree garden. Classical music concerts are hosted in the summer months. Other activities include tennis, horseback riding, or swimming in one of the two lovely hillside pools. *Directions*: From Perugia take N220 toward Citta di Pieve. After Fontignano (3 km), turn right at San Paolo to the villa (4 km).

VILLA DI MONTESOLARE
Hosts: Rosemarie & Filippo Strunk Iannarone
Localita: Colle San Paolo
Panicale (PG) 06064, Italy
Tel: (075) 832376, Fax: (075) 8355462
www.karenbrown.com\italy\ villadimontesolare.html
13 rooms & 7 suites with private bathrooms
Lire 200,000–240,000 double B&B
* 135,000–155,000 per person half board*
Breakfast & dinner served
Open all year, Credit cards: MC, VS
English spoken very well, Region: Umbria

For British couple, Scarlett and Colin, the fantasy of restoring a farmhouse in the hills of Tuscany and blending into the slower-paced life of local farmers became reality eight years ago when they found the property of their dreams. Remotely set amongst the lush green mountains separating Tuscany and Umbria, the ancient stone farmhouse was meticulously restored and tastefully appointed with country antiques and matching fabrics. Within are the hosts' quarters plus two lovely guestrooms on the first floor. Scarlett, an excellent cook, prepares light lunches or, by prior arrangement, dinners accompanied by top-choice local wines. Two kilometers away is a four-bedroom residence that the couple rents out weekly. This is an ideal place for those who like to combine leisurely local touring with pure relaxation, taking advantage of the lovely swimming pool with the most incredible views over the valley. *Directions*: Exit from the A1 autostrada at Val di Chiana and follow the highway towards Perugia. Exit at the second turnoff for Cortona, pass the city, and continue for Citta del Castello on a small winding road. After 5 km turn left at Portole and call the hotel for instructions on how to find the unmarked dirt road to the house. Thirty minutes from Cortona.

STOPPIACCE
Hosts: Scarlett & Colin Campbell
Localita: San Pietro a Dame
Cortona (AR) 52044, Italy
Tel & fax: (0575) 690058
www.karenbrown.com\italy\stoppiacce.html
2 bedrooms with private bathrooms
1 house (4 bedrooms)
Lire 170,000 double B&B
  1,200,000–2,200,000 weekly (house)
2-day minimum stay
Breakfast served—lunch & dinner upon request
Open all year
Fluent English spoken, Region: Tuscany

The Antica Fattoria came highly recommended by several readers who stayed there in the first year it opened. It is indeed a delightful combination of pretty countryside, strategic touring position, comfortable rooms, excellent meals, and warm hospitality. Following the increasingly popular lifestyle trend of abandoning the city for a rural pace, Roman couple Alessandro and Anna left their offices to become, essentially, farmers. They bought and restored two connected stone farmhouses and incorporated seven rooms, decorated pleasantly with a characteristic country flavor, for guests. While Alessandro tends to the crops, Anna lives out her passion for cooking, much to guests' delight. Meals are served either outside at one long table or in the transformed horse stalls below with cozy sitting area and fireplace. At times the *allegria* and good food keep guests at the table until the wee hours. A lovely swimming pool looks over the wooded hills to the valley. The busy hosts take time to assist guests with the many local itineraries and organize a wide variety of games. Perfect for families and a great base for exploring Umbria. The town of Deruta is world famous for its painted ceramic pottery and is lined with shop after shop. *Directions*: From Perugia (18 km), exit from route 3bis at Casalina. Take the first right and follow signs to the Fattoria.

ANTICA FATTORIA DEL COLLE
Hosts: Anna & Alessandro Coluccelli
Strada Colle delle Forche 6
Deruta (PG) 06053, Italy
Tel & fax: (075) 972201
www.karenbrown.com\italy\anticafattoriadelcolle.html
7 rooms with private bathrooms
Lire 110,000 double B&B (low season only)
 105,000–115,000 per person half board (June to September)
1-week minimum stay July & August
All meals served
Open all year
English spoken well, Region: Umbria

An excellent choice as a base for visiting the villas of Palladio and the stunning historical centers of Verona and Padova (plus being 20 minutes from Venice), is the newly opened Villa Goetzen. With a long tradition in hospitality, the local Minchio family bought the peach-colored home (dating from 1739) sitting on the Brenta Canal in town, and transformed it into an elegant bed and breakfast accommodation. Although bordering the main road, silence reigns within. One enters the iron gates into a courtyard, where on the right is a miniature coachhouse with two of the twelve rooms. These are the favorites and most romantic, with beamed mansard ceilings, parquet floors, and canal view. All rooms are decorated with classic good taste in the selection of antique pieces, wrought-iron beds, and coordination of fabrics and individual color schemes. Immaculate bathrooms have black-and white checked tiles. Fortunate guests can sample delectable Venetian meals prepared by Paola and her son, Massimiliano, in one of the three intimate dining rooms. Brother Cristian receives guests and attends to their needs with great charm and finesse. It would be virtually impossible to find a hotel with similar standards in Venice at this rate. *Directions*: Exit at Dolo from the A4 autostrada and go straight into town until you arrive at the canal. Turn left and follow signs for Venezia. The villa is on the right.

VILLA GOETZEN   *New*
Hosts: Minchio family
Via Matteotti 6
Dolo (VE) 30031, Italy
Tel: (041) 5102300, Fax: (041) 412600
12 rooms with private bathrooms
Lire 180,000 double B&B
All meals served
Open all year
Credit cards: all major
English spoken well, Region: Veneto

Picturesque Courmayeur, on the Italian side of the tunnel cutting through Mont Blanc into France, is a popular ski and summer resort. In the summer months comfortable temperatures and spectacular mountain scenery along with activities such as hiking, golf, horseback riding, and kayaking attract many visitors. The warm Berthod family have been offering hospitality to guests for some time, greeting them by name as they return "home" year after year. The old stone chalet and barn, squeezed between other houses in the center of the centuries-old village, Entreves, outside Courmayeur, has been recently restored using old and new materials. The cozy reception area maintains its original rustic flavor with flagstone floors and beams, hanging brass pots, typical locally made pine furniture, and homey touches like dried flower arrangements and lace curtains. The 23 simply appointed rooms have been divided between two buildings and offer amenities of a standard hotel. A hearty breakfast is the only meal served; however, half-board arrangements can be made with local restaurants for longer stays. La Grange is an efficiently run bed and breakfast right at the foot of the snow-capped Alps. *Directions*: From Aosta where autostrada A5 ends, continue on route 26 to Courmayeur. Entreves is 5 km beyond.

LA GRANGE
Hosts: Berthod family
Fraz. Entreves
Courmayeur (AO) 11013, Italy
Tel: (0165) 869733, Fax: (0165) 869744
www.karenbrown.com\italy\lagrange.html
23 rooms with private bathrooms
Lire 150,000–200,000 double B&B
Breakfast only
Closed: May, June, October, November
Credit cards: AX, VS
English spoken well, Region: Valle d'Aosta

Best friends Luciano, Simona, and Tommaso, refugees from city life, have over the past eight years or so transformed the 1,000-acre property, La Casella, made up of woods, rivers, and valleys, into a veritable countryside haven for vacationers. Foremost attention has been given to the 28 rooms which are divided between three separate stone houses. The *Noci* house contains seven doubles upstairs appointed with country antiques, and a large vaulted room downstairs used for small meetings or dining. *La Terrazza*, originally a hunting lodge, has nine rooms, one with namesake terrace looking over the poplar woods. On the highest point sits *San Gregorio*, with small chapel, where guests revel in the utter silence and a spectacular 360-degree view over the entire property. The lively dining room offers delectable cuisine, whose ingredients come directly from the farm. A cozy bar with stone fireplace is another favorite spot to relax. The many sports facilities include a beautiful big swimming pool, tennis, archery, and an equestrian center where many special outings and events are organized. Well marked trails lead the rider, biker, or hiker to such marvels as Todi, Orvieto, or even Perugia. *Directions*: Exit at Fabro from the Rome-Firenze A1 autostrada. Follow signs for Parrano (7 km), turning right at the Casella sign, and continue for another 7 km on a rough gravel road.

LA CASELLA
Hosts: Simona & Luciano Nenna
  Tommaso & Marta Campolmi
Localita: La Casella
Ficulle (TR) 05016, Italy
Tel: (0763) 86075, Fax: (0763) 86684
www.karenbrown.com\italy\lacasella.html
28 rooms with private bathrooms
Lire 130,000–140,000 per person half board
1-week minimum stay July & August
All meals served
Open all year Credit cards: all major
Fluent English spoken, Region: Umbria

The Hotel Aprile, owned by the Cantini Zucconi family for the past 35 years, is located in a 15th-century Medici palace behind the Piazza Santa Maria Novella, near the train station and many fine restaurants and shops. The historical building was restored under the strict ordinance of Florence's Commission of Fine Arts. The small and charming hotel is full of delightful surprises: from 16th-century paintings and a bust of the Duke of Tuscany to the frescoed breakfast room and quiet courtyard garden. The old-fashioned reception and sitting areas are invitingly furnished with Florentine Renaissance antiques, comfy, overstuffed red armchairs, and Oriental carpets worn with time. The wallpapered bedrooms include telephone and mini-bar, and feature parquet floors and high vaulted ceilings, but vary widely in their size and decor; some are too basic and modern. There are twenty-eight doubles, all now with private bathrooms after a recent restoration. Request one of the quieter rooms at the back of the hotel, overlooking the garden. At the desk is manager Roberto Gazzini looking after guests' needs. *Directions*: Use a detailed city map to locate the hotel, three blocks north of the Duomo. There is a parking garage.

HOTEL APRILE
Hosts: Valeria Cantini Zucconi family
Via della Scala 6
Florence 50123, Italy
Tel: (055) 216237, Fax: (055) 280947
28 rooms with private bathrooms
Lire 240,000 double B&B
Breakfast only
Open all year
Credit cards: all major
English spoken well, Region: Tuscany

The relaxed and friendly Ariele Hotel has been in the Bertelloni family for the past 40 years. Located in a quiet residential section across from the Opera House, it is within a short walking distance to the center of town. The entrance and reception area is made up of several old-fashioned-style sitting rooms, giving an immediate sense of the private home it used to be (dating back to 14th century). These spaces include a breakfast room and wallpapered sitting room with antique reproductions, gold velvet armchairs, fireplace, and Oriental carpets on tiled floors. A pleasant side garden with white iron-wrought tables and chairs offers a shady spot for breakfast. Hidden off in a corner is an unusual independent double room.There is also space here for parking at a minimal charge. The spacious, high-ceilinged rooms are individually decorated using a mix of old and new furnishings and have either wood parquet or marble floors. Unfortunately the fluorescent lighting does not help brighten up the sometimes drab color scheme. Guests can depend on the kind assistance of the staff for restaurant and itinerary suggestions. *Directions*: Between Piazza Vittorio Veneto and the Arno river. Use a detailed city map to locate the hotel.

HOTEL ARIELE
Hosts: Bertelloni family
Via Magenta 11
Florence 50123, Italy
Tel: (055) 211509, Fax: (055) 268521
40 rooms with private bathrooms
Lire 210,000 double B&B
Breakfast only
Open all year
Credit cards: VS
English spoken well, Region: Tuscany

The Hotel Hermitage is a dream of a small, well-manicured hotel with efficient service and breathtaking views over the city's most famous monuments. The location could not be more central—on a small street between the Uffizzi gallery and the River Arno. Housed in a 13th-century palazzo, the fifth-floor reception area looking out to the Ponte Vecchio bridge has a cozy living-room feeling with selected antique pieces, Oriental rugs, and corner fireplace. Across the hall is the veranda-like breakfast room dotted with crisp yellow tablecloths and topped with fresh flowers where privileged guests view the tower of Palazzo Signoria. Color-coordinated, separate air-conditioned rooms, some with hydrojet baths, have scattered antiques, framed etchings of the city, and more views. However, the highlight of a stay at the Hermitage is spending time dreaming on the rooftop terrace. The view embraces not only the previously mentioned marvels of Florence, but also the famous dome of the Duomo cathedral and Giotto's tower. Guests are served a Continental breakfast under the ivy-covered pergola and among the many flower-laden vases lining its borders. Reserve well in advance. *Directions*: Consult a detailed city map. There is a parking garage in the vicinity. Call for instructions as car traffic in this part of the city is strictly limited.

HOTEL HERMITAGE
Director: Vincenzo Scarcelli
Piazza del Pesce
Florence 50122, Italy
Tel: (055) 287216, Fax: (055) 212208
E-mail: hermitage@italyhotel.com
www.karenbrown.com\italy\hotelhermitage.html
29 rooms with private bathrooms
Lire 310,000 double B&B
Breakfast only
Open all year
Credit cards: MC, VS
English spoken well, Region: Tuscany

It is not hard to find accommodations in a 15th-century palace in downtown Florence; the historical center of the city has little else. The Residenza is no exception, but it features the added attraction of being situated on Florence's most elegant street, with its famous boutiques, the Tornabuoni. For the last two generations the gracious Giacalone family has owned the palazzo's top three floors and operated them as a three-star hotel. An antique mahogany elevator takes you up to the reception area, which opens onto a pretty dining room with pink tablecloths and shelves lined with a collection of bottles, vases, and ceramics. Twenty-four tastefully furnished rooms with amenities including air conditioning are divided between three floors, capped with a rooftop terrace burgeoning with flowerpots and surrounded by city views. A comfortable sitting room with high, beamed ceilings and a satellite television for guests is located on the upper floor. La Residenza is one of the few small hotels offering dinner on the premises, and Signora Gianna is justifiably proud of their reputation for serving authentic Florentine cuisine. *Directions*: Use a detailed city map to locate the hotel in the heart of Florence next to the Palazzo Strozzi.

LA RESIDENZA
Hosts: Gianna & Paolo (son) Giacalone
Via Tornabuoni 8
Florence 50123, Italy
Tel: (055) 218684, Fax: (055) 284197
24 rooms, 20 with private bathrooms
Lire 280,000 double B&B
Breakfast & dinner served
Open all year
Credit cards: all major
English spoken well, Region: Tuscany

The newly refurbished Hotel Silla is located on the left bank of the River Arno opposite Santa Croce, the famous 13th-century square and church where Michelangelo and Galileo are buried. This position offers views from some of the rooms of several of Florence's most notable architectural attractions—the Duomo, the Ponte Vecchio, and the tower of Palazzo Vecchio. Housed on the second and third floors of a lovely 15th-century palazzo with courtyard entrance, 39 very new and spotless double rooms with private baths are pleasantly decorated with simple dark-wood furniture and matching bedspreads and curtains. Air conditioning was a recently added necessity. The fancy, cream-colored reception area is appointed in 17th-century Venetian style, with period furniture, chandelier and large paintings. Breakfast is served on the splendid and spacious second-floor outdoor terrace or in the dining room overlooking the Arno. The Silla is a friendly, convenient, and quiet hotel, near the Pitti Palace, leather artisan shops, and many restaurants. It offers tourists a good value in pricey Florence. A parking garage is available. *Directions*: Refer to a detailed city map to locate the hotel.

HOTEL SILLA
Host: Gabriele Belotti
Via dei Renai 5
Florence 50125, Italy
Tel: (055) 2342888, Fax: (055) 2341437
www.karenbrown.com\italy\hotelsilla.html
39 rooms, 30 with private bathrooms
Lire 230,000 double B&B
Breakfast only
Open all year
Credit cards: all major
English spoken well, Region: Tuscany

The Hotel Splendor is exactly as its name implies—splendid. Off on a quiet side street, the Splendor manages to miss most of the city center's traffic and street noise, yet guests are still able to walk almost everywhere, since the hotel is only three blocks from the Duomo and near the Accademia museum with its *David*. The prim, centuries-old palazzo, of the pale-yellow hue characteristic of Florence, has geranium-filled boxes at every window. The ambiance is reminiscent of a time-worn elegant private home, with its frescoed foyer and sitting rooms graced with portraits, chandeliers, overstuffed armchairs, and Oriental carpets. In summer, the perfume of the family's own garden roses—found throughout the hotel—fills the air. On the second and third floors are the 31 spacious guestrooms (a few can sleep a family of four), most with air conditioning, recently redecorated with lovely matching armoires and beds in typical Florentine painted, pastel style. Perhaps the architectural highlight is the gracious breakfast room (breakfast is a superb buffet), with high ceilings, parquet floors, and frescoed panels all around. French doors lead from this area to an outdoor terrace with white iron chairs and tables where guests may take in a lovely view of San Marco church and where afternoon beverages are served. Garage service is also available at a charge. *Directions*: Rely on a detailed city map to locate the hotel.

HOTEL SPLENDOR
Hosts: Vincenzo Masoero family
Via San Gallo 30
Florence 50129, Italy
Tel: (055) 483427, Fax: (055) 461276
www.karenbrown.com\italy\hotelsplendour.html
31 rooms, 25 with private bathrooms
Lire 220,000 double B&B, 160,000 without bath
Breakfast only
Open all year Credit cards: all major
English spoken well, Region: Tuscany

On the border of Umbria and the Marches regions, within reach of the unforgettably romantic towns of Spoleto, Todi, Assisi, and Perugia, is Francesco Rambotti's 18th-century stone farmhouse, beautifully situated atop a hill overlooking the peaceful countryside. Aside from wine-producing grapes, the farm raises deer, sheep, and mountain goats, which roam freely on the property. The University of Perugia conducts research here as a model of farm activity perfectly in tune with the conservation of the environment. The tavern-like dining room has a fireplace, exposed-beamed ceiling, long wood tables, and walls lined with wine casks. Hearty regional fare is served here, complemented by the farm's own wine. Guest accommodation in the main house includes six double rooms all with private bath, or alternately, two, two-bedroom apartments with bath and kitchenette. The furnishings are spartan and utilitarian, some with bunkbeds for families, and the baths are new and immaculate. They are now producing natural creams and cosmetics at the farm using soil which is said to have been used in ancient times. This part of the country is loaded with must-see destinations, and La Valle offers an inexpensive base from which to explore them. *Directions*: From the Spoleto-Foligno road, turn right at La Valle 7 km after the town of Nocera.

VILLA DELLA CUPA
Host: Franco Rambotti
Via Colle di Nocera Umbra 141
Gaifana (PG) 06020, Italy
Tel: (0742) 810329, Fax: (0742) 810666
www.karenbrown.com\italy\villadellacupa.html
6 rooms with private bathrooms, 2 apartments
Lire 70,000–80,000 double B&B
* 65,000 per person half board*
All meals served
Open all year Credit cards: AX
Very little English spoken, Region: Umbria

The Castello di Tornano, a strategically situated hilltop tower dating back almost 1,000 years, has a 360-degree vista of the surrounding valley and has been of great historical significance in the seemingly endless territorial battles between the Siena and Florence. The current owners are the Selvolini family, whose lovely daughters, Fabiola and Barbara, opened the wine estate to guests nine years ago. Weekly stays begin with meeting other guests around the exquisite pool cut into the rock and spanned by a bridge. Eight simply appointed apartments, each with living area, kitchen, one or two bedrooms, and garden, are situated in a stone farmhouse in front of the tower. The living room in the villa is one of the common areas where guests can gather together. The *pièce de résistance*, however, is the three-floor apartment within the monumental tower, impeccably furnished in grand style and featuring three bedrooms, two living rooms with fireplace, dining room, kitchen, and tower-top terrace with a view not easily forgotten. Meals can be taken at the restaurant on the property. Tennis courts and riding facilities are now available. *Directions*: At 19 km from Siena take route 408 towards Gaiole. A sign for Tornano to the right is indicated 5 km before Gaiole.

CASTELLO DI TORNANO
Hosts: Fabiola & Barbara Selvolini
Localita: Lecchi
Gaiole in Chianti (SI) 53013, Italy
Tel: (0577) 746067 or (055) 6580918
Fax: (0577) 746094
www.karenbrown.com\italy\castelloditornano.html
9 apartments
Lire 750,000–3,700,000 (tower) weekly
Trattoria on premises
Open Easter to October & Christmas
Credit cards: AX
English spoken very well, Region: Tuscany

The heel of Italy offers a wealth of natural beauty, but, because its remoteness, few really charming places to stay. The Masseria Lo Prieno is run by the delightful Castriota family, whose crops are representative of the staples of the Apulia region, and include olives, almonds, fruits, and grains. Spartan accommodations are offered in bungalows scattered among the pine woods and palms on the family property. Each guesthouse includes two bedrooms, kitchen, bathroom, and an eating area containing basic necessities. Nine simply decorated rooms with bathrooms are now available within a newly constructed house on the property. What were formerly animal stalls have been converted into a large dining space rustically decorated with antique farm tools and brass pots. Along with warm hospitality, the family makes the kitchen's offerings a top priority and it is the food that makes the stay here special. For an exquisite and authentic traditional meal, the restaurant here is incomparable. Both Maria Grazia, the energetic daughter who runs the show, and her charming mother take pride in demonstrating how local specialties are prepared. This is a budget choice for touring this area. *Directions*: From Taranto take N174 to Galatone, then follow signs for Secli. Turn right on Via Gramsci, then left on Via San Luca. Follow signs for Lo Prieno. 80 km from Brindisi.

MASSERIA LO PRIENO
Hosts: Francesco Castriota family
Localita: Contrada Orelle
Galatone (LE) 73044, Italy
Tel & fax: (0833) 865443 or 865898
www.karenbrown.com\italy\masserialoprieno.html
5 bungalows, 9 rooms with private bathrooms
Lire 70,000 double B&B
  60,000 per person half board
Breakfast & dinner served
Open April to September
Some English spoken, Region: Apulia

For the fortunate travelers with time to explore the rich treasures of Florence and the spectacular surrounding countryside as well, innumerable surprises await them. On the extreme outskirts of the city, the Fattoressa offers the ideal location for this type of "dual" exploration. One of the many marvelous attractions of Florence is how the countryside comes right up to the doors of the city. Just behind the magnificent Certosa monastery is situated the 15th-century stone farmhouse of the delightfully congenial Fusi-Borgioli family. With loving care, they have transformed the farmer's quarters into guest accommodations: four sweetly simple bedrooms plus two triples, each with its own spotless bathroom. Angiolina and Amelio, natural bed-and-breakfast hosts, treat their guests like family and, as a result, enjoy receiving some of them year after year. The arrival of daughter-in-law, Laura, who speaks English, has been a great help in assisting guests with local itineraries. Visitors take meals *en famille* at long tables in the cozy, rustic dining room with a large stone fireplace. Here Angiolina proudly serves authentic Florentine specialties using ingredients from her own fruit orchard and vegetable garden. *Directions*: Entering Florence from the Certosa exit off the Siena superstrada, turn left one street after the Certosa Convent. After the bridge, turn right behind the building (Via Volterrana—slightly hidden). The house is just on the left.

LA FATTORESSA
Hosts: Angiolina Fusi & Amelio Borgioli
Via Volterrana 58
Galluzzo (FI) 50124, Italy
Tel & fax: (055) 2048418
www.karenbrown.com\italy\lafattoressa.html
6 rooms with private bathrooms
Lire 140,000 double B&B
Breakfast & dinner served
Open all year
English, French, & German spoken well, Region: Tuscany

A very pleasant alternative to hotels in Florence is a stay at the Milione wine estate in the hills overlooking the city. Jessica Brandimarte oversees this expansive farm property with its large olive oil and wine production as well as a successful silver-making operation, the pride of her late husband. All the sculptures seen on the property are his own creations. Rooms and apartments, many equipped with kitchenette and eating area, are divided among the main villa and another complex of stone farmhouses a short distance down the road. Those attached to the villa are decorated with lovely country antiques, terra-cotta brick floors, beamed ceilings, and dried flower bouquets. Other rooms and apartments are located in various farmers' houses on the property, with each room varying in size and décor (some very simple). Most have wonderful views over the soft hills lined with vineyards. The swimming pool is surrounded by flower-filled terra-cotta vases and bordered by a wood-paneled house with changing rooms for the convenience of guests. Dinner is served upon request, and is taken together around one long table. *Directions*: Exit from the autostrada at Certosa. Follow signs for Firenze city center and turn left at Galluzzo. Follow the road for 2 km and turn a sharp right at the sign for Giogoli Rossi Ristorante.

FATTORIA IL MILIONE
Hosts: Brandimarte family
Via di Giogoli 14
Galluzzo (FI) 50124, Italy
Tel: (055) 2048713, Fax: (055) 2048046
www.karenbrown.com\italy\fattoriailmilione.html
4 rooms with private bathrooms
5 apartments
Lire 150,000 double
3-day minimum stay
No breakfast, dinner served upon request
Open all year
English spoken well, Region: Tuscany

The Casa Nova bed and breakfast, in relation to our other more remote selections in the area, has the advantage of being on the edge of Greve, the center of the Chianti region. Although right next to the newer section of town, the large hilly property covered with vineyards seems deep in the countryside. Any new construction is absolutely invisible from the house. Sandra Taccetti and her husband offer their stone farmhouse with six bedrooms for guests, while they live in the converted barn. There is a simple and casual feel to the place and guests can be right at home in the downstairs living room with its floral-print sofas, breakfast room, or out on the back porch overlooking the garden and lush green landscape. The clean and uncluttered bedrooms, all with bathrooms except one, are appropriately decorated with country antiques. The beamed ceilings and brick floors naturally make up the rest of the decor. The two adjoining rooms with shared bathroom are ideal for a family of four, while two other doubles each have their own terrace. From Casa Nova you are equidistant to Florence and Siena. *Directions*: From Florence coming into town, turn left at the first stoplight, Via Gramsci, and follow the curve up to the left. The road ends at the house. Note: Via di Uzzano has nothing to do with signs for Castello di Uzzano.

CASA NOVA
Hostess: Sandra Taccetti
Via di Uzzano 30
Greve in Chianti (FI) 50022, Italy
Tel & fax: (055) 853459
www.karenbrown.com\italy\casanova.html
6 rooms, 5 with private bathrooms
Lire 110,000–120,000 double B&B
Breakfast only
Open all year
Very little English spoken, Region: Tuscany

An outstanding alternative to the city hotels of Venice is the perfectly charming Gargan bed and breakfast situated in the countryside just 30 kilometers from Venice. The Calzavara family renovated the family's expansive 17th-century country house and opened the restaurant and guestrooms, offering four sweetly decorated bedrooms each with its own bathroom on the top floor plus two suites consisting of two bedrooms and one bathroom. Signora Antonia enjoys making her guests feel as "at home" as possible by having fresh flowers in the cozy, antique-filled bedrooms. The downstairs sitting and dining rooms display the family's country antiques as well as a large fireplace and nice touches such as lace curtains and paintings. Guests are treated to a full breakfast of home-baked cakes and exceptional five-course dinners prepared by Renzia, a renowned chef of Treviso with her own cooking school, using all ingredients from their farm. The Gargan is an ideal choice in this area, being a short drive from such marvels as Padova, Venice, Treviso, Vicenza, Verona, and Palladian Villas plus many smaller medieval villages. *Directions*: From Venice take route 245 to Scorze, turning right for Montebelluna at the stoplight 1 km after town. After the town of S. Ambrogio turn left at the stoplight. Turn right at the church in Levada up to the house.

GARGAN
Hosts: Calzavara family
Via Marco Polo 2
Levada di Piombino Dese (PD) 35017, Italy
Tel: (049) 9350308, Fax: (049) 9350016
www.karenbrown.com\italy\gargan.html
4 rooms, 2 suites, all with private bathrooms
Lire 95,000 double B&B
  87,000 per person half board
All meals served
Open all year
Some English spoken, Region: Veneto

When Lois Martin, a retired language professor, spotted the lovely restored farmhouse at San Martino, she knew it literally had her name on it and immediately purchased it. She has been running a bed and breakfast for the past two years and offers travelers all possible amenities of home. The house is completely open to guests, from the upstairs cozy living room with large stone fireplace which divides the four bedrooms to the downstairs country kitchen and eating area. A full breakfast is served either outside on the patio or in the kitchen with its impressive display of Deruta ceramics. One bedroom with king mattress is joined by a bathroom to a small room with twin beds, ideal for a family. The other two doubles each has a bathroom, with one being en suite. Besides a swimming pool overlooking the wooded hills and valley, other extras are satellite TV, American washer and dryer, guest bathrobes, and dinner upon request, served out on the back porch where tobacco was once hung to dry. Being right on the border of Umbria and Tuscany, towns such as Gubbio, Perugia, Cortona, Assisi, Deruta, and Lake Trasimeno are all easily accessible, plus an itinerary including some ten local castles. Lois, a most accommodating hostess, is a wealth of information on the area. *Directions*: From Lisciano square, pass the bar and turn left for San Martino, continue for 2 km and take a right up the hill at the sign for San Martino for iust over 1½ km to the house.

CASA SAN MARTINO   *New*

Hostess: Lois Martin
Localita: San Martino 19
Lisciano Niccone (PG) 06060, Italy
Tel: (075) 844288, Fax: (075) 844309
www.karenbrown.com\italy\casasanmartino.html
4 rooms, 3 with private bathrooms
Lire 160,000 double B&B
2-day minimum stay
Breakfast, dinner upon request
Open all year
English spoken fluently, Region: Umbria

The Luz family of Luino (see following page) just recently refurbished another home, creating a second, more economical accommodation just 2 kilometers up the road from their hotel on Lake Maggiore. The Colmegna is run by their young and energetic daughter Lara and caters well to families. The two pale-yellow buildings run right along the waterfront bordered by an old stone port. There are several terraces for dining outdoors and another with a lawn for sunning or relaxing and enjoying the view. Beyond this is a gorgeous shaded park with romantic trails, tall trees, and wildflowers at one of the prettiest points of the lake. Simply appointed bedrooms are all situated lakeside on the two floors and accommodate from two to four persons. Swimming, sailing, and windsurfing sports can be arranged. Luino is famous for its open market on Wednesdays, a long-standing tradition since 1541. Within touring distance are the lakes of Lugano and Como, the ferry from Laveno across Lake Maggiore, and the Swiss border. *Directions*: Luino is halfway up the lake on the eastern side near the Swiss border. Heading north, Colmegna is on the left-hand side of the main road just past the town of Luino.

CAMIN HOTEL COLMEGNA   **New**
Hostess: Lara Luz
Localita: Colmegna
Luino (VA) 21016, Italy
Tel: (0332) 510855, Fax: (0332) 537226
www.karenbrown.com\italy\caminhotelcolmegna.html
22 rooms with private bathrooms
Lire 150,000–190,000 double B&B
Breakfast & dinner served
Open March to November
Credit cards: all major
English spoken well, Region: Lombardy

Although a hotel, the Camin is the best alternative on Lake Maggiore where bed and breakfasts are virtually non existent. The Luz family bought and restored the lovely turn-of-the-century villa across from the lake 30 years ago. It retains its "liberty"-style decor throughout the several sitting and dining rooms with high frescoed ceilings, stained glass and lead windows, and ornate chandeliers. The reception area has an old-fashioned wooden bar with leather stools, velvet sofas and armchairs, Oriental carpets, and an enormous stone fireplace. Bedrooms upstairs vary in size (single, double, or suite) and are in keeping with the general decor of the accommodation. Many amenities are offered such as air conditioning and hydrojet baths in suites. A garden surrounds the villa where in the summer months tables and umbrellas are set up for dinner or buffet breakfast. Gracious Signora Renate runs the show, assisting her guests with various itineraries around the lake area. Guests have access as well to the family's other lakefront hotel, with alternative restaurant, park, and swimming. This place exudes old-world charm. *Directions*: Luino is halfway up the eastern side of the lake and the hotel is easily found right in town.

CAMIN HOTEL LUINO　　　New
Hosts: Luz family
Via Dante 35
Luino (VA) 21016, Italy
Tel: (0332) 530118, Fax: (0332) 537226
12 rooms with private bathrooms
Lire 230,000–260,000 double B&B
Breakfast & dinner served
Open all year
Credit cards: all major
English spoken very well, Region: Lombardy

The noble Albertario family have four large coutryside properties in Umbria and Tuscany which they have recently opened up to accommodate travellers. Macciangrosso is decidedly the most beautiful, with its hilltop position overlooking the sweeping valley, and bordered by ancient cypress trees. The large stone villa, which has been added on to at various times throughout its long history (15th-century origins), belonged to the noble Piccolomini ancestors. You enter through the side gate, walk over a large patio looking onto the precious rose garden with its 62 varieties, and climb an external stairway up to the six bedrooms. These are all accessed by a main living room, more like a museum with its rare antique pieces and gilded frame paintings. Bedrooms are simpler, appointed with wrought-iron beds and coordinated bedspreads and curtains, and each with a small bathroom. Other common living areas are the transformed cantina and dining and game rooms. The swimming pool is bordered by a stone wall from the Etruscan period. Ten apartments of various sizes are in the rest of the home and in a nearby house next to the chapel. Close to the thermal spas, Macciangrosso is on the edge of both Umbria and Tuscany. *Directions*: From Chiusi take route 146 towards Chianciano. Take the road on the right to the end—marked Macciano on the map—3 km before reaching Chianciano.

MACCIANGROSSO   New
Hosts: Sonia & Luigi Albertario
Localita: Macciano
Chiusi (SI) 53044, Italy
Tel & fax: (0578) 21459 or (06) 35451372
E-mail: mc4198@mclink.it
6 bedrooms with private bathrooms, 10 apartments
Lire 220,000 double B&B
 800,000–1,900,000 weekly per apartment
3-day minimum stay 1 week for apartments
Breakfast only
Open all year
English & French spoken well, Region: Tuscany

Ca'delle Rondini opened its doors first as a local restaurant and then last year as a bed and breakfast establishment. The typical rectangular-shaped white farmhouse and incorporated barn, built in 1800, faces out to the main road in town and at the back to acres of flat fields, fruit orchards, and horse stables. In a section of the long house live gregarious host, Ilo, and his brother, Alessandro, who helps Mamma in the kitchen with the creation of delectable local fare whose ingredients come directly from the farm. Entering the lofty restaurant with pale-yellow walls, fireplace, brick floors, beamed ceilings, and large arched windows, one has the sense of being part of a truly authentic local gathering place—especially for Sunday lunch. Guests sit at long, rustic, wood tables in one of the two rooms and are offered a variety of inventive antipasti served on cutting boards. The six comfortable rooms above and one below (with access for the handicapped) each have telephone, television, and air conditioning, and are very pleasantly appointed in typical country style with mansard beamed ceilings, rose-colored walls, and canopy beds. Outings by bike or horseback are arranged in the nearby nature park reserve. Ca'delle Rondini has a friendly, informal ambiance and provides a great base for visiting Venice, Padova, Treviso, Verona, and Vicenza. *Directions*: Ca'delle Rondini is in the town of Maerne, just 10 km from Venice and northwest of Mestre.

CA'DELLE RONDINI   New
Hosts: Silvestri family
Via Ca' Rossa 26
Maerne (VE) 30030, Italy
Tel & fax: (041) 641114
7 rooms with private bathrooms
Lire 110,000 double B&B
All meals served for guests
Open all year, Restaurant open Thurs to Sun
No English spoken, Region: Veneto

We are delighted to include the La Biancarda bed and breakfast, the beautiful country home of the Florio family of Ancona, overlooking the colorful hilly coutryside. Just south of Ancona begins one of the prettiest coastlines of the eastern side with a combination of seaside villages, hilly countryside, and dramatic mountains cascading into the sea. Signora Giovanna had the salmon-colored farmhouse dating to 1760 restored ten years ago to provide her family with a relaxing country retreat, and adorned it with many of the family's precious antiques. The impressive stone-walled living room upstairs with enormous fireplace, plus cozy library and billiard room are all open to guests. Six guest bedrooms include a suite with sitting room. A real treat is waking up to breakfast in the delightful country kitchen with fireplace, long family table, beamed ceilings, and collection of hanging brass pots. Exquisite dinners based on fresh fish and local produce and wines can also be arranged. Outdoor activities in the area include golf, tennis, horseback riding, and swimming (beaches are ten minutes away), plus the historical towns of Macereto, Loreto, and Urbino. *Directions*: From the A14 autostrada, exit at Ancona Sud and follow signs for Numana. Follow this road for several kilometers to Coppo, turning left onto a dirt road just behind a gas station—follow it to the end.

LA BIANCARDA
Hosts: Giovanna Florio & family
Via Biancarda 129, Localita: Coppo
Massignano (AN) 60125, Italy
Tel: (071) 2800503 or 34331, Fax: (071) 2077624
Tel (off-season): (071) 203219
6 bedrooms, 5 with private bathrooms
Lire 160,000–220,000 double B&B
2-day minimum stay
Breakfast, dinner upon request
Open May to October 15
English spoken wel, Region: Marches

The very simple but economical Oasi Verde or "green oasis" is just that: a convenient roadside stop for those traveling between Umbria and the Marches region. Carla and Andrea Rossi inherited the sprawling 200-year-old stone farmhouse and surrounding land, ideally located midway between Perugia and Gubbio (a not-to-be-missed medieval stone village set high up in the hillside), and decided to convert it to a bed and breakfast and restaurant. The eight rooms in the main house, each with own bathroom, have been decorated like model room number 3, with its original beamed ceiling and country-antique bed and armoire. White-tiled floors may be out of character, but give a sense of cleanliness nonetheless. Another wing of the complex houses three simply furnished suites (two bedrooms and a bathroom) for longer stays, perfect for a family of four. Renovation work is being completed on another wing which will offer an additional ten rooms, each with separate ground-floor entrance. The windows at the back of the house open out to green hills with alternating patches of woods and sunflower fields. The facilities have recently been enhanced by the addition of a swimming pool and bikes available for rent. *Directions*: From Perugia on route 298 after 25 km, you find the bed and breakfast on the left-hand side, at Mengara, 10 km before Gubbio.

OASI VERDE
Hosts: Andrea & Carla Rossi
Localita: Mengara 1
Gubbio (PG) 06024, Italy
Tel: (075) 920156 or (0336) 633534, Fax: (075) 920049
www.karenbrown.com\italy\oasiverde.html
8 rooms with private bathrooms, 3 suites
Lire 75,000–95,000 double B&B
  65,000–75,000 per person half board
3-day minimum stay (high season)
All meals served
Open March 20 to Nov 3, Credit cards: MC, VS
Very little English spoken, Region: Umbria

Florentine sisters Francesca and Beatrice Baccetti eagerly accepted the challenge of converting the family's country home and vineyards into a bed and breakfast. Restoration work began immediately on the two adjacent stone buildings dating back to 1400. All original architectural features were preserved, leaving the five guestrooms and ten apartments (for two to four people) with clay-tiled floors, wood-beamed ceilings, mansard roofs, and generous views over the tranquil Tuscan countryside. The very comfortable and tidy rooms are furnished with good reproductions and feel almost hotel-like, with telephone, television, and modern bathrooms in each. A beautiful swimming pool with hydro-massage, tennis courts, billiards room, and nearby horse stables are at the guests' disposal, although finding enough to do is hardly a problem with Florence only 18 kilometers away and practically all of Tuscany at one's fingertips. Breakfast is served at wood tables in the stone-walled dining room or out on the terrace. Readers give Salvadonica a high rating. *Directions*: From Florence take the superstrada toward Siena for 20 km, exiting at San Casciano Nord. Follow signs for town, turning left at the sign for Mercatale. Salvadonica is on this road and well marked.

SALVADONICA
Hosts: Francesca & Beatrice Baccetti
Via Grevigiana 82
Mercatale Val di Pesa (FI) 50024, Italy
Tel: (055) 8218039, Fax: (055) 8218043
www.karenbrown.com\italy\salvadonica.html
5 rooms with private bathrooms, 10 apartments
Lire 150,000–190,000 double B&B
2-day minimum stay, 1 week high season
Breakfast only
Open March to October
Credit cards: all major
English spoken very well, Region: Tuscany

In a city where the word "charm" is practically non existent, the Hotel Regina came as a pleasant surprise among the rather nondescript choice of modern hotels in the city. For those flying in and out of Milan, with a desire to catch a glimpse of the city center, this is an ideal selection. The attractive, typically 18th-century façade and entrance invite guests into a luminous reception area converted from the original courtyard with stone columns, arches, marble floors, and a small corner bar. Completely refurbished rooms include all modern amenities and are very quiet, being set off the street. Decorated comfortably and uniformly with identical furniture, warmth is given to rooms with soft pastel-colored walls, parquet floors, and scattered Oriental rugs. A full buffet breakfast is served below and is included in the room rate. Manager Michela is helpful in satisfying guests' requests. Linate airport is easily reached by cab in 20 minutes, while the Malpensa airport can be reached by bus from the train station. *Directions*: Via Correnti is just off the Via Torino which leads to Milan's famous cathedral and shopping area, and is between the Basilicas of San Lorenzo and San Ambrogio.

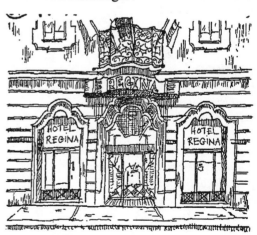

HOTEL REGINA
Hostess: Michela Barberi
Via Cesare Correnti 13
Milan 20123, Italy
Tel: (02) 58106913, Fax: (02) 58107033
E-mail: hotel.regina@traveleurope.it
www.karenbrown.com\italy\hotelregina.html
43 rooms with private bathrooms
Lire 360,000 double B&B
Breakfast only
Open all year
Credit cards: all majo.
English spoken well, Region: Lombardy

Just 20 kilometers from Siena, at the foot of Chianti is the Godiolo stone farmhouse with its double loggia and cupola dating back to 1350. Red geraniums cascade from every one of the balconies and terra-cotta urns. While Signor Giuliano tends to the vineyards and wine-production, Signora Bianca dedicates her time to making their guests feel very much at home. What used to be the children's rooms are now four charming guestrooms with nice touches—embroidered linen sheets and dried flower arrangements. Breakfast in the typical tiled kitchen consists of homemade baked goods to which guests help themselves. Signora, with her Roman-Tuscan origins, is an excellent cook and guests can treat themselves to a delightful dinner with the family. Their son, Stefano, when not studying, is often around to assist and is eager to practice his English. Nearby are the thermal baths of Rapolano where massages, mud baths, and other spa services are available—true relaxation. *Directions*: Exit from the A1 autostrada at Val di Chiana and head towards Siena on route 326 towards Serre di Rapolano, but turn right, up to Godiolo rather than left into town.

GODIOLO
Hosts: Giuliano & Bianca Perinelli
Localita: Modanella
Serre di Rapolano (SI) 53040, Italy
Tel: (0577) 704304, Fax: none
www.karenbrown.com\italy\godiolo.html
4 rooms with private bathrooms
Lire 200,000 double B&B
Dinner served upon request
Open all year
Some English spoken, Region: Tuscany

On the same road as the Godiolo bed and breakfast, a more independent type of accommodation is offered at the 13th-century Castello di Modanella. It is a sprawling stone complex complete with towers and turrets, several separate houses where the farmers of the vast wine estate once lived, a church, and even a school. The castle is in a constant state of restoration and along the way 33 rental apartments have been incorporated in various sections. Some apartments can be found in the old schoolhouse just outside the castle walls on two floors with one, two, or three bedrooms, bathrooms, kitchen, and living room. They maintain a true rustic flavor with original beams, mansard ceilings, worn brick floors, stone walls, and a mix of old and new wood furniture. All have lovely views over the countryside. Other comfortable apartments are located in four separate houses all about 800 meters from each other and the castle on the vast property. Although currently there are no accommodations in the castle itself, it is worth a visit with its arched entrance, iron gates, stone courtyard, and clock tower. The estate is under the direction of Gabriella Cerretti who assists guests with their every need. Guests also enjoy sports facilities such as tennis courts, two swimming pools, and two lakes for fishing. *Directions*: Travel for 30 km from Siena on route 326 towards the autostrada, then turn left at the sign for the Castello, opposite Serre di Rapolano.

CASTELLO DI MODANELLA
Hostess: Gabriella Cerretti
Serre di Rapolano (SI) 53040, Italy
Tel: (0577) 704604, Fax: (0577) 704740
www.karenbrown.com\italy\castellodimodanella.html
33 apartments for 2 to 9 persons
Lire 170,00–350,000 daily
2-day minimum stay
No meals served
Open all year
Some English spoken, Region: Tuscany

While many agritourism farms are run by transplanted urbanites, many are still owned and operated by farmers whose families have worked the land for generations. Such is the case with Onofrio Contento and his family, proprietors of Masseria Curatori, not far from the city of Monopoli and the Adriatic Sea, where, for five generations, the family has produced olives, almonds, and cattle. Inside the main coral-color house are modest and immaculate quarters for guests, consisting presently of a large three-bedroom apartment with kitchen and living room on the second floor, plus a double with private bath on the ground floor. Old and new family furniture has been combined to decorate the rooms. The view is pleasingly pastoral, overlooking olive-tree studded hills. Four apartments for two to four persons were built several years ago in a nearby one-story building overlooking a lovely stone-walled garden and fruit orchard. Breakfast and extra meals are taken together with the hospitable family in their dining room. Horseback riding is also arranged for guests. This lodging is recommended for visitors with some command of the Italian language. *Directions*: 40 km from Brindisi. Take coastal route N16, exiting at Monopoli-San Francesco da Paola. Take the road back across the highway and take the first left. Follow Via Conchia for 2 km to the pink house.

MASSERIA CURATORI
Hosts: Onofrio Contento family
Contrada Cristo delle Zolle 227
Monopoli (BA) 70043, Italy
Tel: (080) 777472, Fax: none
5 apartments, 1 room with private bathroom
Lire 80,000 double B&B
  65,000 per person half board
2-day minimum stay
All meals served
Open all year
Very little English spoken, Region: Apulia

A well-kept secret among off-the-main-road travelers is the countryside north of Rome known as "Sabina" after the mountain range. It is unusual that agritourism has not developed close to Rome compared to what has occurred around Florence, but locals are beginning to wake up. Ancestors of the Gabutti family—adopted Romans—came from this area and the principal palazzos in both medieval towns of Casperia and Montasola, plus a large farm with olive groves, have been in the family for generations. One of the daughters, Letizia, decided to leave a law career in Rome to work on restoration of these properties and offer hospitality in the form of apartments. Guests began arriving last year and were comfortably situated in quaint Montasola. Spacious apartments include one or two bedrooms, living room, kitchen, and bathrooms, all well decorated with the family's own antiques. Characteristic architectural features have been preserved, and two apartments have terraces with a breathtaking countryside panoramic view (our favorite is the mansard *Le Stelle*). There is something very special indeed about being a "resident" of an intact medieval village with its narrow stone alleyways. Guests can lounge under the shady trees of a stone-walled garden close by. Other charming villages dot the area, Umbria is at a short distance, and Rome is just a 45-minute train ride away. *Directions*: Arrangements to be met should be made at the time of reservation.

MONTEPIANO   New
Hostess: Maria Letizia Gabutti
Via dei Casalini 8
Montasola (RI) 02045, Italy
Tel & fax: (0765) 63252
4 apartments
Lire 145,000–300,000 daily per apartment
2-day minimum stay, No meals served
Open all year
Very little English spoken, Region: Lazio

As you travel southwest toward Florence through the foothills of the Appenines, the scenery transforms itself dramatically from the flatlands of the *padana* into soft green hills textured with alternating fields of wheat and grape vines. From Bologna, the Tenuta Bonzara farm and vineyard is a half-hour drive up a road that winds through scented pine forest, arriving at a group of houses owned by several farming families. The wine estate is owned by Dottor Lambertini of Bologna, and is run by warm-hearted Mario and his family, whose main responsibility is overseeing the wine production. Guest accommodation on the estate consists of two small houses containing two apartments, each with one or two bedrooms, bathroom, kitchenette, and sitting room—the nicest are the one-bedroom apartments in the older house with small corner fireplaces, redbrick floors and beamed ceilings, rustically furnished with simple pinewood pieces. A trattoria on the premises serves meals, and a museum has been set up in the old barn displaying antique farm tools, carts, and agricultural machines. A tennis court is available, and participation in the grape harvesting is encouraged. *Directions*: Take the Bologna/Casalecchio exit from the A1 autostrada and continue to Gesso, Rivabella, Calderino, Monte San Giovanni, and left up the hill to San Chierlo.

TENUTA BONZARA
Host: Dottor Francesco Lambertini
Via San Chierlo 37
Monte San Pietro (BO) 40050, Italy
Tel: (051) 6768324, Fax: (051) 225772
4 apartments
Lire 680,000–830,000 weekly
2-day minimum stay in low season
* 145,000–195,000 daily*
Trattoria on premises (dinner only)
Open May to October
Some English spoken, Region: Emilia-Romagna

The scenic approach to the Fattoria di Vibio passes through lush green hills, by picturesque farms, and is highlighted by a romantic view of the quaint town of Todi, 20 kilometers away. Two handsome brothers from Rome run this top-drawer bed and breakfast consisting of several recently restored stone houses. The houses sit side by side and share between them ten double rooms with private baths. Common areas for guests include a cozy, country-style living room with fireplace, games room, and country kitchen. The accommodations are enhanced by preserved architectural features such as terra-cotta floors and exposed-beam ceilings, and typical Umbrian handicrafts such as wrought-iron beds, renovated antiques, and *Deruta* ceramics. On the assumption that guests may find it difficult to leave this haven, the hosts offer only half board, along with a beautiful swimming pool, tennis, hiking, horseback riding, and biking (at an extra charge). Signora Gabriella, with a passion for cooking, gets all the richly deserved credit for the marvelous meals served either poolside or on the panoramic terrace. *Directions*: From either Todi or Orvieto follow route S448 until the turnoff for Vibio just outside Todi. Follow the well-marked dirt road for 10 km.

FATTORIA DI VIBIO
Hosts: Giuseppe & Filippo Saladini
Localita: Buchella-Doglio
Montecastello di Vibio (PG) 06057, Italy
Tel: (075) 8749607, Fax: (075) 8780014
www.karenbrown.com\italy\fattoriadivibio.html
10 rooms with private bathrooms
Lire 105,000–140,000 per person half board
2-day minimum stay, 1 week August
Breakfast & dinner served
Open March to December
Credit cards: AX, VS
Very little English spoken, Region: Umbria

Surprisingly, one of the least visited regions in Italy is the Marches, an area rich in culture, nature, and history bordering on the Adriatic. Just 15 kilometers from the coast in the heart of this gentle, hilly countryside, is the Campana farm, run by 10 families of professionals and artists who came here from Milan in search of an alternative lifestyle. The farm, made up of four pale-peach stone houses dating from 1700, has been restored with great care and taste, making space for private quarters, a refined restaurant, wine cellar, studio, music room, and, for guests, eleven rooms, a few large enough for a family of four. Some have lovely terraces looking across vineyard-covered hills to the distant sea, and are decorated with a combination of old and new furnishings. Other rooms are situated within a separate two-story, recently renovated farmhouse. Drawing on the considerable pool of available talent, an unusual variety of activities is offered—from courses in painting, theater, sculpture, and photography to workshops in crafting leather, silk, and wool. A swimming pool and tennis courts were recently added, as well as bikes for local touring. *Directions*: From Ancona go south on the A14 autostrada, exit at Pedaso and continue south to Carassai, then turn right. After 5 km, turn right for Montefiore, then left at the small sign for La Campana.

LA CAMPANA
Hosts: Co-op Agricola
Via Menocchia 39
Montefiore dell'Aso (AP) 63010, Italy
Tel: (0734) 938229, Fax: (0734) 938484
E-mail: campana@agricoop.it
www.karenbrown.com\italy\lacampana.html
11 rooms with private bathrooms
Lire 140,000–150,000 double B&B
  80,000–105,000 per person half board
Breakfast & dinner served
Open all year, Credit cards: MC, VS
English spoken well, Region: Marches

La Loggia, built in 1427, was one of the Medici estates during the centuries they ruled over Florence and surrounding territories. Owner Giulio Baruffaldi, weary of urban life in Milan, transplanted himself and his wife here and succeeded in reviving the estate's splendor while respecting its past, enhancing its architectural beauty while giving utmost attention to comforts and warmth. Their informal yet refined hospitality is reflected in the care given to the decor of the apartments, each containing one to three bedrooms, living room, kitchen, fireplace, and many lovely antiques and original paintings from the Baruffaldis' own art collection. In fact, many important bronze and ceramic sculptures by international artists are displayed throughout the gardens of the villa. Four double rooms have been added with fireplace, hydro-massage bath, and steam room. Apart from just basking in the pure romance and tranquillity of this place, there is a swimming pool, horseback riding, and nearby tennis and golf facilities. Other activities include the occasional cooking or wine-tasting lesson, and impromptu dinners in the cellar. The hosts and their absolutely charming guest assistant, Ivana, seem to exist merely to pamper their guests' every whim. This is the stuff dreams are made of. *Directions*: From the Florence-Siena autostrada, exit after San Casciano at Bargino. Turn right at the end of the ramp, then left for Montefiridolfi (3½km). La Loggia is just before town.

FATTORIA LA LOGGIA
Hosts: Giulio Baruffaldi & Cuca Roaldi
Via Collina, Montefiridolfi in Chianti
San Casciano Val di Pesa (FI) 50020, Italy
Tel: (055) 8244288, Fax: (055) 8244283
10 apartments, 4 rooms with private bathrooms
Lire 180,000–250,000 double
3-day minimum stay
Occasional dinner & wine tastings
Open all year
Fluent English spoken, Region: Tuscany

One result of increasing interest in the singular attractions of the *maremma*, or southern Tuscany, is the opening or expansion of several noteworthy places to stay. The Villa Acquaviva, once owned by nobility, has been a small family hotel for the past nine years. The ambitious proprietors, Serafino and Valentina, completed extensive remodeling to include seven guestrooms named for and painted in the colors of local wildflowers. The bedrooms all have private baths, and are decorated with country antiques and wrought-iron beds. The charming breakfast room has sky-blue tablecloths and looks out arched windows to a lush flower garden with alternating palms and umbrella pines, and on to a view over the gently rolling landscape up to the village of Montemerano—a quaint, medieval town with excellent restaurants and artisan shops. Breakfast of homemade cakes, breads, and jams can be taken inside or out on the patio. Just completed last year are eight additional rooms in a stone farmhouse on the property. These are our new favorites, with beautiful local antiques and colorful matching fabrics adorning beds and windows. The farmhouse has its own spacious breakfast room and living area downstairs. *Directions*: From Rome, take the Aurelia road, exiting at Vulci. Follow signs for Manciano, then for Montemerano. Approximately 1½ hours from Rome.

VILLA ACQUAVIVA
Hosts: Valentina di Virginio & Serafino d'Ascenzi
Localita: Acquaviva
Montemerano (GR) 58050, Italy
Tel: (0564) 602890, Fax: (0564) 602895
15 rooms with private bathrooms
Lire 150,000–300,000 double B&B
3-day minimum stay in high season
Breakfast only
Closed February
English spoken well, Region: Tuscany

The Fontanelle country house sits in the heart of the Maremma area of Tuscany where, besides being pleasant and well run, it fills a need for the growing interest in this off-the-track destination. Signor Perna and his two lovely daughters, originally from Rome, searched and found this peaceful haven from the stress of city life, promptly transferring themselves and undertaking major restoration work. Looking over a soft green valley up to the nearby village of Montemerano, the stone farmhouse with its rusty red shutters offers two comfortable rooms with spotless private bathrooms. The converted barn houses the remaining five rooms. Sunlight pours into the front veranda-like breakfast room where coffee and cakes are taken together with other guests at one large table. The Pernas assist guests in planning local itineraries including visits to artisan workshops. With due notice, guests can find a wonderfully prepared dinner awaiting them under the ivy-covered pergola in the rose garden. The property is part of a reserve where deer, wild boar, and various types of wildlife can be observed. *Directions*. From Rome, take the A12 autostrada. Continue north on Aurelia route 1, turning off at Vulci after Montalto. Follow signs for Manciano then Montemerano. Turn left at the bed-and-breakfast sign before town and follow the dirt road for 4 km.

LE FONTANELLE
Hosts: Daniela & Cristina Perna
Localita: Poderi di Montemerano
Montemerano (GR) 58050, Italy
Tel & fax: (0564) 602762
www.karenbrown.com\italy\lefontanelle.html
7 rooms with private bathrooms
Lire 120,000 double B&B
Breakfast & dinner upon request
Open all year
Some English spoken, Region: Tuscany

Lucia Ann Luhan, whose parents are from Italy, grew up in a family rich in Italian tradition. After years of living in California and running a restaurant and catering business, she and her family have moved over permanently to Villa Lucia, the 500-year-old stone farmhouse, now a bed and breakfast, which she bought on a whim while on holiday in Italy many years ago. Son, Jason, assists with the general running of the place while Lucia is busy with her Italian language courses. All of the seven rooms are decorated in a homey, comfortable way; nothing contrived, just naturally pleasing and in keeping with the rustic nature of the old stone farmhouse. Two lovely apartments in the former barn are also available. When the weather is mild, a bountiful breakfast is served outside on the terrace where guests congregate again in late afternoon to sip cool drinks and socialize. Lucia has an "open house" policy, with a homemade pot of soup always on the burner plus snacks of cheese and salami on hand when guests return in the afternoon. Guests can also enjoy a sumptuous dinner when requested in the morning. Besides being close to most of Tuscany's highlights, the famous spa town of Montecatini is just a six-minute drive down the hill with a golf course. The inn also offers a small swimming pool. *Directions*: Exit from autostrada A11 at Montecatini and follow signs for Monsummano (52 km west of Florence). Montevettolini is 3 km southwest of here.

VILLA LUCIA
Hostess: Lucia Ann Luhan
Via dei Bronzodi 144
Montevettolini (PT) 51010, Italy
Tel & fax: (0572) 628817
www.karenbrown.com\italy\villalucia.html
2 apartments, 7 rooms, 6 with private bathrooms
$150 (US) double B&B, 2-night minimum stay
Breakfast & dinner served upon request
Open April 15 to November 15
English spoken very well, Region: Tuscany

Signora Novella and her family, delightful and gregarious hosts, have been welcoming guests for over 13 years, ever since they moved to Emilia-Romangna from the south. Having agricultural experience, they were able to set up a farm, with Novella, a retired schoolteacher, overseeing the kitchen. She is an excellent cook and guests return time and time again for her handmade pasta, joining the family at the long wood table in their rustic dining room with its hanging brass pots and ox harnesses. Daughters Alessandra and Donatella recently returned home to help run the business. Guest accommodations have been transferred from upstairs in the white 18th-century farmhouse (one room remains) to the horse stalls, which have been converted into seven simple double rooms with private baths. The rooms are immaculate, if rather plain with basic modern furnishings. Guests tend to their own rooms and are even apt to help clear the table in the very informal *en famille* atmosphere at Le Radici. The sea, just 15 kilometers away, can be seen in the distance, and several medieval towns and castles dot the hills in the surrounding countryside besides, of course, "must sees" Ravenna and Ferrara. A unique experience, best enjoyed if you speak some Italian. *Directions*: On route 9 from Rimini to Cesana, follow signs for Calisese and Montiano. Turn left at the Esso gas station for Le Radici, or call for assistance.

LE RADICI
Hostess: Novella Piangatelli
Localita: Montenovo
Via Golano 808
Montiano (OF) 47020, Italy
Tel: (0547) 327001, Fax: (0547) 327168
7 rooms with private bathrooms
Lire 75,000 per person half board
Breakfast & dinner served
Open March to December
Some English & French spoken
Region: Emilia-Romangna

In the northern Piedmont region, leading into the foothills of the Alps, is the peaceful countryside where Piercarlo Novarese, Il Mompolino's cordial host, decided to establish his inn and equestrian center. Run more like a small hotel, the sixteen guestrooms are divided between two mustard-color buildings. Each room has a private bath and balcony, and is complemented with rustic furnishings. The larger suites feature sitting rooms and are the nicest, furnished with the occasional antique. A large, open dining room serves breakfast, lunch, and dinner, and boasts delectable regional dishes skillfully prepared by local women. Il Mompolino makes an ideal stopover on the way to the Alps, the lake region, or Milan. It also provides an appealing spot to relax for a few days between more demanding tourist destinations. Sports activities abound, including horseback riding, tennis, swimming, and a gym with sauna. A variety of horseback-riding lessons is offered at the equestrian center, as are mounted excursions into the adjacent national park. Perhaps a good idea between bowls of pasta! *Directions*: Take the Carisio exit from the Milan-Turin A4 autostrada. From Carisio Mompolino is 7 km and well marked.

IL MOMPOLINO
Host: Piercarlo Novarese
Localita: Mompolino
Mottalciata (VC) 13030, Italy
Tel: (0161) 857668 or 669, Fax: (0161) 857667
www.karenbrown.com\italy\ilmompolino.html
16 rooms with private bathrooms
2 apartments
Lire 100,000 double B&B
All meals served
Open all year
Credit cards: all major
Very little English spoken, Region: Piedmont

The Gasthof Obereggen, located in the Ega Valley is very simple, but its location and price are hard to match. The inn is situated on the side of a hill overlooking a gorgeous valley in one of the most beautiful mountain regions of northeastern Italy. The town of Obereggen is a ski resort and the lift is just a few minutes' walk away. From the sun-drenched deck, which extends generously from the hotel, there is an absolutely glorious vista across the meadows to the mountains. Behind the hotel even more majestic peaks rise jaggedly into the sky. Inside there is a cozy dining room with hunting trophies lining the walls and a typical tiled stove against one wall to keep the room toasty on a cold day. The inn has at present twelve basically uninspired bedrooms, with those on the second floor opening out onto balconies with lovely views. Major renovation work currently underway (completion early 1997) will add four more rooms. The Gasthof's greatest asset is Signora Pichler who runs her little inn with warmth and gaiety. She speaks no English, but her hospitality overcomes all language barriers, and her abundant and delicious home-style cooking speaks to all who love to eat. *Directions*: Obereggen is almost impossible to find on any map, although the Val d'Ega and the town of Ega (San Floriano on some maps) are usually indicated. Obereggen is 3 km south of Nova Levante and 25 km southeast of Bolzano.

GASTHOF OBEREGGEN
Hosts: Pichler family
Via Obereggen 8 (San Floriano)
Nova Ponente (BZ) 39050, Italy
Tel: (0471) 615722, Fax: (0471) 615889
16 rooms (1997), several with private bathrooms
Lire 85,000–95,000 double B&B
* 63,000–75,000 per person half board*
All meals served
Open December to Easter & June to mid-October
No English spoken (German)
Region: Trentino-Alto Adige

The location of La Chiocciola bed and breakfast, minutes from the main tollway from Rome to Florence and on the border of the Lazio and Umbria regions, is ideal. Added bonuses are the warm hospitality, deliciously prepared regional meals, and lovely country-style bedrooms. Roberto and Maria Cristina from Rome bought the stone farmhouse dating back to 1400 several years ago and began restoration work while living in the newer house next door. The results of their efforts are four perfectly neat and spotless bedrooms in each of the two houses, a living room area for guests, and a large rustic dining room with outdoor veranda. Obvious care and attention has been put into the decorating of the bedrooms with wrought-iron canopy beds, crisp, white linen curtains, and botanical prints. The 50-acre property with fruit orchards and vineyards is part of the Tiber river valley and woods. There are bicycles and a swimming pool for guests' use. Innumerable day trips and itineraries of special interest are offered in the area of Umbria and Lazio. *Directions*: From Rome or Florence on the A1 autostrada, exit at Orte and turn immediately left, passing under the tollway. Go in the direction of Amelia and repass over the tollway, taking the first left towards Penna in Teverina. La Chiocciola is 5 km along this road.

LA CHIOCCIOLA
Hosts: Roberto & Maria Cristina de Fonseca Pimentel
Localita: Seripola
Orte (VT) 01028, Italy
Tel & fax: (0761) 402734
www.karenbrown.com\italy\lachiocciola.html
8 rooms with private bathrooms
Lire 150,000 double B&B
* 100,000 per person half board*
All meals served
Open all year
Credit cards: MC, VS
English spoken well, Region: Lazio

The apartments at Torre Amena, the Valente family's hilltop countryside property, offer an alternative to the more classic bed-and-breakfast-type accommodation of La Chiocciola. As owners of one of our favorite hotels in Rome, the Locarno (page 140), hospitality comes quite naturally to brother and sister team, Alfredo and Caterina. Alfredo has overseen most of the restoration work of the wooded property which is composed of the main stone house and surrounding "cottages" for guests, including a three-story mini tower. Named the *Olive Turret*, the latter includes a living room and kitchen on the first floor and a bedroom on each of the next two floors. Opposite the tower is *Pine Tree*, a cozy two-bedroom independent house built around an enormous umbrella pine. A living room and kitchen open out to a front porch. Apartments are pleasantly decorated with the family's country furniture and a breakfast basket is left at the beginning of your stay. Orte is within reach of three regions and offers an hourly train to Rome or Florence. Close by, activities such as horseback riding, tennis, and golf are available as well as a swim in thermal waters. *Directions*: Exit from the A1 autostrada at Orte and follow signs for Viterbo. From this highway, take the first exit and follow it to Vasanello. Before town and after approximately 4 km, you find the unmarked entrance on the left up to the Torre. Best to call first to be met.

TORRE AMENA
Hosts: Caterina & Alfredo Valente
Localita: Torre Amena
Orte (TR) 01028, Italy
Tel: (06) 3610841, Fax: (06) 3215249
3 apartments
Lire 140,000–230,000 daily per apartment
3-day minimum stay, one week in high season
No meals served
Open all year
English spoken well, Region: Lazio

Fattoria La Cacciata is an authentic family farm close to Orvieto, a fascinating and popular tourist destination, famous for its magical cathedral. The cordial Belcapo family actually owns two adjacent farms on the outskirts overlooking the majestic town on its limestone perch. The property also commands a dramatic view of the rich Umbrian valley below. The 200-acre farm/vineyard, in competent Belcapo-family hands for five generations, produces top-rated *Orvieto Classico* on a large scale, as well as a red and a rosé wine and olive oil. The primary turn-of-the-century villa and one small stone house are reserved for the family (although at times guests are roomed within the home), while four other rustic houses scattered around the property accommodate guests. In the 15 rooms, each different from the next in size and decor, an eclectic mix of rustic country furniture fits in with original architectural features of farmers' quarters. An airy dining room overlooking the countryside and horse stables serves up sumptuous dinners. A spectacular swimming pool has just been added looking up to picturesque Orvieto perched on its rock, and horses are available for lessons or scenic outings. *Directions*: Exit from the autostrada at Orvieto and turn left at the first stoplight on Viale 1 Maggio; follow signs for Porano, then signs to La Cacciata.

FATTORIA LA CACCIATA
Hosts: Settimio Belcapo family
Localita: Canale, Via La Cacciata 6
Orvieto (TR) 05010, Italy
Tel: (0763) 92881 or 300892, Fax: (0763) 341373
www.karenbrown.com\italy\fattorialacacciata.html
15 rooms, 13 with private bathrooms
Lire 90,000–110,000 double B&B (extra for pool use)
75,000–85,000 per person half board
All meals served
Open all year
Very little English spoken, Region: Umbria

A very high rating goes to the newly opened Locanda Rosati on the border of Umbria and Lazio, and just steps away from Tuscany. Giampiero and sister, Alba, with their respective spouses, Luisa and Paolo, sold their cheese production business in Lucca and returned to Orvieto to transform the family farmhouse into a bed and breakfast. The results are splendid and guests, taking priority over the agricultural activity in this instance, are treated with extra-special care. The downstairs common areas include two cozy living rooms with fireplace and a large stone-walled dining room divided by a brick archway leading down to the "tufo" stone cellar. Seven bedrooms upstairs (one with access and bathroom for the handicapped) have been decorated with an animal theme evident in the carvings on bedboards and lamps. The third floor is reserved for the two families. Although the *locanda* is right on the road, most rooms face the countryside to the back where a large open space leads to the swimming pool. Alba delights guests with her cooking, while affable Paolo has taken over the project of landscaping. Energetic Giampiero advises guests on fascinating local itineraries, including a number of artisans' workshops. *Directions*: Exit from the A1 autostrada at Orvieto and follow signs for Viterbo-Bolsena. Skirt town and continue towards Bolsena for about 8 km on route 71. After a series of sharp curves, the *locanda* comes up on the right.

LOCANDA ROSATI
Hosts: Rosati Family
Localita: Buonviaggio
Orvieto (TR) 05018, Italy
Tel & fax: (0763) 27314
www.karenbrown.com\italy\locandarosati.html
7 rooms with private bathrooms
Lire 160,000 double B&B
* 120,000 per person half board*
Closed January & February
Very little English spoken, Region: Umbria

A convenient stopover while heading either north or south along the main artery—A1 autostrada—is the Villa Ciconia inn. Located below the historical center of Orvieto, in the newer commercial outskirts, the property maintains its tranquil setting thanks to the fortress of trees protecting the 16th-century stone villa. The first floor includes reception area, breakfast room, and two large high-ceilinged dining rooms. These latter, with their somber gray-stone fireplaces, tapestries, heavy dark-wood beams, and subdued-color frescoes depicting allegorical motifs and landscapes, give the place a medieval castle's air. The ten bedrooms on the second floor, all with en-suite bathrooms, are appointed in appropriate style, with antique chests and wrought-iron beds and all the amenities of a four-star hotel. Most rooms are quiet and look out onto the woods behind the villa. There are also two enormous beamed sitting rooms on this floor for guests. The restaurant has a solid reputation for creating excellent Umbrian specialties. Manager Luigi Falcone is always on hand to assist guests. *Directions*: Exiting from the autostrada, turn right towards Orvieto and right again where marked Arezzo, Perugia, passing under the tollway. The Ciconia is just after the river on the left-hand side of the road.

VILLA CICONIA
Hosts: Petrangeli family
Via dei Tigli 69
Orvieto (TR) 05018, Italy
Tel: (0763) 92982, Fax: (0763) 90677
www.karenbrown.com\italy\villaciconia.html
10 rooms with private bathrooms
Lire 200,000–230,000 double B&B
All meals served. Restaurant closed Mondays
Open all year
Credit cards: all major
English & French spoken well, Region: Umbria

Claudia Spatola does a superb job of running a bed and breakfast in the complex of stone houses known as Borgo Spante which dates back to the 15th century and has been in her family since 1752. Consisting of a main villa, connecting farmers' houses, chapel, barns, swimming pool, and garden, it is isolated in 500 acres of woods and hills, yet only 16 kilometers from Orvieto and not far from Assisi, Todi, and Perugia. Guests stay in a combination of rooms and apartments in the former farmers' quarters with their irregular-sized rooms, sloping worn-brick floors, and rustic country furnishings—very charming in its way. Authentically Umbrian meals, prepared by local women, are served in the dining room with long wood tables and fireplace. A larger dining area has been added in the former barn, along with four additional mini-apartments—simply and characteristically decorated. Memorable evenings are spent in the garden or poolside conversing with other guests or listening to an impromptu concert. *Directions*: From the A1 autostrada exit at Orvieto and follow signs for Arezzo on route 71. After 7 km, turn right at Morrano and proceed for 12 km to the sign for Spante. Turn left and continue for 2 km.

BORGO SPANTE
Hostess: Claudia Spatola
Localita: Ospedaletto
San Venanzo (TR) 05010, Italy
Tel & fax: (075) 8709134 or fax: 8709201
5 rooms with private bathrooms
8 apartments
Lire 90,000 per person half board
2-day minimum stay
Breakfast & dinner served
Open all year
Some English spoken, Region: Umbria

Lo Spagnulo gives us a good idea of how the *masseria* farms of Apulia functioned in the 1600s. They were self-sufficient agricultural production centers, described as "factories," which included the proprietor's villa, housing for farmers, common dining area, church, administrative offices, animal shelters, and work areas. The Spagnulo still cultivates animals, fresh produce, almonds, and olives. Fortress-like in appearance, its white-stone exterior leads inside to a courtyard garden, off which the guest quarters are located. These vary in size and shape, many comprising two or three bedrooms, living/eating area, and kitchen. Featuring the vaulted ceilings, exposed beams, terra-cotta floors and stone walls of the original building. The rooms display charm despite the somewhat spartan furnishings. These accommodations are recommended over the nondescript rooms which have been added in a modern building nearby. The stalls have been converted into a restaurant for guests serving typical local dishes family style. Proprietor Livino Massari, a professor, and his family are present on weekends and during the summer. *Directions*: Heading south on route 379, exit at Marina di Ostuni. Follow signs to Rosa Marina, turning left at the sign for the farm.

MASSERIA LO SPAGNULO
Host: Livino Massari
Localita: Rosa Marina-Contrada Spagnulo
Ostuni (BR) 72017, Italy
Tel: (0831) 350209, Fax: (0831) 333756
www.karenbrown.com\italy\masserialospagnulo.html
26 apartments
Lire 80,000 double B&B
  70,000–85,000 per person half board
All meals served
Open all year
Credit cards: AX, VS
English spoken well, Region: Apulia

With her children grown and traveling around the world, Cristina, an expatriate from England, decided to offer hospitality to travelers in her country home. Situated an hour north of Rome by train or car, the pretty countryside home made of typical local tufo brick is a short distance from the ancient village of Otricoli with its pre-Roman origins. It is one of many villages centered in the Tiber river valley, historically an important area for trade and commerce with Rome. A long wing off the main house, reserved for guests, offers three beamed bedrooms decorated with country furniture and overlooking the garden and hills. An order-as-you-like breakfast is served either in the kitchen or out on the patio. The cozy living room with gray-stone fireplace invites guests to relax after a day in the city. Besides keeping up with the duties of her bed and breakfast activity, Cristina teaches English in one of Rome's many international schools. Being at the edge of Umbria and Lazio, she can suggest a myriad of local itineraries and destinations, known and not so well known, for guests to explore. This is a very informal, at-home accommodation just 7 kilometers from the main autostrada between Rome and Florence. *Directions*: Exit at Magliano Sabina and turn left for Otricoli-Terni. Turn off for Otricoli and take the first gravel road to the right—Via Crepafico. Gates to Casa Spence are on the curve.

CASA SPENCE   **New**
Hostess: Cristina Spence
Via Crepafico 29
Otricoli (TR) 05030, Italy
Tel & fax: (0744) 719758
3 rooms, 1 with private bathroom
Lire 100,000–120,000 double B&B
Breakfast only
Open all year
Fluent English spoken, Region: Umbria

Paciano, situated on the border of Umbria and Tuscany, south of Lake Trasimeno, is an intriguing medieval village, perfectly intact, and recently named the most ideal village in Italy. Here father and son team Giuseppe and Luigi Buitoni, of the famous pasta producing family, decided to put to use their refined culinary skills. The old olive oil press, part of the family's 12th-century residence, now functions as a restaurant with summer garden and bed and breakfast accommodation upstairs. Seven lovely bedrooms are decorated in refined country style, each with its own color scheme noted in the rich fabrics of the bedspreads and curtains. The palazzo was meticulously restored preserving all original architectural features while adding an extra floor and converting arched doorways to closets. The breakfast and sitting room is soft and inviting with splendid antiques, floral tapestry armchairs, fresh flowers, and crystal bottles lining shelves. A full buffet breakfast is served. Caterina, Luigi's darling wife, now helps welcome guests to the home. A part of the family's residence in the attached medieval tower is rented weekly—a special treat for a group of ten. *Directions*: Exit at Chiusi-Chianciano from the A1 autostrada; take the road towards Trasimeno and Perugia and turn right up to the town of Paciano where indicated.

LOCANDA DELLA ROCCA
Hosts: Buitoni family
Viale Roma 4
Paciano (PG) 06060, Italy
Tel: (075) 830236, Fax: (075) 830155
www.karenbrown.com\italy\locandadellarocca.html
7 rooms with private bathrooms, 1 apartment
Lire 150,000–170,000 double B&B
All meals served
Credit cards: MC, VS
Open: March to December
English spoken well, Region: Umbria

Ideally located at the edge of Chianti and just 20 minutes from the main A1 autostrada, the Fattoria Montelucci property is made up of over 1200 acres of woods, olive groves, vineyards, and pastures. In the heart of this working farm sits the pale-yellow villa with its ten second-floor guestrooms, each decorated in simple country style with eyelet curtains, wrought-iron beds, and antique chests. Downstairs are several common sitting rooms including billiard and music rooms. A luminous, beamed dining room, where a buffet breakfast is served, opens out to a large terrace looking over the breathtaking wooded hills. Other meals are served next door in the converted olive mill, with its original press, stone fireplace, and arched windows looking out over the same spectacular view. A typical Tuscan meal in this marvelous setting is alone worth the visit. Host Stefano's true passion is revealed at the riding stables, with its 30 horses, indoor/outdoor rings, and jumping course, offering lessons and country outings. Easily reached are the two ancient cities of Arezzo and Cortona. *Directions*: Exit the autostrada at Valdarno and follow signs for Montevarchi, Bucine, and then Pergine. Follow signs in town up to the Fattoria (5 km).

FATTORIA MONTELUCCI   **New**
Host: Stefano Balzanelli
Localita: Le Ville
Pergine Valdarno (AR) 52020, Italy
Tel: (0575) 896525, Fax: (0575) 896315
E-mail: montelucci@val.it
10 rooms with private bathrooms
5 apartments
Lire 120,000–180,000 double B&B
80,000–120,000 per person half board
Apartments 550,000–1,500,000 weekly
All meals served
Open all year, Credit cards: VS, MC
English spoken well, Region: Tuscany

The southernmost, "heel-side" of Italy's boot-shaped peninsula, known as *Puglia*, presents another facet of the country's many-sided culture. It is a land with spectacular coastlines, villages with distinct Greek and Turkish influence, endless lines of olive groves, fields of wild flowers, and a rich history of art including baroque (Bari's Santa Nicola church is exquisite). All of this plus exquisite cuisine and a warm and open people await in *Puglia* (Apulia), as does the Masseria Salamina, a 16th-century fortified farmhouse between Bari and Brindisi covering 100 acres of land and producing primarily olive oil. The driveway leads to the sand-colored castle with turreted tower with expansive vistas sweeping to the sea. The seven suites, each with a separate entrance and freshly decorated with reproductions and wicker furniture, are found through the courtyard. Host Gianvincenzo and family live in the main wing and run their masseria with hotel efficiency and service. A large lofty restaurant with terra-cotta floors provides all meals for guests. Eight additional apartments are available for longer stays and in the low season a fascinating week-long organized stay including Mediterranean cooking lessons and local excursions for small groups is arranged. *Directions*: From the SS16 exit at Pezze di Greco. Just before town take the first right for 1 km to the masseria.

MASSERIA SALAMINA
Host: Gianvincenzo De Miccolis Angelini
Pezze di Greco (BR) 72010, Italy
Tel & fax: (080) 727307 or 728582
E-mail: salamina@mailbox.media.it
www.karenbrown.com\italy\masseria.html
7 suites with private bathrooms, 8 apartments
Lire 120,000–160,000 double B&B
 90,000–110,000 per person half board
1-week minimum stay in July & August
All meals served
Open all year, Credit cards: MC, VS
Some English spoken, Region: Apulia

Right along the road connecting the hilltowns of Pienza and Montepulciano is the conveniently positioned farm of Felice and Giulia, transplanted from their hometowns in the regions of Marches and Campania respectively. The 18th-century stone farmhouse forms a U with inner courtyard from which you gain access to the breakfast room, restaurant, living room, and upstairs bedrooms divided on both sides. Bedrooms are luminous and spacious, with immaculate bathrooms, pretty bedspreads, and country furniture. The bedrooms on the right side overlook the hilly countryside and the 100-acre property of woods and fields which produces its own wine and olive oil. Ancient Pienza can be seen at a distance. The real treat here is Giulia's cooking using fresh farm produce. She has a flair for combining local traditional recipes with her own personal inventions, having homemade pastas as her base. This is an easy-access touring base for the endless itineraries available, including Siena Montalcino and tours of the d'Orcia wine valley, with an exceptionally low rate. *Directions*: Exit from the autostrada at Chiusi and follow signs for Montepulciano, then Pienza. After a total of 25 km, well before Pienza, the iron gates of the Santo Pietro are on the left.

SANTO PIETRO   *New*
Hosts: Felice d'Angelo & Giulia Scala
Strada Statale 126, No. 29
Pienza (SI) 53026, Italy
Tel & fax: (0578) 748410
9 rooms with private bathrooms
Lire 120,000 double B&B
Breakfast & dinner served
Open all year
Some English spoken, Region: Tuscany

L'Olmo just opened its doors to guests last year and already holds great promise. Francesca and her parents moved to Pienza from northern Turin and had the lovely 16th-century stone country home restored down to the last detail, preserving original terracotta floors and wood-beamed ceilings. With superb taste and guests' comfort in mind, five suites were created and appointed with antique chests, locally made wrought-iron beds, and pretty floral fabrics for color. Each has its own travertine marble bathroom and two have a fireplace. The two suites on the ground floor have their own garden and whirlpool tubs. Francesca, the charming hostess, lives in a part of the house and tends to guests in a warm and highly professional manner. Common rooms downstairs include two cozy sitting rooms with fireplace and invitingly soft armchairs, leading out to the stone courtyard with tables and large pots of flowers. A full buffet breakfast or gourmet candlelit dinner prepared by women from the village are served in the luminous dining room. Outdoors is the heated swimming pool with a 360-degree view over the soft green countryside. A romantic spot for a special splurge. *Directions*: From Pienza continue straight southward out of town and after 6 km turn left for Montichiello. Signs indicate the bed and breakfast before Montichiello.

L'OLMO   New
Hostess: Francesca Lindo
Localita: Montichiello
Pienza (SI) 53020, Italy
Tel: (0578) 755133, Fax: (0578) 755124
6 rooms with private bathrooms
Lire 320,000 double B&B
Breakfast & dinner served
Open March to November
Credit cards: MC, VS
English spoken very well, Region: Tuscany

After welcoming many Karen Brown travelers to their previous home—the Podere Capretto—the Zito family, from the States, have happily started up another bed and breakfast in a lesser-known area of Tuscany, south of the stunning Etruscan town of Volterra. Their new home was actually that of the priest of the adjacent church, dating to the 1600s. The front entrance hall filled with potted plants leads to the dining and living room with a variety of antiques and a grand piano. Upstairs are two guest bedrooms, each with en-suite bathroom and appointed with the family's antique beds and armoires. Between the two rooms is a cozy sitting room with video library off which are Rose and Alfred's bedroom and that of their son, David. The garden surrounding the house and looking on to the woods has been restored to its original state following the replanting of shrubs and flowers. Also available for longer stays are two separate houses within the nearby medieval stone village of San Dalmazio. Each has been renovated almost entirely by Alfred and David, keeping all characteristic features such as beams and sloping brick floors intact. Residents of Italy for over 10 years, the Zitos are a rich source of information for Tuscan itineraries. Alfred and daughter Lisa manage several other country properties in the area. *Directions*: Take route 68 at Cecina from the coast highway route 1 to Pomarance and call to be met. The house is out of town at S. Ippolito.

CASA ZITO   New
Hosts: Zito family
Localita: S. Ippolito
Pomarance (PS) 56045, Italy
Tel & fax: (0588) 67789
2 rooms with private bathrooms, 2 apartments
Lire 130,000 double B&B
Lire 800,000 weekly apartments
Breakfast only
Dinner upon request
Open all year
Fluent English spoken, Region: Tuscany

Forty-five kilometers northeast of Florence, in a beautiful, hilly area of Tuscany, lies the Rufina valley, famous for its robust red wine. Crowning a wooded slope is one of the many residences of the noble Galeotti-Ottieri family. The 15th-century main villa, where the family lives when not in Florence, was once a convent. The interior reveals spacious high-ceilinged halls with frescoes depicting family history. The family has also restored several stone farmhouses on the vast property, one of which is the Locanda Praticino (run by daughter-in-law Antonella) whose upper floor contains seven lovely, simple double rooms, each with private bath and named after its color scheme. Downstairs is a large dining and living room with vaulted ceiling, enormous stone fireplace, and family antiques. A unique loft bedroom in the third-floor cupola offers a sweeping view of the lush countryside. The addition of a swimming pool and tennis courts, plus enchanting landscape, makes it difficult to tear oneself away for touring. Available for longer stays are five very tastefully decorated apartments (two in the main house). The Petrognano is a tranquil spot where guests may enjoy the gracious hospitality of this historically important Florentine family. *Directions*: From Florence head toward Pontassieve. Continue to Rufina, turning right at Castiglioni-Pomino. The farm is just before Pomino.

FATTORIA DI PETROGNANO
Hosts: Cecilia Galeotti-Ottieri family
Localita: Pomino
Rufina (FI) 50060, Italy
Tel: (055) 8318812 or 8318867
Fax: (055) 242918
7 rooms, 6 with private bathrooms
5 apartments
Lire 110,000 double B&B
All meals served
Open March to October
English & French spoken well, Region: Tuscany

Annabel and Cesare Taticchi heartily welcome guests to their corn and horse-breeding farm, a rambling Renaissance villa, above Perugia. The former stables near the main house contain a breakfast room and the eight guestrooms with wood-beamed ceilings and brick floors, furnished in simple country style. Ceramic bathroom tile (and lamps), handmade by their talented daughter, depicts horses, ducks, roses, butterflies, and the like, for which the rooms are named. The main villa's dramatic entrance foyer with arched stairway leads up to a glassed-in veranda overlooking a lush flower garden and woods through which the River Tiber flows. Annabel serves her specialties in the elegant old-style dining room with chandelier and frescoes. Time stands still in the original library/billiard room and the two living rooms with grand piano, Oriental carpets, and period paintings where guests may lounge. Twenty horses are available for lessons in the indoor/outdoor ring or excursions in the area. Week-long courses with special all-inclusive rates are now available in cooking, ceramics, and riding. *Directions*: Take route E45 from Perugia and exit at Ponte Pattoli. Turn right at the T intersection and continue for 1 km. The farm is just after the tennis/sport complex.

IL COVONE
Hosts: Annabel & Cesare Taticchi
Strada della Fratticiola 2
Ponte Pattoli (PG) 06085, Italy
Tel: (075) 694140, Fax: (075) 694503
www.karenbrown.com\italy\ilcovone.html
10 rooms with private bathrooms
Lire 120,000 double B&B (3-day minimum stay)
  95,000–115,000 per person half board
Breakfast & dinner served
Open all year
Credit cards: all major
English spoken well, Region: Umbria

Gennarino a Mare is primarily a restaurant—one of the best known in Ponza both for its seafood specialties and its prime location right on the waterfront. It even has a large deck that stretches out over the water, built upon large wooden pilings. Gennarino a Mare is a favorite place to dine, especially in summer when boats of all shapes and sizes dock at the adjacent pier and the merry yacht set comes to eat and drink. The restaurant has hosted many of the world's rich and famous, so there's no telling who might be sitting at the next table. It is no wonder the restaurant is so popular: as you enjoy dinner, you can watch the reflection of the fishing boats shimmering in the water and, behind them, the gaily painted houses of Ponza stepping up the hill like brightly painted blocks. The property's gracious owner, Francesco Silvestri, was born right in the same house where the restaurant now stands—his parents lived here and ran a small *pension*. The 12 simple bedrooms, located on the floors above the restaurant, are all decorated similarly with colorful matching drapes and bedspreads setting off white walls. Although small, each room has its own little step-out balcony with a romantic view. Remember, Gennarino a Mare is basically a restaurant, but a real winner for a simple, reasonably priced place to stay in Ponza. *Directions*: Take either the ferry or hydrofoil from Anzio to Ponza. The hotel is on the opposite side of the port, so it is best to take a taxi if you have luggage.

GENNARINO A MARE
Hosts: Tilla & Francesco Silvestri
Via Dante, 64
Isola di Ponza (LT) 04027, Italy
Tel: (0771) 80071, Fax: (0771) 80140
12 rooms with private bathrooms
Lire 200,000 double B&B
 125,000–215,000 per person half board
All meals served
Open all year Credit cards: all major
English spoken well, Region: Lazio

The Vecchio Convento is a real gem, offering quality accommodation for a moderate price. Its several dining rooms are brimming with rustic country charm and serve delicious meals prepared from local produce. There are 20 guestrooms tastefully decorated with antiques—most have private bathrooms. The town of Portico di Romagna is like the inn, inviting yet unpretentious—an old village surrounded by wooded hills and clear mountain streams. A stroll through medieval pathways which twist down between the weathered stone houses leads you to an ancient stone bridge gracefully arching over a rushing stream. The inn, too, is old, but was not (as you might expect from its name) originally a convent. According to its gracious owner, Marisa Raggi, it was named for a restaurant located in a convent that she and her husband, Giovanni (the chef) used to operate—when they moved here they kept the original name. The restaurant (closed Wednesdays) is still their primary focus, as its fine, fresh cuisine reflects. Because of the winding, two-lane mountain highway which leads to the village, it takes about two hours to drive the 75 km from Florence. *Directions*: The inn is located 34 km southwest of the town of Forli.

ALBERGO AL VECCHIO CONVENTO
Hosts: Marisa Raggi & Giovanni Cameli
Via Roma 7
Portico di Romagna (FO) 47010, Italy
Tel: (0543) 967053, Fax: (0543) 967157
20 rooms, 15 with private bathrooms
Lire 140,000 double B&B
All meals served (except Wednesdays)
Open all year
Credit cards: all major
Some English spoken, Region: Emilia-Romagna

On the outskirts of historical Mantua sits the Villa Schiarino, one of the magnificent estates formerly belonging to the Gonzaga family, once among the most powerful nobility in Lombardy. The cordial Lena Eliseo family, the present owners, have taken on the enormous task of restoring the 15th-century palace room by room. With high vaulted ceilings, completely frescoed rooms, wrought-iron chandeliers, and original terra-cotta floors, the seemingly endless parade of rooms reveals one delight after another. Besides being a museum, the villa is also used for large parties, weddings, and business affairs, plus offers three unique bedrooms sharing baths. Surrounding the villa are small houses, once inhabited by farm hands, which are now available to travelers on a daily or weekly basis. The three modest but spacious and comfortable apartments are appointed with a mixture of antique and contemporary furniture and can accommodate up to four persons. Each apartment has its own living area and one includes a kitchenette. This location is the ideal spot to base yourself while exploring less-touristy Ferrara, Cremona, Verona, and Mantua, which are filled with medieval and Renaissance buildings (Palazzo del Te and Palazzo Ducale are "must-sees"). *Directions*: From Mantua take route N62 past the church and turn left on Via Gramsci. Follow it for 1 km to the villa.

VILLA SCHIARINO LENA
Hosts: Lena Eliseo family
Via Santa Maddalena 7
Porto Mantovano (MN) 46047, Italy
Tel & fax: (0376) 398238
www.karenbrown.com\italy\villaschiarinolena.html
3 apartments for 2 to 4 persons, 3 rooms
Lire 140,000–180,000 daily per room or apartment B&B
Breakfast only
Open all year
English spoken well, Region: Lombardy

High above the strip of shore holding the Fortino Napoleonico hotel sits the Hotel Emilia, owned by the Fiorini Dubbini family. Grandmother Emilia opened a small restaurant right on the beach 50 years ago, gaining an excellent reputation for fresh seafood dishes. That successful undertaking was followed by the hotel which, not surprisingly, has a restaurant known for seafood. It is surrounded by an extensive lawn sweeping to the edge of a cliff which drops 150 meters straight down to the sea below. Truly breathtaking views of Mount Conero and the dramatic, rugged coast can be enjoyed from this point as well as from any of the guestrooms. The hotel itself is rather stark and modern, with interiors softened by wicker couches topped by plump, yellow floral-print pillows, paintings, and flower bouquets. The all-white rooms are basic but comfortable, with wicker and rattan beds and clean, tiled bathrooms. This is primarily a summer resort with swimming pool and tennis available on the premises, plus a nearby golf course. Art shows and concerts are frequently held here and enthusiastic son Maurizio has just opened a quaint bar/trattoria down the road, where jazz music is featured. *Directions*: Exit at Ancona Sud off autostrada A14 and follow signs for Camerano, then Portonovo. Watch for signs indicating the hotel's entrance.

HOTEL EMILIA
Hosts: Maurizio Fiorini family
Localita: Collina di Portonovo
Portonovo (AN) 60020, Italy
Tel: (071) 801145, Fax: (071) 801330
www.karenbrown.com\italy\hotelemilia.html
31 rooms with private bathrooms
6 apartments
Lire 150,000–250,000 double B&B
All meals served
Open all year
Credit cards: all major
English spoken well, Region: Marches

For those travelers wishing to explore the lesser-known Marches region, or about to embark on a ferry to Greece, the unique Fortino hotel offers comfortable and relaxing accommodations. Five kilometers along the coast from the city of Ancona, the hotel boasts a beachfront location. Originally a fortress, the vantage point it affords must have been considered strategic by Napoleon in 1811, when he ordered it constructed. Fifteen guestrooms, four suites, and a restaurant are housed within the low white, stone structure while the remaining 15 rooms are in a new building nearby. The restaurant specializes in fresh seafood dishes and looks so directly out to sea, it gives the impression of being on a ship. At the heart of the fort is a courtyard, complete with cannons, where breakfast is served, and a separate building contains a bar and a spacious living room with fireplace, decorated in neoclassic style. Rich period antiques appoint the three lovely suites, while simpler wicker furniture is found in the double rooms. Just two steps away is the beach, and up on the roof of the one-story fort is a deck with a spectacular coastal view. A swimming pool is also available for guests. *Directions*: From Ancona, follow signs for Camerano. Take a left at Portonovo, heading down to the sea. Watch for signs indicating the hotel's entrance.

FORTINO NAPOLEONICO
Hosts: Amleto Roscioni family
Via Poggio
Portonovo (AN) 60020, Italy
Tel: (071) 801450, Fax: (071) 801454
30 rooms & 4 suites with private bathrooms
Lire 260,000–320,000 double B&B
All meals served
Open all year
Credit cards: all major
English spoken well, Region: Marches

Accommodation of all levels is available in Positano's many hotels: from five-star luxury to simple bed and breakfasts. Casa Cosenza, with its sunny yellow façade, fits into the latter category. Sitting snug against the cliff side, halfway down to the beach, it is reached by descending one of the variety of stairways found in this unique seaside town. The front arched entranceway, lined with terra-cotta pots overflowing with colorful local flora, leads to an enormous tiled terrace overlooking the pastel-color houses of Positano and the dramatic coastline. Seven guestrooms on the second floor, each with private bathroom and balcony, enjoy the same breathtaking panorama. The residence dates back 200 years, as evidenced by the typical cupola ceilings in each room, originally designed to keep rooms cool and airy. Rooms have bright, tiled floors and are simply and sweetly decorated with old-fashioned armoires, desks, and beds. Room 7 (at a slightly higher rate), although smaller and with an older bathroom, has a lovely large terrace, as do two newly added rooms behind the main house. A Continental breakfast is served on the terrace. The helpful and very friendly Cosenza family assures visitors a pleasant stay. *Directions*: Park your car in a garage in town and ask for directions for the *scalinatella* stairway where there are signs to Casa Cosenza. Remember to pack light!

CASA COSENZA
Hosts: Cosenza family
Positano (SA) 84017, Italy
Tel & fax: (089) 875063
9 rooms with private bathrooms
Lire 175,000–195,000 double B&B
3-day minimum stay in high season
Breakfast only
Open all year
Very little English spoken, Region: Campania

The spectacular Amalfi coast offers a wide variety of accommodation, yet few as special as La Fenice—as fantastic as the mythological bird for which it is named. Guests leave their cars on the main road and climb the arbored steps to discover the idyllic white villa hidden amid the lush Mediterranean vegetation. The incredibly hospitable proprietors, Costantino and Angela, heartily welcome new arrivals on the shady front terrace, where breakfast is served each clement morning, accompanied by classical music. Six luminous bedrooms, three with terrace and marvelous sea views, the others with lateral sea or garden view, are simply decorated with scattered antiques in a wing off the family's home. Seven more rooms, most with terraces, reached by *many* steps down from the road, are built separately into the side of the cliff and have colorful, tiled floors and similar furnishings. Descending yet *more* steps (always surrounded by incredible coastal views), you'll come across the curved sea-water pool and Jacuzzi carved against the rock, where a fresh Mediterranean lunch is served, at an extra cost, during summer months, prepared primarily with home-grown ingredients. A fishing boat picks up guests on the beach for a delightful tour of the coast and lunch on board. This property is a natural wonder, cascading down to the sea and a small private beach. *Directions*: Located on the coastal highway south of Positano in the direction of Amalfi. Two curves after the town, watch for gates on the right.

LA FENICE
Hosts: Angela & Costantino Mandara
Via Marconi 4
Positano (SA) 84017, Italy
Tel: (089) 875513, Fax: none
www.karenbrown.com\italy\lafenice.html
15 rooms with private bathrooms
Lire 160,000 double B&B
Breakfast & lunch served (extra charge for lunch)
Open all year
Some English spoken, Region: Campania

Villa Rosa opened its doors last year after some restoration work by local couple Virginia and Franco who own a clothing store and ceramic store in town. The 150-year-old house, hidden behind bougainvillea vines high above the road, is on three levels and has always been in Virginia's family. Taking the stairs up to the middle level, you find the reception area and large common living room where hostess Camilla greets and assists guests to their rooms. The 12 rooms are divided up among the three floors, each having access to the large front terraces which are divided by plants and grapevines for privacy. Picturesque views of Positano's colorful houses and the spectacular coastline are enjoyed from any point. Breakfast is served either in rooms or out on individual terraces adorned with large terra-cotta vases laden with cascading pink and red geraniums, in sharp contrast with pure white walls. Bedrooms maintain original tiles and vaulted ceilings and are furnished with simple antiques, while bathrooms display typical yellow and blue handpainted tiles from Vietri. Air conditioning is an exceptional amenity offered. *Directions*: Following the main road through town, you find Villa Rosa almost at the end just before the famous Sirenuse Hotel. Parking is in public garage only.

VILLA ROSA   *New*
Hosts: Virginia & Franco Caldiero
Via C. Colombo 127
Positano (SA) 84017, Italy
Tel & fax: (089) 811955
www.karenbrown.com\italy\villarosa.html
12 rooms with private bathrooms
Lire 150,000 double B&B
Breakfast only
Open March to October
Some English spoken, Region: Campania

The Villa Rucellai rates high among Italian bed and breakfasts, due to its setting, style, and gracious proprietors, the Rucellai Pique family. From the moment you enter the grand foyer looking out over the classical Italian Renaissance garden of this 16th-century country villa, all sense of time and place is lost. The Rucellais' devotion to their "farm" (in the family since 1759) is apparent, as is their warm and enthusiastic hospitality. Guests are given the run of the charming old home: from the cozy bedrooms, varying in size and decor, antique-filled library, and spacious living room with fireplace, plump floral sofas, and family portraits to the country kitchen and breakfast room overlooking a 14th-century pool, where guests are served *en famille* at a long wooden table. Members of the family enjoy suggesting itineraries of particular interest for their guests, as well as cultural events such as art courses, concerts, and art exhibits. The Villa Rucellai provides truly special accommodation as well as serving as an excellent base from which to visit Florence, Siena, Lucca, and Pisa. *Directions*: From Florence take the A11 autostrada, exiting at Prato Est. Turn right on Viale della Repubblica, then left on Borgo Valsugana, following signs for Trattoria La Fontana, and proceed on Via di Canneto for 2 km up to the Villa.

VILLA RUCELLAI DI CANNETO
Hosts: Giovannu Rucellai Pique family
Via di Canneto 16
Prato (FI) 50047, Italy
Tel & fax: (0574) 460392 or (0574) 464986
11 rooms with private bathrooms
Lire 150,000 double B&B
Breakfast only
Open all year
Fluent English spoken, Region: Tuscany

One option (among at least 20 possibilities) for in-home accommodations in the Radda area is at the home of a gregarious Florentine couple, Giuliana and Enis Vergelli, whose stone house sits on a long, winding road, just before the castle/village of Volpaia. The guest quarters are actually found in another stone house a few steps away in the quaint 14th-century village. The wood-shuttered residence can be rented entirely or as two separate apartments. One apartment is just like a doll house, comprised of a mini living area with minuscule fireplace, kitchenette, and a ladder staircase leading up to the bedroom and bath—an absolutely adorable love nest for two. The other apartment, also on two floors, has a good-sized living room with kitchen, bathroom, and two bedrooms, simply and very comfortably furnished. Giuliana also offers accommodation in a bedroom with bathroom, garden, and separate entrance in her own home. Guests are welcome to wander through the Vergellis' garden and enjoy the terrace with sweeping views over Chianti country. Giuliana adores pampering her guests and appears now and then with jams, honey, or a freshly made soup. *Directions*: Driving through the town of Radda, turn right at signs for Volpaia castle. Follow uphill for several kilometers to the first house before entering town, marked Vergelli.

AZIENDA AGRICOLA VERGELLI
Hosts: Enis & Giuliana Vergelli
Localita: Volpaia
Radda in Chianti (SI) 53017, Italy
Tel & fax: (0577) 738382
www.karenbrown.com\italy\aziendaagricolavergelli.html
2 apartments, 1 room with private bathroom
$450 (US) weekly for 2 persons
$650 (US) weekly for 4 persons
$80 (US) double room (no breakfast)
No meals served
Open all year
No English spoken, Region: Tuscany

Another addition to the group of house rentals in Radda is Le Selve, owned by a young couple who transferred to this serene countryside from Milan a few years ago. Their stone farmhouse is perched on a hilltop dominating the sweeping lush green landscape below—a truly heavenly 360-degree panorama. Sonia and Nando divided the house into two apartments, the top floor for themselves and their son, and the bottom floor for their guests. This downstairs apartment has a bedroom, bathroom, and living room with fully equipped kitchenette, eating area, and garden, furnished very simply but comfortably for independent travelers. Sonia's great passion for horses has her spending most of her time down at the stables, where outings in the gorgeous countryside are organized. The couple is happy to advise guests on various itineraries here in the heart of Tuscany. A nice and very quiet retreat, and a great base for exploring the scenic roads of Chianti. *Directions*: Coming from the west, just before Radda, turn right for San Sano and follow road until the sign S. Giusto in Salcio and turn right up hill to the farmhouse.

LE SELVE II
Hosts: Sonia & Nando Danieli
Localita: Le Selve-San Giusto
Radda in Chianti (SI) 53017, Italy
Tel: (0577) 738196, Fax: none
1 apartment
$450 (US) weekly for 2 persons
No meals served
Open all year
Some English spoken, Region: Tuscany

For its combination of idyllic location, charming ambiance, and delightful hosts, the Podere Terreno is an example of the best in Italian bed and breakfasts, with Sylvie and Roberto, a Franco-Italian couple, along with gregarious son, Francesco, dedicating themselves to pampering their guests. The 400-year-old house is surrounded by terra-cotta flower vases, a grapevine-covered pergola, a small lake, and sweeping panoramas of the Chianti countryside. Within are seven sweet double bedrooms with bath, each decorated differently with country antiques and the family's personal possessions; a wine cellar loaded with the proprietors' own Chianti Classico; and a billiard room/library. Guests convene in the main room of the house around the massive stone fireplace on fluffy floral sofas for hors d'oeuvres before sitting down to a sumptuous candlelit dinner prepared by your hosts. This is a cozy, stone-walled room, filled with country antiques, brass pots and dried-flower bouquets hanging from the exposed beams, and shelves lined with bottles of wine—absolutely delightful. *Directions*: From Greve follow signs to Panzano, then go left for Radda and on to Lucarelli. After 3 km turn right at Volpaia. After 5 km, turn right at the sign for Podere Terreno.

PODERE TERRENO
Hosts: Marie Sylvie Haniez & Roberto Melosi
Via della Volpaia
Radda in Chianti (SI) 53017, Italy
Tel & fax: (0577) 738312
www.karenbrown.com\italy\podereterreno.html
7 rooms with private bathrooms
Lire 130,000–140,000 per person half board
2-day minimum stay
Breakfast & dinner served
Open all year
Credit cards: MC, VS
English spoken very well, Region: Tuscany

Both Radda and Greve are excellent bases from which to explore scenic Chianti wine country with its regal castles and stone villages, in addition to Siena, Florence, and San Gimignano. Radda in particular offers a myriad of possibilities for accommodation, including private homes whose owners have coordinated a booking service: if space is not available at one, similar arrangements can be made elsewhere. The Val delle Corti is the home and vineyard estate of the ex-mayor of Radda, Giorgio Bianchi (who runs the booking service) and his lovely wife, Eli. The cozy pale-stone house with white shutters tops a hill overlooking town. The hosts, who moved here 25 years ago from Milan, are extremely active in community affairs and are a superb source for area information. They offer guests a quarter of their stone farmhouse: a rustic two-bedroom apartment with a separate entrance, a large bathroom, kitchen, and living room with fireplace, all furnished simply with family belongings. On request, Eli will supply coffee and jam for the weekly stay, while other meals can be taken at their nephew's newly opened restaurant in town, Le Vigne. *Directions*: Equidistant from Florence and Siena off the N222 Chianti road. Before entering Radda, turn right toward Lecchi-San Sano, then take the first left at Val delle Corti.

PODERE VAL DELLE CORTI
Hosts: Eli & Giorgio Bianchi
Localita: La Croce
Radda in Chianti (SI) 53017, Italy
Tel & fax: (0577) 738215
www.karenbrown.com\italy\poderevaldellecorti.html
1 apartment
$650 (US) per week
Half board available at Le Vigne restaurant
Open Easter to October
English spoken very well, Region: Tuscany

On the opposite side of town from the Podere Val delle Corti (see preceding page), live Giorgio Bianchi's sister and family, who offer a two-bedroom apartment in a stone tower dating from 1832. This unique accommodation, perfect for a family of four, has an enchanting view of Radda and the countryside. The three-story tower has terra-cotta floors and beamed ceilings, a living room/kitchenette on the ground floor, one bedroom and a bath on the second floor, and a second bedroom on top. Furnishings are simple and in keeping with tower's rustic features. A small olive grove separates the tower from the Vitalis' lovely home, where a swimming pool awaits road-weary guests and a double bedroom with bathroom is offered. Lele is a vivacious hostess who divides her time between guests; a small in-house weaving business; and helping out her son and daughter-in-law, a young and ambitious couple who converted a farmhouse into the most authentic regional restaurant in town—Le Vigne. A half-board meal plan can be arranged for guests of the tower. *Directions*: From either Siena or Florence, follow signs for Radda off the spectacular Strada del Chianti N222. Go through town until you reach the hotel/restaurant Villa Miranda (not recommended), after which turn right at the sign for Canvalle and follow the dirt road up to the tower.

TORRE CANVALLE
Hosts: General & Lele Bianchi Vitali
Localita: La Villa
Radda in Chianti (SI) 53017, Italy
Tel & fax: (0577) 738321
1 apartment, 1 room with private bathroom
$700 (US) weekly (heating extra)
$100 (US) double B&B (heating extra)
Half board available at Le Vigne restaurant
Open all year
English spoken very well, Region: Tuscany

The southeast corner of Tuscany offers a rich variety of sites to explore for those who seek the road less traveled, from the Amiata mountains for nature lovers, to the hilltowns of Montepulciano, Pienza, Montalcino for wine and art lovers, to Chianciano and Vignoni for thermal baths. La Palazzina, adoringly run by mother and daughter team, Bianca and Nicoletta, serves as the perfect base from which to visit these treasures. The restaurant is very special indeed. All the freshest, most natural ingredients from the farm are used in recipes originating from the Renaissance. The refined meals are served in two elegant dining rooms, accompanied by baroque music. The unusual checked tiled floors throughout the villa give it a cool, clean look and mix well with the many antique pieces. The 12 dainty bedrooms with immaculate bathrooms have women's names, each having its own color scheme. A swimming pool hugs the side of a hill overlooking the sweeping valley. Week-long courses are now offered in a variety of fields (Tuscan cooking, herbs and plants, astronomy). There are five lovely apartments for two to four persons in a nearby stone farmhouse for weekly stays. *Directions*: From Florence on the A1 autostrada, exit Chiusi and follow for Sarteano on route 478, turning left for Radicofani. After 14 km turn left for Celle Sul Rigo then right at the sign for La Palazzina.

LA PALAZZINA
Hosts: Innocenti family
Localita: Le Vigne
Radicofani (SI) 53040, Italy
Tel: (0578) 55771, Fax: (0578) 53553
12 rooms with private bathrooms
* 3 apartments for 4 persons*
Lire 98,000–112,000 per person half board
All meals served
Open April to October
Credit cards: all major
Some English spoken, Region: Tuscany

The Villa Maria is perhaps best known for its absolutely delightful terrace restaurant which has a bird's-eye view of the magnificent coast. Whereas most of Ravello's hotels capture the southern view, the Villa Maria features the equally lovely vista to the north. The Villa Maria is two minutes by foot from the main square on the path winding to the Villa Cimbrone. After parking in the square (or at the Hotel Giordano), look for signs for the Villa Maria, perched on the cliffs to your right. The building is a romantic old villa with a garden stretching to the side where tables and chairs are set, a favorite place to dine while enjoying the superb view. Inside, there is a cozy dining room overlooking the garden. The bedrooms are air conditioned and furnished with antique pieces including brass beds. The bathrooms have been freshly remodeled and some even have Jacuzzi tubs. The hotel is owned by Vincenzo Palumbo whose staff speak excellent English and go out of their way to assist guests. Vincenzo also owns the nearby more modern Hotel Giordano which has a heated pool that you can use. Guests at the Villa Maria enjoy a wonderful view and location in a charming villa with a fine restaurant. *Directions*: Ravello is about 6 km north of Amalfi on a small road heading north from the highway.

VILLA MARIA
Host: Vincenzo Palumbo
Via San Chiara 2
Ravello (SA) 84010, Italy
Tel: (089) 857255, Fax: (089) 857071
www.karenbrown.com\italy\villamaria.html
17 rooms with private bathrooms
2 apartments
Lire 220,000–260,000 double B&B
  160,000–180,000 per person half board
  (required in high season, June to September)
All meals served
Open all year, Credit cards: all major
English spoken very well, Region: Campania

The area of Tuscany south of Siena is a delightful discovery for those wanting to explore the lesser known. Besides the charming hilltowns of Montepulciano, Pienza, and Montalcino, there are the abbeys of Monte Oliveto and Sant'Antimo, plus the thermal baths of Bagno Vignoni. The variety of landscapes within an 8-kilometer stretch of road makes it one of the most fascinating driving excursions in the region. And while touring this richly historical and natural area, a perfect base is the magnificent castle of the Aluffi Pentini family, theirs for the past 400 years or so. The family resides in the main villa while guests are accommodated in several separate houses along the internal road in a combination of apartments with one or two bedrooms, living room and kitchenette, plus six simply and characteristically appointed bedrooms with country furniture. Rooms facing out have some of the most breathtaking views imaginable. Downstairs is the dining room with wood tables covered with cheery checked cloths, where breakfast and dinner are served using home-grown products. Farm products such as wine, olive oil, grappa, and jams are sold. *Directions*: The castle is well marked at 5 km from San Quirico d'Orcia. Ripa d'Orcia is actually marked on most maps.

CASTELLO DI RIPA D'ORCIA
Hosts: The Aluffi Pentini family
Localita: Ripa d'Orcia
Via della Contea 1
San Quirico d'Orcia (SI) 53023, Italy
Tel: (0577) 897376, Fax: (0577) 898038
www.karenbrown.com\italy\castellodiripadorcia.html
7 apartments, 6 rooms with private bathrooms
Lire 135,000–160,000 double B&B
  750,000–1,300,000 weekly for apartments
2-day minimum stay (rooms)
Breakfast & dinner served (except Mondays)
Open March to January 7, Credit cards: AX, VS
English spoken well, Region: Tuscany

With passion and determination, Daniela and her architect husband, Piero, brought back to life the family's ancient property with total respect for its 9th-century origins. The place is very special indeed and rich with historical events. A nature lover's paradise, the complex of stone houses is surrounded by lush vegetation, woods, and olive groves from which the family's prestigious oil comes, and the perfume of lavender and jasmine is divinely intoxicating. Hospitality is offered within six apartments attached to the main house accommodating from two to five persons, impeccably decorated with the family's refined antiques which live harmoniously with their perfectly preserved centuries-old environment. The dwellings feature living room with fireplace, balconies taking in either the sweeping countryside views down to the sea or out to the woods and a 200-year-old oak tree, wrought-iron beds, and original paintings by Daniela's father, a renowned fresco painter. Daniela, a world traveler, is a hostess *par excellence* and her contagious enthusiasm makes a stay at Caminino nothing less than splendidly memorable. Besides Siena and Montalcino, there are plenty of off-the-beaten-track sights to see. *Directions*: From Grosseto take Aurelia route 1 north and exit at Braccagni. Continue straight towards Montemassi and before town turn right for Caminino (listed on most maps) and Roccatederighi. After 1 km turn right at the gate for Caminino.

FATTORIA DI CAMININO
Hosts: Daniela & Piero Marrucchi Locatelli
Via Provinciale di Peruzzo
Roccatederighi (GR) 58028, Italy
Tel: (0564) 569737, Fax: (055) 2345999
6 apartments
Lire 500,000–1,300,000 weekly
No meals served
Open all year
English spoken well, Region: Tuscany

Tuscany is the most visited region in Italy—mostly between Siena and Florence—but it nonetheless contains many other treasures off the beaten track. Heading west from Florence toward the coast are the lovely towns of Lucca and Pisa, and just north of them is the beautifully scenic area known as Garfagnana, which features two nature reserves and the Apuan Alps. Here in the northernmost tip of Tuscany is evidence of how Italian culture varies not only from one region to another, but within a region itself. In the heart of these mountains, the genial Coletti family runs a lively local restaurant and cultivates cereals, wild berries, and chestnuts. Hospitality is offered within seven double rooms with a mountain-cabin feeling, having pinewood floors and ceilings, in a restored three-story building within the stone village of Roggio. Most have a balcony and all have modern bathrooms. Meals are taken around the corner at the family restaurant where Gemma Coletti prepares her special lasagna and polenta with porcini mushrooms, among other local specialties. A true value and a way to see a slice of village life. *Directions*: From Lucca, take route 445 toward Castelnuovo and on to Vagli di Sotto then right for Roggio. Take a winding road up to Roggio, where a sign indicates the Coletti restaurant in the village.

LA FONTANELLA
Hosts: Gemma & Severino Coletti
Localita: Vagli Sotto
Roggio (LU) 55100, Italy
Tel: (0583) 649179, Fax: none
www.karenbrown.com\italy\lafontanella.html
7 rooms with private bathrooms
Lire 60,000 double
All meals served
Open all year except Christmas
Very little English spoken, Region: Tuscany

A delightful alternative to our group of accommodations in Rome is Casa Stefazio, the only true in-home bed and breakfast. The location and setting are as perfect as the dedication and warm hospitality offered by Stefania and Orazio in their large, ivy-covered suburban home, just 30 minutes from the city center, surrounded by several acres of manicured garden and utter silence. On the lower level, with a separate entrance, are three bedrooms and one spacious "suite" accommodating a family of four (this has a sauna), each with its own immaculate bathroom, satellite TV, air conditioning, and mini bar. On the first floor near the hosts' quarters is an additional bedroom with its own bathroom. The main areas include living room, large American-style kitchen, where both Stefania and Orazio work wonders (he has a Cordon Bleu diploma), and eating area overlooking the expansive lawn and distant woods. Dinner is served on request under the pergola. Sports activities such as horseback riding, tennis, golf, and swimming are easily arranged. The hosts also organize excursions for groups of friends throughout Italy. Highly recommended by readers. *Directions*: Located north of Rome just outside the circular highway around the city (GRA), close to the tollway north to Florence and south to Naples. Call one day ahead to receive detailed directions. Pickup at the station or airport can be arranged with advance notice.

CASA STEFAZIO
Hosts: Stefania & Orazio Azzola
Via della Marcigliana 553
Rome 00138, Italy
Tel: (06) 87120042, Fax: (06) 87120012
www.karenbrown.com\italy\casastefazio.html
2 rooms, 2 suites with private bathrooms
$170–220 (US) double B&B
Breakfast only, Dinner served upon request
Open March 15 to December
English spoken very well, Region: Lazio

It is truly refreshing to have found such an efficiently run, friendly, and well-priced accommodation as the Hotel Celio in a centrally located area of Rome, not overrun by tourists. Just around the corner from the Colosseum, the Celio is part of an authentic Roman neighborhood. Plans to restore the façade of the turn-of-the-century building are currently in the process; however, the cheery side entrance covered with jasmine vines, along with the lovely interiors, immediately erase the first misleading impression. Brothers Roberto and Marcello, also owners of the Santo Stefano in Venice (page 203), are attentive to guests' comfort. The small entrance, painted with scenes of Roman monuments, leads to a cozy reception/sitting area and bar with large lit paintings. Eleven rooms of varying dimensions are each named after the famous artist whose fresco reproduction adorns the wall over the bed. Each is traditionally decorated with rich fabrics in royal blue and yellow, and has a small, but very modern and well-equipped bathroom with mosaic tiles. Breakfast is served in rooms, and other extras include nearby garage facilities, air conditioning, video library, tourist information, and, above all, silence, a rarity in Rome. This affordable accommodation is a delightful combination of the personal attention guests receive in a private home and the amenities of a 4-star hotel. *Directions*: Consult a city map.

*HOTEL CELIO   **New***
Hosts: Quatrini family
Via SS. Quattro 35/C
Rome 00184, Italy
Tel: (06) 70495333, Fax: (06) 7096377
11 rooms with private bathrooms
Lire 200,000–280,000 double B&B
Breakfast only
Open all year
Credit cards: all major
English spoken well, Region: Lazio

The Due Torri is a good example of a small and charming city hotel, a breed not easy to find in today's urban centers. The building, dating from the early 1800s, is tucked away on a tiny, narrow street in the historical section of Rome between the Spanish Steps and Navona Square. Renovated several years ago, the 26 very small bedrooms are decorated with care and taste, featuring spotless bathrooms, period antiques, and peach-colored fabric walls matching bedspreads and draperies. Many amenities are offered, including elevator and air conditioning, which provides welcome relief on Roman hot summer days. The cozy, newly renovated reception and sitting area have Oriental carpets, cream-color draperies, gilt-framed mirrors and paintings, and elegant tapestry chairs. The fifth-floor mansard room 503 is especially appealing, as are the fourth-floor rooms with balconies. Breakfast is served off in a room made cheery with trellis- and ivy-covered paper. A courteous staff assists in making suggestions for local sightseeing and restaurants. Due Torri is a popular hotel, so be sure to reserve your room at least one month in advance. *Directions*: Use a detailed city map to locate the hotel, north of Navona square in a maze of winding streets.

HOTEL DUE TORRI
Hostesses: Lidia Aperio Bella & Cinzia Pighini
Vicolo del Leonetto 23
Rome 00186, Italy
Tel: (06) 6876983 or 6875765
Fax: (06) 6865442
www.karenbrown.com\italy\hotelduetorri.html
26 rooms with private bathrooms
Lire 302,000 double B&B
Breakfast only
Open all year
Credit cards: all major
English spoken well, Region: Lazio

Many hotels in Rome can boast panoramic views over the city, but few have such a close-up view of a world-famous monument as the Fontana Hotel. Located directly on the square containing the magnificent Trevi fountain, the Fontana's windows look out on to its gushing waters, where you can practically toss a coin from your room. The sleek black-and-white breakfast room with wrought-iron chairs and tables is situated on the top floor of the 14th-century building, giving a bird's-eye view over the square from an enormous picture window. The small rooms are sweetly done with pastel-floral wallpaper, bedspreads, and white curtains and vary in size and decor. Bathrooms were incorporated into each room later, and are quite small. Narrow, vaulted-ceilinged halls leading to the guestrooms are adorned with antique prints of Rome. A very gradual updating of rooms is in progress and the initial results are splendid. Signora Elena and her staff at the desk attend to guests' every need. The noise commonly associated with a city hotel is not a problem here as the square is closed to traffic, although loud voices of tourists lingering into the early hours can be a problem in the summer when the fountain closes at midnight. *Directions*: Use a detailed city map to locate the hotel in the Piazza di Trevi off the Via Tritone.

FONTANA HOTEL
Hostess: Elena Daneo
Piazza di Trevi 96
Rome 00187, Italy
Tel: (06) 6786113 or 6791056, Fax: (06) 6790024
27 rooms with private bathrooms
Lire 300,000 double B&B
Breakfast only
Open all year
Credit cards: all major
English spoken well, Region: Lazio

The Locarno Hotel is centrally located on the corner of a rather busy street, only two blocks from bustling Popolo Square. Its downtown location makes noise unavoidable, so it is advisable to request a room away from the street, even though the installation of thermal windows has helped. Even with the extensive renovations it has undergone, the hotel, dating from 1925, retains the art-deco flavor it had originally. The red-carpeted reception area leads to a cozy bar and long, mirrored sitting room lined with cushioned banquettes and café tables. There is also a side patio with shady canvas umbrellas where guests can take breakfast in warm weather, if not in the new and cheery breakfast room looking out to the patio. Another fabulous addition is the opening of the rooftop garden where you can gaze over Rome's tiled roofs and terraces to St. Peter's dome and Villa Borghese park. The rooms, decorated with antiques, gold-framed mirrors, and pretty floral wallpaper, are air conditioned. Two apartments (no kitchen) are offered to guests in the building directly across the street. The Locarno features such extras as a parking garage and free use of bicycles with which you might tour the Villa Borghese park. It is no wonder that this has always been a favorite among artists and writers. Reserve well in advance. *Directions*: Use a detailed city map to locate the hotel one block east of the Tiber River at Flaminia square sign.

HOTEL LOCARNO
Hostess: Caterina Valente
Via della Penna 22
Rome 00186, Italy
Tel: (06) 3610841 or (06) 3610842, Fax: (06) 3215249
www.karenbrown.com\italy\hotellocarno.html
48 rooms, 2 suites with private bathrooms, 2 apartments
Lire 305,000 double B&B
Breakfast only
Open all year, Credit cards: all major
English spoken well, Region: Lazio

A welcome addition to the group of family-run city hotels is the Venezia, efficiently run and owned by young and gracious Patrizia Diletti. Although hotels near train stations are generally less desirable, the area around Rome's Termini station has experienced dramatically positive changes, thanks to the city's new mayor—there is a high concentration of hotels and offices within the turn-of-the-century-style buildings. Although the Venezia has 61 rooms, it has the feeling of a small and friendly place from the moment one enters its doors. Patrizia inherited the hotel from her Swiss grandparents and has made it her priority to maintain their reputable tradition in hospitality. Her passion for collecting antiques such as Orientals rugs and rich period paintings is evident throughout the spacious sitting rooms. A buffet breakfast is served in a room with peach tablecloths and fresh flowers topping tables. Upstairs the spotless rooms are decorated uniformly in white and rose hues with Venetian glass chandeliers, and offer all modern amenities. Patrizia has purposely decorated predominantly with white (even bedspreads), so that any sign of dirt can be spotted immediately. The corner rooms are the most spacious and those on the top floor have small balconies lined with geranium pots. Centrally located, the hotel is a 15-minute walk to Rome's historical center. *Directions*: Consult a detailed city map to locate the hotel to the right of the station.

HOTEL VENEZIA
Hostess: Patrizia Diletti
Via Varese 18
Rome 00185, Italy
Tel: (06) 4457101, Fax: (06) 4957687
E-mail: venezia@flashnet.it
61 rooms with private bathrooms
Lire 305,000 double B&B
Breakfast only
Open all year, Credit cards: MC, VS
English spoken well, Region: Lazio

Behind the city gates of Porta Pinciana, whose ancient walls lead from the Via Veneto, is tranquil, tree-lined Via Nomentana, once a luxurious residential street. Many elegant pastel-colored villas remain (including that of Mussolini), but most have been converted into embassy-owned apartments over the years. The Villa del Parco has been transformed into a lovely and quiet hotel with a bed-and-breakfast feel to it. A flower-edged driveway leads to the villa, passing by tables set up for breakfast in the small front garden. When you enter the pleasant lobby scattered with antiques and comfy sofas, you feel that you've arrived home. Three cozy sitting rooms invite guests to sit and relax. All of the thirty guestrooms, each with private bath, have been renovated and vary greatly in size and decor, which tends to be a mixture of old and new furnishings. Request one of the larger rooms facing out the back of the hotel just in case the street noise might be disturbing. The very cordial Bernardini family and friendly staff are happy to make restaurant and itinerary suggestions. Just completed last fall is the addition of an elevator and five nice new bedrooms on the top floor with beamed mansard ceilings. *Directions*: Rely on a detailed city map to locate the hotel in a residential district, a 15-minute walk from the city center.

HOTEL VILLA DEL PARCO
Hosts: Bernardini family
Via Nomentana 110
Rome 00161, Italy
Tel: (06) 44237773, Fax: (06) 44237572
30 rooms with private bathrooms
Lire 245,000 double B&B
Breakfast only
Open all year
Credit cards: all major
Some English spoken, Region: Lazio

An alternative to staying in Rome's busy city center, especially for families, is the Santa Rufina farm on the very outskirts of Rome. For a capital city of its size, it is truly amazing to find this enormous oasis of green farmland emerging just at the cutoff point of urban developments. Sophisticated hosts Gianni and Giulia happily settled back in the inherited family farm after many years of working abroad and after recently renovating and converting the stalls and barn into four independent apartments, began their bed-and-breakfast business. Guests stay in various-sized lodgings with one or two bedrooms, nice new bathrooms, fully equipped kitchenettes, and luminous living rooms, each with its own front garden. They are pleasantly furnished with the family's antiques, paintings, and drawings. Breakfast fixings are left at the beginning of guests' stay. Although the Remedias work in the city, Gianni's brothers still manage the farm and live just across the road within the property. A small pool is available to guests as an added plus and reduced rates are given for weekly stays. *Directions*: Santa Rufina is located directly west of Rome, just outside the circular highway around the city (GRA)—exit at Boccea to number 1115 (iron gate entrance). Thirty-five km from Fiumicino airport, 20 km from city center. A car is recommended to reach public transportation to the city.

TENUTA SANTA RUFINA
Hosts: Giovanni Remedia family
Via Boccea 1115
Rome 00167, Italy
Tel & fax: (06) 61909138 or Tel: (0335) 246977
www.karenbrown.com\italy\tenutasantarufina.html
4 apartments for 2 to 5 persons
$120–150 (US) daily per apartment
3-day minimum stay
No meals served
Open all year
English spoken very well, Region: Lazio

It came as a great surprise when Sarah Townsend announced that she had sold her beautiful bed and breakfast property "Il Bacchino," which had welcomed so many readers. However, Sarah, an artist and decorator with a passion for restoring historic buildings, had found her greatest challenge: the stunning Terranova Palace. Set in the remote hills of central Umbria, the early-18th-century palace with remarkable views over the entire Upper Tiber Valley was most probably the summer residence of nobility. Extensive restoration work began six years ago on the building, Italian garden, and general grounds, with plans to open formally in 1999. In the meantime, while the finishing touches are being worked on, accommodation is offered in the sumptuous guesthouse "la Palazzina" which contains two luxurious bedrooms each with its own bathroom, living rooms on both floors with fireplaces and French doors opening out to the garden, and kitchen with a terrace looking out over the breathtaking countryside with woods, olive groves, vineyards, lakes, and swimming pool. Fortunate guests have a unique opportunity to witness a palace in the remaking. A very romantic retreat—not to be missed. *Directions*: A detailed description will be sent to guests at the time of reservation.

PALAZZO TERRANOVA   New
Hosts: Sarah & Johnny Townsend
Localita: Ronti
Citta di Castello (PG) 06012, Italy
Tel & fax: (075) 8526046 or (075) 8574536
4 rooms with private bathrooms
$300 (US) double B&B
3-day minimum stay
Breakfast only
Dinner upon request
Open all year
English spoken fluently, Region: Umbria

The spectacular 3,000-acre hilltop farm property of Montestigliano, with its splendid full valley and plain views, is a rich combination of woods, cultivated fields, olive groves, and open meadows all surrounding the hamlet dating from 1730. British-born hostess Susan makes sure guests are comfortable in one of the ten independent apartments within the various houses scattered about the property. All retain their original Tuscan character in furnishings and have a combination of one to three bedrooms, kitchen, living room with fireplace, and essential modern amenities like washing machines. The granary has been restored and converted into a farm shop, recreation room, and dining room. Groups of up to 12 persons have the opportunity to reside in the main villa, once owned by nobility. Two swimming pools are at guests' disposal, plus many paths and trails for long countryside walks. Montestigliano is a marvelous base for getting to know in depth a part of Tuscany whose traditions and lifestyles have remained intact. While still having Siena, San Gimignano, Pienza, Montalcino, and the Chianti area at one's fingertips, there's a chance to explore the many nearby medieval villages of this culturally rich region. Plenty of shops and places to dine are available in the towns of Rosia and Sovicille. *Directions*: From Siena (12 km) take route 73 to Rosia, turning left at the sign for Orgia/Torri. The road up left to Montestigliano is immediately after Stigliano.

MONTESTIGLIANO
Hostess: Susan Pennington
Rosia (SI) 53010, Italy
Tel: (0577) 342013, Fax: (0577) 342100
10 apartments, 1 house
Lire 95,000–273,000 daily per apartment
5-day minimum stay, 1 week July & August (apts)
Breakfast & occasional dinners served
Open all year
Fluent English spoken, Region: Tuscany

Parma is without doubt the city most internationally known for its cheese and prosciutto, which you should not fail to sample while you're in the region. Thirty kilometers from Parma are found the curative thermal waters of Salsomaggiore and just beyond town is the Antica Torre, the ancient 13th-century tower which majestically crowns a hilltop overlooking the soft green countryside. The Pavesi family, proprietors of the surrounding farm, offer warm hospitality to its guests within the tower. One bedroom with bath is located on each of the tower's four floors and, in addition, the family has a large two-bedroom apartment available in the main house, ideal for a family. There are four additional apartments recently added within the stone residence. Rooms are simply decorated, and have lovely views over the valley. The barn has been converted into a pleasant dining room where fortunate guests sit down together to a hearty, homemade, Emiliana-style meal, including fresh pastas, vegetables, meat, and poultry direct from the farm (drinks not included). Amenities include a swimming pool, bicycles, and horses. *Directions*: From Salsomaggiore, go through town, following signs for Cangelasio and then Antica Torre, 3½ km from Salsomaggiore.

ANTICA TORRE
Hosts: Francesco Pavesi family
Localita: Cangelasio-Case Bussandri 197
Salsomaggiore Terme (PR) 43039, Italy
Tel & fax: (0524) 575425
www.karenbrown.com\italy\anticatorre.html
4 rooms with private bathrooms
5 apartments
Lire 100,000 double B&B
* 75,000 per person half board*
2-day minimum stay, 1 week in July & August
All meals served
Open March to November
Very little English spoken, Region: Emilia-Romagna

Though near both Verona and Lake Garda, the Ca'Verde farm feels far away from civilization, immersed in a wooded valley in the Veneto wine country. Nine families got together 13 years ago to purchase the unusual stone Provence-style farmhouse, originally a 15th-century convent, and turned it into a busy dairy farm producing cheese and yogurt. They adhere to traditional production methods without additives or preservatives. Five attic rooms are available for guests in the enormous U-shaped house where three of the families live. Rooms for two to four people are small and utilitarian, with rustic wood beds, beamed ceilings with skylights, and one clean, modern bathroom for every two rooms. Four new more comfortable rooms with bathrooms have been added (at a slightly higher rate) to another wing. Meals, prepared by a professional chef using regional recipes and homemade wine, are served in three informal dining rooms with red-checked tablecloths and large fireplaces. Guests dine in or out on the patio, and in the summer are treated to outdoor concerts and cinema. *Directions*: From Verona take the A12 autostrada toward Brennero. Exit at Verona Nord, and follow signs for San Ambrogio. Go through town and start up the hill, watching for a small sign for Ca'Verde on the left side of the road. (Total of 15 km.)

CA'VERDE (Co-op 8 Marzo)
Hostess: Vilma Zamboni
Azienda Agricola 8 Marzo
San Ambrogio Valpolicella (VR) 37010, Italy
Tel: (045) 6861760, Fax: (045) 6861245
Tel: (02) 66802366, Fax: (02) 66802909 when closed
www.karenbrown.com\italy\caverde.html
9 rooms, 4 with private bathrooms
Lire 64,000–79,000 double B&B
* 52,000–62,000 per person half board*
All meals served, Open May to October
Some English spoken, Region: Veneto

In the southeastern corner of Tuscany, bordering Umbria and Lazio, is a delightful yet-undiscovered pocket of absolutely stunning countryside. It was only natural that Andrea, with his expert culinary skills, and his lovely wife, Cristina, a born hostess, should open a bed and breakfast close to their vast countryside property. La Crocetta, as its name implies, sits right at the crossroads leading up to the charming town of San Casciano. While the hosts live up in the village, eight guestrooms are offered above the restaurant within the three-story stone house built in the 1930s. You enter the small restaurant by way of a front porch, where meals are also served, into the cozy reception area set around a large sit-in fireplace. Here within the two dining rooms with soft-pink-colored walls Andrea presents his delectable creations featuring homemade pastas with vegetable fillings. Small guestrooms with varying color schemes, each with a new bathroom, are pleasantly appointed with canopy beds and fresh country fabrics used for bedspreads and curtains. Thermal hot springs and horseback riding facilities are located in the vicinity. Orvieto, Perugia, Siena, and the hilltowns of Montepulciano and Montalcino are all at easy touring distance. *Directions*: From the A1 autostrada, exit at Fabro from the south or Chiusi from the north, traveling towards Sarteano-Cetona, then San Casciano.

LA CROCETTA
Hosts: Cristina & Andrea Leotti
Localita: La Crocetta
San Casciano dei Bagni (SI) 53040, Italy
Tel: (0578) 58360 Cellphone: (0330) 549775
Fax: (0578) 58353
8 rooms with private bathrooms
Lire 140,000 double B&B
* 100,000 per person half board*
All meals served
Open Easter to November
English spoken well, Region: Tuscany

Perched atop a hill and enjoying a 360-degree view of perfectly unspoiled landscape as far as the eye can see, including a stunning medieval castle, sits the Le Radici farmhouse. Partners and ex-urbanites, Marcello and Alfredo, carefully chose this peaceful spot with the intention of offering accommodation to those who truly appreciate nature, and opened the doors to guests in 1995. The two houses have been restored, maintaining most of the original rustic flavor, and divided into five separate six-person apartments. They include one or two bedrooms, living room with fireplace, kitchenette, and bathroom on either the ground or first floors. Wrought-iron beds and country furnishings adorn rooms, complemented by wood-beam and brick ceilings. Special attention has been given to landscaping around the immediate property which includes vineyards and olive groves. The real treat is the absolutely gorgeous "borderless" swimming pool with cascading water which fits harmoniously into its surroundings. The hosts suggest many interesting itineraries in this seemingly remote area, yet only a short distance from the autostrada and bordering Umbria. One can relax in the thermal waters of San Casciano or venture out to the towns of Orvieto, Todi, or Pienza, among others. *Directions*: From the town of San Casciano follow signs for Le Radici (4 km).

LE RADICI
Hosts: Alfredo Ferrari & Marcello Mancini
San Casciano dei Bagni (SI) 53040, Italy
Tel & fax: (0578) 56038 or Tel: (0578) 56033
5 apartments
Lire 140,000–216,000 daily per apartment*
*Utilities extra
2-night minimum stay
No meals served
Open all year
Credit cards: MC, VS
English spoken very well, Region: Tuscany

Agritourism and bed-and-breakfast-type accommodations are virtually non-existent in the northern lake district, so coming across the enchanting Villa Simplicitas was a special treat. The pale-yellow country house of Milanese family Castelli, run by sister-in-law Ulla, sits isolated high up in the hills between Lakes Como and Lugano and is surrounded by thick woods. There is a wonderful old-fashioned charm to the place, enhanced by many heirloom turn-of-the-century antiques scattered about the cozy living and dining rooms. Pretty floral fabrics cover sofas and armchairs, in perfect harmony with the soft yellow walls bordered with stenciled designs. The same warmth is spread among the ten guest bedrooms with their pinewood floors and *trompe l'oeil* paneled walls, antique beds, and lace doilies adorning dressers. Innovative meals prepared by local chef Maurizio are served either inside or out on the veranda with green and white striped awnings and matching director's chairs. In the evening, impeccably set tables are candlelit for a romantic dinner for two—simply heavenly. *Directions*: From Como head north to Argegno. Turn left, passing through S. Fedele, then just after town at the first bus station, turn left—it is just 2 km up to the house. Alternatively, call from town.

VILLA SIMPLICITAS
Hosts: Curzio Castelli family
Localita: Simplicitas
San Fedele d'Intelvi (CO) 22028, Italy
Tel: (031) 831132 or (02) 66802366
Fax: (02) 66802909
www.karenbrown.com\italy\villasimplicitas.html
10 rooms with private bathrooms
Lire 180,000 double B&B
* 115,000 per person half board*
All meals served
Open: June to October
English spoken well, Region: Lombardy

San Gemini, in the southwest corner of Umbria, is a jewel of a medieval village, so perfectly preserved that one can easily imagine what life was like in those times. Home also of the famous mineral water, just outside town there are the fascinating Roman ruins of Carsulae (3rd century B.C.). A very special place from which to explore the area is within one of the apartments of the Medici family, who have divided up the 17th-century palazzo where neoclassical sculptor Antonio Canova once lived. Congenial hosts Paolo and Nelly, both artisans, live above the spacious guest apartment which contains two bedrooms, two new bathrooms, kitchen, living room with fireplace, and dining room. Pleasantly decorated with country antiques, rooms are enhanced by the high-beamed ceilings, tiled brick floors, and pastel-colored walls. The bedrooms look out through noble cypress trees towards the main square while the living room opens out to a courtyard where you can have a meal or just relax. The apartment accommodates from four to eight persons and there is an extra charge for cleaning and linens. *Directions*: From the A1 autostrada, exit at Orte and follow signs for Narni, then San Gemini. Palazzo Canova dominates the main square from above.

PALAZZO CANOVA   **New**
Hosts: Paolo & Nelly Medici
Via Scuole Vecchie 42
San Gemini (TR) 05029, Italy
Tel & fax: (06) 9987358
1 apartment
Lire 700,000–900,000 weekly
* (high season)*
2-day minimum stay
No meals served
Open all year
English spoken well, Region: Umbria

Even though Il Casale opened its doors to guests just two years ago, it already gives the impression of being highly efficient and well seasoned, thanks to warm and dedicated host, Alessandro, who has combined his extensive hospitality experience with a desire to see his great-grandfather's lovely country property restored properly. Six double rooms and two small apartments including bedroom, kitchen/eating area, and bathroom are all housed within the extended stone farmhouse. Another section is reserved for the family who looks after the wine estate. Access to the guest entrance is through a well-kept garden around the back with a small chapel and lovely views over the soft hills. Main areas include a sitting room and beamed breakfast room with fireplace where a varied Continental breakfast is served, if not outside. The spotless home is appointed with scattered antiques, and very comfortable guestrooms, each with a different color scheme, have new bathrooms and either countryside views or garden or interior patio entrance. Alessandro has given infinite care to details in both the esthetics and service offered to his guests. His formula of offering all the services of a hotel with the rates and warmth of a bed and breakfast seems to work perfectly. Plenty of tourist information on vineyard itineraries and local cultural events is available. *Directions*: From San Gimignano follow signs for Certaldo for 3 km. Il Casale is on the left and well marked.

IL CASALE DEL COTONE
Host: Alessandro Martelli
Localita: Cellole 59
San Gimignano (SI) 53037, Italy
Tel & fax: (0577) 943236, Cellphone: (0338) 6257417
6 rooms with private bathrooms, 2 apartments
Lire 160,000–180,000 double B&B
Lire 160,000–208,000 daily per apartment
Breakfast only
Open all year Credit cards: AX, VS
English spoken very well, Region: Tuscany

Due to the ever-increasing popularity of the stunning medieval village of San Gimignano, accommodations in the surrounding countryside have flourished. La Casanova is a typical square stone farmhouse with wood shutters and red-tile roof, which you'll grow accustomed to seeing throughout Tuscany. The bed and breakfast's exceptional feature is that it enjoys a privileged view of the towers of San Gimignano, an ancient town referred to as the "Manhattan" of the year 1000. Marisa and Monica Cappellini are jovial hostesses who pride themselves on offering comfortable and immaculate accommodations to their international clientele. Breakfast is served on the outside patio where guests are immersed in breathtaking scenery, before heading out to visit intriguing San Gimignano and the many surrounding villages. This is an authentic and simple wine-producing farm with eight double rooms with private baths. Country furniture characteristic of the region decorates the rooms, whose original architectural features have been preserved. When Marisa is fully booked guests are offered accommodation in her sister's nearby bed and breakfast. *Directions*: From San Gimignano take the road toward Volterra. After 2 km, turn left at the sign for Casanova, **not** Hotel Pescille.

CASANOVA DI PESCILLE
Hostess: Marisa Cappellini
Localita: Pescille
San Gimignano (SI) 53037, Italy
Tel & fax: (0577) 941902
www.karenbrown.com\italy\casanovadipescille.html
8 doubles with private bathrooms
Lire 110,000 double B&B
Breakfast only
Open all year
No English spoken, Region: Tuscany

Accidentally coming upon the Casolare, tucked away in the unpopulated hills 8 kilometers past medieval San Gimignano, was a delightful surprise. Just before reaching the bed and breakfast, you'll see a half-abandoned stone convent dating back to 1100 where the hosts reside. The attractive renovated farmhouse, hosted by Andrea, a former art and antique dealer, and his Spanish wife, Berta, retains all the features characteristic of the original structure. The five double rooms are extremely comfortable and tastefully appointed. Rooms are divided among the two floors of the house, with one being an independent structure poolside. The two suites for two to four persons with terrace and living room have been decorated with refined antiques as well. Original watercolor paintings of a local artist depicting various local sites adorn an entire wall in the inviting double living room. An extra bonus is the breathtaking swimming pool, with sweeping coutryside panorama, surrounded by a manicured lawn, fruit trees, and terra-cotta pots overflowing with pink geraniums. It provides refreshment after a hot day of sightseeing, while you anticipate another appetizing candlelit meal at dusk under the pergola. Berta is an excellent cook and prepares very special Tuscan menus accompanied by an impressive wine list. This is a truly tranquil haven. *Directions*: From San Gimignano follow signs for Montaione. Staying left at the fork, turn left for Libbiano and take the dirt road to the end.

CASOLARE DI LIBBIANO
Hosts: Andrea & Berta Bucciarelli
Localita: Libbiano 3
San Gimignano (SI) 53037, Italy
Tel & fax: (0577) 946002
www.karenbrown.com\italy\casolaredilibbiano.html
5 rooms & 2 suites with private bathrooms
Lire 135,000–165,000 per person half boara
Breakfast & dinner served
Open Easter to November, Credit Cards: MC, VS
English spoken well, Region: Tuscany

The increasing popularity of this perfectly intact medieval town and the resulting availability of accommodations has made San Gimignano a hub from which tourists fan out to visit nearby, less-well-known treasures such as Volterra, Colle Val d'Elsa, and Monteriggioni. A pleasant stay is very likely at the Podere Villuzza, run by friendly young Sandra and Gianni Dei who opened the doors of their 150-year-old stone farmhouse to guests after extensive modification. Chairs are set up in front where visitors can enjoy the view of vineyard-covered hills leading up to the impressive multi-towered town. A hearty dinner may be shared with other guests in the rustic dining room where Sandra prepares tantalizing, fresh specialties from the family recipe book. Her husband occupies himself with the production of top-quality Vernaccia wine. Five double rooms are furnished in true country style with a mix of wrought-iron beds and antique armoires, complemented by mansard beamed ceilings and stone walls. The larger double has a private terrace overlooking the back hills. Also available are three small apartments within the house that include a living area and kitchen for weekly stays. Ongoing renovation work of new rooms and a swimming pool should be completed sometime in early 1998. *Directions*: Go through town and follow signs for Certaldo. After 2 km turn right and follow signs for Villuzza.

PODERE VILLUZZA
Hosts: Sandra & Gianni Dei
Strada 25
San Gimignano (SI) 53037, Italy
Tel: (0577) 940585, Fax: (0577) 942247
www.karenbrown.com\italy\poderevilluzza.html
5 rooms with private bathrooms, 3 apartments
Lire 120,000–150,000 double B&B
Breakfast & dinner served
Open all year
English spoken well, Region: Tuscany

In the heart of the wine valley of Piedmont, between the principal cities of Piedmont: Alessandria, Alba, and Asti, you find a typical farmhouse and vineyard run cooperatively by several local families. There are simple and very neat guest bedrooms upstairs, decorated with country furniture typical of the area. One of the five bedrooms has an en-suite bathroom. The farm work seems to be evenly divided among these energetic families, whose members convene along with locals at lunch time in the spacious and rustic restaurant on the premises. Here they can count on a hearty multi-course meal prepared from the freshest possible ingredients directly off their land. This provides a convenient and very economical location from which to launch excursions to some of the delightful villages in the immediate vicinity, and of course, to Alba and Asti, which should not be missed. You can also take shorter trips on horseback from nearby stables into the scenic surrounding countryside. Or alternatively, you could visit the Italian Riviera, just an hour and a half away. Advance reservations are required. *Directions*: Coming from the direction of Nizza Monferrato, take the middle road at the triple fork just before San Marzano. La Viranda is just up the road on the left.

LA VIRANDA
Hostess: Lorella Solito
Localita: Corte 64
Piazza Martiri Liberta 2
San Marzano Oliveto (AT) 14042, Italy
Tel: (0141) 856571, Fax: none
5 rooms, 1 with private bathroom
Lire 56,000 double B&B
  40,000 per person half board
All meals served
Closed August & January
Some English spoken, Region: Piedmont

From the sheer monumental size of the Cavaglioni villa, erected from the original 14th-century fortress, one has an idea of just how important an agricultural center this farm property was in its heyday. The property was just one of many owned by the noble Galeotti-Ottieri family since the 18th century and today Signora Anna Maria opens up the third floor of the villa to guests, offering accommodation within six double and three single rooms, all down a long hall divided by a large living area. Rooms are simply appointed with wrought-iron beds and old family antiques. Wood beams divide fresco designs on some of the ceilings while worn terra-cotta bricks cover floors. A definite sensation that time has stood still pervades. New bathrooms, each with colored tiles coordinating with bedrooms, are either en suite, shared, or private but outside rooms. The nicest room is the one at the end, considered a suite for its size. A basic breakfast is served in a small uninspired room on this floor. To the back is a large garden where two separate apartments are available for longer stays. Gracious Signora Anna Maria adores assisting guests with local itineraries and suggestions. *Directions*: From Siena take route 223 towards Grosseto. After 10 km turn right for San Rocco then in 1 km, before town, turn left at the sign for Cavaglioni. Pass an iron gate to the side entrance.

FATTORIA DI CAVAGLIONI
Hostess: Anna Maria Galeotti-Ottieri
Via del Poggetto 1
San Rocco a Pilli (SI) 53010, Italy
Tel: (0577) 347723, Fax: (0577) 348364
www.karenbrown.com\italy\fattoriadicavaglioni.html
9 rooms, 4 with private bathrooms
2 apartments
Lire 110,000–120,000 double B&B
Breakfast only
Open all year
English spoken well, Region: Tuscany

In the olive-strewn countryside around the magical town of Ostuni is the Tenuta Deserto farm, where the Roman Lancelloti family has summered for centuries. This *masseria* was built in several periods dating back to the 1600s, and is made up of the main house, a chapel, a 16th-century stone tower, and several houses which were once farmers' quarters. The main brick villa has been divided into sections—a large part reserved for a three-bedroom apartment with three bathrooms, fully equipped kitchen, and living room. Six more two- and three-bedroom apartments have been created in outlying white houses, one being of actual *trullo* construction, with cone-shaped stone roof, typical of the Alberobello area. Young and gracious Sveva and Riccardo have been hosting travelers for many years and are most attentive to their needs. The spacious rooms are decorated with taste and care, using family antiques, botanical prints, local handicrafts, and brightly colored floral bedspreads. Some apartments have fireplace, kitchen, and small terrace. Guests convene poolside or in the lovely "clubhouse" living room with fireplace and vaulted ceilings. Meals can be arranged upon request. *Directions*: From Bari take coastal route N379, exiting at San Vito. Cross through town, following signs for Ceglie. After 3½ km turn right on a dirt road at the bed-and-breakfast sign.

TENUTA DESERTO
Hosts: Sveva & Riccardo Lancellotti Delfino
San Vito dei Normanni (BR) 72019, Italy
Tel: (0831) 983062, Fax: (06) 3219566
www.karenbrown.com\italy\tenutadeserto.html
7 apartments
Lire 300,000–1,400,000 weekly per apartment
* (2 to 7 people)*
Weekly stay required in July & August
Dinner served upon request
Open April to October
English spoken very well, Region: Apulia

Right in the heart of the chic (and expensive) Italian Riviera is a small jewel of a bed and breakfast, hugging the hillside above the ports of Portofino and Santa Margherita. The young and pleasant host, Roberto, has completely restored the two small stone farmhouses on a piece of his grandfather's property. Eight tastefully decorated double rooms are divided between the two houses, each with private bath, scattered antiques, and lovely panoramic views over the olive trees and fruit orchards and down to the sea. A cozy high-ceilinged living room, inviting one to curl up with a book or converse, gives visitors the feeling of being at the home of friends. The ambiance is intimate and welcoming. A peaceful garden is another relaxing spot. In the small beamed dining room, breakfast and dinner (featuring local specialties such as the famous fresh pesto sauce) are served and prepared by Roberto himself. From Genoa to the marvels of Cinque Terre, the Ligurian coast holds some very special treasures, and the Gnocchi makes a perfect and very reasonable place from which to discover them. *Directions*: From Santa Margherita follow signs to Genova/S. Lorenzo uphill for about 4 km until you see a blue sign indicating an intersection. Just after the sign, about 90 meters before the intersection, take the narrow road on the left with the red and white gate.

VILLA GNOCCHI
Host: Roberto Gnocchi
Via Romana 53
Santa Margherita (GE) 16038, Italy
Tel & fax: (0185) 283431
Cellphone: (0330) 486432
8 rooms with private bathrooms
Lire 120,000 double B&B
  80,000 per person half board
Breakfast & dinner served
Open Easter to October
English spoken well, Region: Liguria

As more travelers realize just how close together destinations of interest throughout Italy are, weekly house rentals to use as a home base from which to explore have become more popular. One such ideal base is La Sovana, bordering Tuscany and Umbria and equidistant to Florence, Chianti, Siena, Cortona, Perugia, and Assisi, plus many other smaller hilltowns. Two stone farmhouses were carefully restored to provide 14 apartments for two to six people. Tastefully decorated with local antique beds and armoires, matching floral bedspreads and curtains, each has a fully equipped kitchenette and eating and living area. Guests can dine upon request in the dining room in the main house, whose enormous arched window takes in the expansive view of vineyards and wheat fields. Giovannella and Giuseppe Olivi, dedicated and amiable hosts, and their two children make their guests feel right at home, dining with them each evening. Potted flowers abound around the farmhouse and poolside, where on Saturday nights a sumptuous barbecue is organized to enable guests to meet one another. Tennis courts, a small fishing lake, and bikes are available. Additional apartments are now available in a converted barn, *Il Granaio*, in the woods a short walk away from the main farmhouse. *Directions*: Just 2 km from the Chiusi exit of the A1 autostrada. La Sovana is just before Sarteano on the right.

LA SOVANA
Hosts: Giuseppe Olivi family
Localita: Sovana
Sarteano (SI) 53047, Italy
Tel: (0578) 274086, Fax: (075) 600197
14 apartments
Lire 600,000–2,400,000 weekly
Lunch & dinner served upon request
Open Easter to November
Some English spoken, Region: Tuscany

Saturnia's thermal waters have been gushing from an underground volcano for over 2,000 years, yet only recently have it and the enchanting surrounding *maremma* area become internationally famous, leading to new accommodations springing up. One such is the charming Villa Clodia, once home to nobility, now run by former restaurateur Giancarlo Ghezzi. The villa is a curiosity, seemingly built out of the limestone rock, one side overlooking the street and the other an expansive valley of grapevines and olive trees. Because of its unusual proportions, each room is unique in size and decor. A small winding stairway takes guests up or down to rooms, some of which have been literally carved out of the rock. All bedrooms feature scattered antiques, new bathrooms, and valley views, and a fortunate few boast a terrace. Breakfast is offered in a sweet, luminous room next to the sitting room. A lush rose garden and fruit orchard surround the inviting star-shaped pool. Advance reservations are a must and weekly stays are preferred. *Directions*: From Rome take the Aurelia highway north, turning off to the right at Vulci where you follow signs for Manciano, Montemerano, and Saturnia. Villa Clodia is in the middle of town.

VILLA CLODIA
Host: Giancarlo Ghezzi
Via Italia 43
Saturnia (GR) 58050, Italy
Tel: (0564) 601212, Fax: (0564) 601305
10 rooms with private bathrooms
Lire 135,000 double B&B
3-day minimum stay
Breakfast only
Closed February
Credit cards: VS
English spoken well, Region: Tuscany

Luciana and Luigi from Rome are pioneers in offering accommodation in Sabina, taking advantage of the lovely inherited piece of property which they have brought back to life in their early retirement. Gregarious Luciana, a former flight attendant, is the hostess par excellence. She goes out of her way to see that guests needs are taken care of and checks their mood and energy level each morning before suggesting one of her many fascinating local itineraries and events—enough to keep one busy touring for a couple of weeks! Accommodation is offered in a variety of apartments divided between the main villa and the well-restored farmhouse down the hill. Each has one or two bedrooms, bathroom, kitchenette, and eating area, while a double living room with enormous stone fireplace is reserved for all guests. The cozy country decor prevalent throughout the rooms, with their stenciled borders and mix of family antiques, is the result of Luciana's good taste combined with her creative talents. Apartments on ground and second floors (some with terraces) take in views of the sweeping valley below. In addition to producing wine, olive oil, and fruit, Luigi oversees the business/hobby of raising thoroughbred horses. Luciana also arranges courses in Italian and cooking. Guests can use the pool and 9-hole golf course at a nearby club or ride at the horse stables in the next town. *Directions*: From the A1 exit Magliano and follow signs for Poggio Mirteto.

VILLA VALLEROSA   *New*
Hosts: Luciana Panciera & Luigi Giuseppi
Via di Vallerosa 27
Selci Sabino (RI) 02040, Italy
Tel & fax: (0765) 519179
6 apartments
Lire 145,000–230,000 per apartment daily
2-day minimum stay, 1 week high season
No meals served
Open all year
English spoken well, Region: Lazio

In centuries past, the property of the noble Pennisi family extended over a vast territory of the coast south of Taormina. What remains today are 12 acres of primarily citrus groves with a 17th-century hamlet in the center. Even though the Signori Pennisi reside in nearby Fiumefreddo, they are present on the farm during the day to attend to their guests. The pale-yellow, ivy-covered, one-story "Villa Ada" has been divided into two comfortable apartments, including two bedrooms, two bathrooms, and a large double living room with fireplace which opens up to a delightful terrace overlooking the groves and encompassing views of the Etna volcano and the sea, marred only by the highway several kilometers away. Pretty floral curtains, wrought-iron beds, and family antiques impart a true country flavor to the setting. Directly across the brick walk is a complex which houses the other two apartments, former barn/present dining room, enormous wine cellar, and even the family chapel. Rooms, here again, are authentically decorated with period pieces and harmonize well with the exposed beam ceilings and terra-cotta brick floors. With advance notice, meals are served at long tables in the cantina or out under the pergola on hot summer evenings. *Directions*: From Taormina on local route 114, pass Fiumefreddo and take the first right where Borgo is well marked.

BORGO VALERIO
Hosts: Piero Pennisi family
Via Civi 2
Fiumefreddo (CT) 95013, Sicily, Italy
Tel: (095) 641234, Fax: (095) 642662
Cellphone: (0330) 694157
5 apartments
Lire 80,000–280,000 per apartment per day with breakfast
Occasional meals served
Open all year
Very little English spoken, Region: Sicily

Tenuta Gangivecchio is far off the beaten path, but well worth a detour. Not only will you discover a jewel of a small inn, but the adventure of finding Gangivecchio leads you through Sicily's beautiful Madonie region. The Tornabene family began by converting a room in their home (a 13th-century Benedettino monastery) into a restaurant serving a set-menu lunch based upon fresh produce from the farm. Although a two-hour-drive, the excellence of the simple, yet delicious meals soon brought guests from as far away as Palermo. The enterprising Tornabene family have now renovated the stables of the monastery into ten tastefully decorated guestrooms—appealing in their simplicity with rustic, red-tile floors, fresh whitewashed walls, hand-loomed scatter rugs, dark wood accents, rough-hewn beamed ceilings, attractively framed old prints on the walls, and pretty cotton floral bedspreads. Delicious, home-cooked meals are served to guests in a pretty dining room on the ground floor of the inn. Plan to arrive on a weekend for a lunch prepared by Signora Wanda and her daughter Giovanna, served in the dining room of the monastery. *Directions:* Drive east through Gangi on SS120. Just outside town, turn right at a small signpost for Gangivecchio. Go for about a kilometer and turn left at a tiny yellow sign. Continue up the hill for about 5 km. Tenuta Gangivecchio is on your right.

TENUTA GANGIVECCHIO
Hosts: Betty & Paolo Tornabene
C. da Gangivecchio
90024 Gangi, (PA), Sicily, Italy
Tel & fax: (0921) 689191
10 rooms with private bathrooms
Lire 100,000 per person half board
All meals served
Closed 1 or 2 weeks end of June
Credit cards: AX, VS
Some English spoken, Region: Sicily

On the southwestern coast between the archaeological ruins of Selinunte and Sciacca with its hot springs, lies the anonymous town of Menfi. Menfi was virtually destroyed in the earthquake of 1968, and consequently is a mix of new construction and devastated areas still awaiting government funds. In the very center of all this sits the splendid 18th-century palazzo of the noble Ravida family, which miraculously survived disaster. One enters the front iron gates from the city street to discover a large stone courtyard with palm trees leading to the U-shaped villa with its solid Doric stone columns. The baron and his wife, who are in residence seasonally as they live in Rome, offer hospitality in lovely rooms within the villa and garden house wing. The bedrooms are in perfect harmony with the general feeling of the home. There is a perfume of the past as you wander through the frescoed sitting rooms filled with period antiques worn by time and ancestral paintings. Fortunately for guests, the gracious hosts are experts in itineraries throughout Sicily. Their large agricultural property at a short distance from town comprises vineyards, and vast citrus and olive groves. With hundreds of years of tradition in producing oil, it is no wonder that Ravida has received national and European recognition. They also host a week-long cooking course combining daily outings. *Directions*: Follow signs to the center of Menfi and ask for Via Roma or Palazzo Ravida.

RAVIDA
Hosts: Nicola & Ninni Ravida
Via Roma 173
Menfi (AG) 92013, Italy
Tel: (06) 3052537, Fax: none
6 rooms, 4 with private bathrooms
Lire 200,000 double B&B
Breakfast & occasional dinner served
3-day minimum stay
Open all year
English spoken well, Region: Sicily

The Alcala farm, made up of citrus and olive groves, vineyards, wheat crops, and a wide variety of fruit trees, extends over 75 acres of fertile plain backdropped by the Etna volcano—a picture-perfect setting. Cordial hostess Anna Sapuppo and her young family have taken over the family's agricultural business (her husband is a university professor) and have added the hospitality activity as well. The main house is a turn-of-the-century *masseria*, built in several sections, while guests are situated nearby in three different apartment setups, housing from two to six guests. Two of them are separate houses and have large open terraces. They include living room areas and kitchenettes and are pleasantly decorated with floral sofas and a mix of modern and old family furniture. Although breakfast is not served, guests can help themselves to plenty of fruits. An occasional typically Sicilian dinner is served in the fascinating rustic wine cantina with its enormous wooden wine barrels or by request in your apartment. Anna, a native Sicilian, gladly assists her guests with touring suggestions which include Catania city (important where **not** to go), the Taormina coast, Siracusa, Etna National Park, and the temples of Agrigento. A superb base at an unbeatable rate. *Directions*: Take autostrada A19 from Catania and exit at the first exit for Motta. Backtrack on the parallel road, passing the US army base and turn left at the sign for Alcala.

ALCALA
Hosts: Anna Sappupo family
Casella Postale 100
Misterbianco (CT) 95045, Sicily, Italy
Tel & fax: (095) 7130029, Cellphone: (0368) 3469206
www.karenbrown.com\italy\alcala.html
3 apartments
Lire 35,000 per person
3-day minimum, 1 week July & August
Dinner served upon request
Open all year
Some English spoken, Region: Sicily

The coastal stretch from Messina to Cefalu has special appeal to the off-the-beaten-track traveler who will find the perfect place to stay at Casa Migliaca, a 200-year-old farmhouse nestling in the wooded hills 7 kilometers off the main road. This stone house just outside town, owned by Maria Teresa and Sebastiano, who left the city several years ago in favor of a rural lifestyle, offers a lovely sweeping view over olive and citrus groves down to the sea. The very congenial hosts love to converse with guests around the kitchen table or down in the cool dining room (originally oil press) around the press wheel. A special effort was made to keep everything possible intact, giving the house its own very distinct charm, maintaining all original floors, ceilings, beams, kitchen tiles, and furniture, although new bathrooms have been incorporated in most of the rooms. There are even extra showers out in the garden! Guests are offered a choice of three double bedrooms upstairs (two with en-suite bathrooms) or five downstairs. For those who desire direct contact with Sicilian culture, Casa Migliaca is a truly memorable experience. *Directions*: From coastal route number 113, just 25 km after Cefalu, turn right at the sign for Pettineo and follow it right past town (7 km). Just after a gas station, turn right on a descending gravel road to the house (unmarked).

CASA MIGLIACA
Hostess: Maria Teresa Allegra
Contrada Migliaca
Pettineo (ME) 98070, Sicily, Italy
Tel & fax: (0921) 336722
www.karenbrown.com\italy\casa migliaca.html
8 rooms, 7 with private bathrooms
Lire 85,000 per person half board
Breakfast & dinner served
Open all year
English spoken well, Region: Sicily

For those who prefer the service of a small pensione, native Salvatore and his amiable Panamanian wife MariSin await you with open arms. The pale-yellow three-story house sits in the quaint town of Scopello with its piazza and three streets. From ancient times this was an important fishing center especially for tuna, and the *Tonnara* stone fishing station down by the sea still stands as proof. The entrance hall is a combination breakfast and dining room with a sitting area in the corner around the fireplace. A central staircase leads up to guestrooms, a few with balconies facing out to the distant sea. The rooms are simply appointed with light-wood armoires, wrought-iron beds, and crocheted white bedspreads. In the evening after a day at the seaside or touring, you come "home" to a delicious home-cooked meal of fresh fish or meat and vegetables from their garden. Enthusiastic MariSin spends time chatting with her guests and advising them what to visit in this culturally rich area. "Must-sees" include the ancient town of Erice, the ruins of Segesta, Selinunte, and Agrigento. Bikes are available to tour the spectacularly beautiful Zingaro Nature Reserve along the northern coast (one of its kind in Sicily). *Directions*: From Palermo, exit from autostrada A29 at Castellammare and follow signs for Scopello. The pensione is found just after the bar with outdoor tables.

PENSIONE TRANCHINA
Hosts: MariSin & Salvatore Tranchina
Via A. Diaz 7
Scopello (TP) 91010, Sicily, Italy
Tel & fax: (0924) 541099
10 rooms with private bathrooms
Lire 75,000 double B&B
* 75,000 per person half board (high season)*
Breakfast & dinner served
Open all year
Credit cards: all major
English spoken fluently, Region: Sicily

The Limoneto was recommended to us by a reader who was "winging it" through the Sicilian countryside (not advisable). He raved about the "open arms" hospitality, the excellent meals, comfortable accommodations, and proximity to fascinating Siracusa. We have to agree. At just 10 kilometers from the historical center of Siracusa with its Greek and Roman influences, the orange- and olive-grove farm is a perfectly delightful, safe, and economical base from which to explore Sicily's southeastern corner. Adelina, Alceste, and their son, Francesco, make sure of this simply by making guests part of their family. Guestrooms are split between the refurbished barn and part of the main house, all with individual entrances. Rooms, some accommodating up to four persons, are new with pleasant modern decor and all have spotless bathrooms. Dinner is served either in the spacious dining room where locals come for a Sunday meal, or out in the back garden. Adelina welcomes the curious into her kitchen to observe and participate in the making of typical regional meals using ingredients fresh from her own garden. The warmth exudes and when the evening is just right, she might even read some poetry. *Directions*: From Catania, take the autostrada to Siracusa sud exit. Turn right, then immediately left for Canicattini. At the end of the road, turn right on route 14 for Palazzolo and, after half a kilometer, turn left for Limoneto.

LIMONETO
Hosts: Alceste & Adelina Norcia
Viale Teracati 142
Siracusa (SC) 96100, Italy
Tel & fax: (0931) 717352 or (0931) 37149
www.karenbrown.com\italy\limoneto.html
6 rooms with private bathrooms
Lire 90,000 double B&B 3-day minimum stay
* 70,000 per person half board*
All meals served
Open all year
Some English spoken, Region: Sicily

Taormina is on what could be referred to as the Amalfi coast of Sicily and, although the town is lovely and rich with history, it is very touristy. This of course means that rates are on the high side, but, happily, the Villa Schuler makes it affordable and its location is superb. The villa was converted from a private residence to a hotel by the Schuler family at the turn of the century and now grandson Gerardo has taken over the reins. The pink façade faces out to the street and has a large raised terrace with potted flowers, palms, and cypresses. A full breakfast is served either here or in the gazebo where you can enjoy views encompassing the coastline and the peak of the Etna volcano. To the back is an enchanting garden—the town's largest besides the nearby public botanical gardens— filled with a profusion of jasmine, bougainvillea, and geraniums with several quiet places to sit in the shade. You can exit from the garden directly onto the main street of town and it is just a short walk to the cable car which takes you down to the beach where guests gain free entrance. Rooms have been updated over the past years, almost all with new bathrooms, and are spacious and simply but pleasantly decorated. Most have some sort of small balcony or terrace with sea views. The rooftop terrace offers yet another head-spinning view. *Directions*: Follow signs through town to the hotel.

VILLA SCHULER
Hosts: Gerardo Schuler family
Via Roma 2
Taormina (ME) 98039, Sicily, Italy
Tel: (0942) 23481, Fax: (0942) 23522
E-mail: schuler@cys.it
www.karenbrown.com\italy\villaschuler.html
35 rooms with private bathrooms
Lire 145,000 double B&B (30% discount in low season)
Breakfast only
Open March to November
English spoken well, Region: Sicily

There is a beautiful stretch of coastline on the Adriatic Sea just south of Ancona, dramatically different from the more flat and uninteresting shoreline to the north and south with its modern hotels and condos. The quaint stone village of Sirolo sits high above the water on a mountainside looking down to the beaches of the Riviera Conero. Delightful seafood restaurants dot the shore, where you might enjoy a plate of pasta with fresh clams while watching the tide come in. Isabella and Giorgio Fabiani decided several years ago to open a bed and breakfast in 14th-century Sirolo, and offer seven guestrooms above their small and quaint peach-colored restaurant with its outdoor tables. The bedrooms are very simply furnished in old-fashioned style, and most have sea views. The young couple is full of ideas to improve the premises, but since this is a historical building (legend has it that St. Francis stayed overnight here), even simple exterior renovations are often restricted—not even the faded green shutters adorning the windows can be touched. Nonetheless, the place exudes a basic charm and fortunately they have just completed renovation of two apartments nearby overlooking the park and sea. True Marchigiano-style meals feature seafood dishes for which Isabella has been highly praised. *Directions*: The Rocco is located at the edge of the town of Sirolo, after Portonovo.

LOCANDA ROCCO
Hostess: Isabella & Giorgio Fabiani
Via Torrione 1
Sirolo (AN) 60020, Italy
Tel: (071) 9330558 or 7823256, Fax: none
7 rooms with private bathrooms, 2 apartments
Lire 150,000–200,000 double B&B
* 80,000 per person half board*
All meals served
Open April to October Credit cards: AX, VS
Some English spoken, Region: Marches

In yet another lesser-known pocket of Tuscany halfway between Siena and the sea is the absolutely stunning 1,000-acre property of the Visconti family. Dating back to the 1400s, in its heyday it was a village in itself, complete with the noble family's main villa, farmers' houses, church, nuns' quarters, oil press, and blacksmith and carpenter's shops. These stone buildings are all attached to the villa in a U-shape formation which has a beautiful formal garden within. Terra-cotta pots with lemon trees and red geraniums give spots of color among the greenery. Vitalino and Vittoria, the gracious hosts, whose home has been in the same family since its origins, welcome guests in the restored part of the villa where 13 new rooms with private bathrooms have been created. Each with beamed ceilings and brick floors, they are simply appointed with beds and armoires, looking out either to the garden or woods at the back. Common areas are the dining and living room with enormous fireplace, and an upstairs loggia with a panoramic view over the pool and countryside that seems to take in all of Tuscany. Also available on the property are two farmhouses for weekly stays. For those who enjoy spectacular scenery in a very special, historical setting, this is the place. *Directions*: From Siena follow route 73 past Rosia to route 541. After 10 km turn left at Pievescola and continue to Radicondoli and then on to Angua and Solaio—marked on most maps.

FATTORIA SOLAIO   **New**
Hosts: Vittoria & Vitalino Visconti
Radicondoli (SI) 53030, Italy
Tel & fax: (0577) 761029
13 rooms with private bathrooms
Lire 140,000 double B&B
Lire 1,000,000–1,200,000 weekly apartments
2-day minimum stay
Breakfast & dinner served
Open all year
English spoken well, Region: Tuscany

The town of Spoleto has gained international fame thanks to the July *Due Mondi* festival, a month-long series of cultural events including ballet, theater, opera, and concerts with renowned artists which attracts a worldwide audience. Accommodations are reserved from one year to the next. For the rest of the year, however, Spoleto holds its own along with nearby Assisi, Spello, Todi, and Perugia as an enchanting medieval stone town, rich in historical past. La Terrazza del Duomo serves as an excellent base from which to explore in depth the entire region of Umbria. Paolo Tamburi, from Rome, bought and restored the 17th-century palazzo, situated within the old walls of the town, ten years ago and created eight spacious apartments for weekly stays. The apartments vary in size and layout, accommodating from two to seven people. All take in views over the tiled rooftops and contain one to three bedrooms, fully equipped kitchen, living area, and one or two bathrooms. The largest, number 4, is spread out on three levels. Rooms are very comfortable, with beds, tables, and armoires made by a local carpenter. Cordial hostess, Daniela, of Spoleto, is on hand to assist guests, including furnishing breakfast upon request. *Directions*: From autostrada A1, exit at Orte and follow route 418 to Spoleto. Best to call from town for directions.

LA TERRAZZA DEL DUOMO
Hostess: Daniela Tulli
Via Vaita de Domo 5
Spoleto (PG) 06049, Italy
Tel & fax: (0743) 223593, Cellphone: (0338) 7210636
8 apartments
Lire 900,000–1,600,000 weekly
Breakfast served upon request
Open all year
English spoken well, Region: Umbria

Halfway between Florence and Siena in the heart of the Chianti region is the Sovigliano farm, recently restored by a handsome couple from Verona, Claudio Bicego and his wife, Patrizia, who delight in welcoming international visitors into their warm home. Guests have an independent entrance to the five bedrooms (only two with private bath), each very much in keeping with the pure simplicity of this typical farmhouse. Exposed-beam ceilings and terra-cotta floors, antique beds and armoires, and bucolic views make time stand still here. There is also a one-bedroom and a two-bedroom apartment within the house, decorated in similar style, with kitchen and dining area. The upstairs living room, sparsely furnished with the family's elegant antiques, kitchen with country fireplace, and surrounding garden are for everyone's use. Signor Bicego is actively involved in the production of top Tuscan wines in conjunction with several other wine estates, and also coordinates with other area residents to organize lessons in language, history, and culinary arts with local professors. *Directions*: From Siena, exit the superstrada at Poggibonsi; from Florence at Tavarnelle. Follow signs for Tavarnelle and, go through town towards Barberino, turning off at the sign for Sovigliano.

SOVIGLIANO
Hosts: Patrizia & Claudio Bicego
Via Magliano 9
Tavarnelle Val di Pesa (FI) 50028, Italy
Tel & fax: (055) 8076217
5 rooms, 3 with private bathrooms
2 apartments (2-day minimum stay)
Lire 135,000–160,000 double B&B
  150,000–175,000 2-person apartment B&B
Dinner upon request
Open all year
Credit cards: AX
English spoken well, Region: Tuscany

With their hearts set on running a bed and breakfast in the Liguria region, young Milanese couple Lucia and Nereo searched hard and long before finding Giandriale. Set high up in the remote mountains above the coast, the 18th-century stone farmhouse is surrounded by acres of low-range mountains covered with thick woods as far as the eye can see. Utter silence prevails. Just three bedrooms are reserved for guests within their home, simply decorated with country-style wood furniture. The one with en-suite bathroom is on the first floor, while the other two share a bathroom on the second floor next to the hosts' quarters. Meals are enjoyed in the downstairs dining room displaying an old-fashioned country stove that is used occasionally in the colder months for making polenta. Lucia prepares coffee cakes and jams for breakfast and uses mostly regional recipes in her cooking. Classic sightseeing destinations in the area include the riviera (Portofino, Santa Margherita, Chiaveri), or the Cinque Terre, 45 minutes away in the opposite direction. Nereo can also suggest several interesting off-the-beaten-track itineraries beyond Giandriale. Hiking trails and mountain bikes are available. *Directions*: From autostrada A14, exit at Sestri Levante and follow signs for Casarza Ligure, Castiglione, then, after 2 km and many curves, Missano. Before the church in town, turn left at the sign for Giandriale. The house is 6 km up the road (15 minutes).

GIANDRIALE
Hosts: Lucia Marelli & Nereo Giani
Localita: Giandriale
Tavarone di Maissana (SP) 19010, Italy
Tel & fax: (0187) 840279
www.karenbrown.com\italy\grandriale.html
3 rooms, 1 with private bathroom
Lire 80,000 double B&B
* 60,000 per person half board*
All meals served
Open all year
Some English spoken, Region: Liguria

Another one of Italy's best-kept secrets is the *Cinque Terre* coastline of southern **Liguria** bordering Tuscany, though this beautiful and quite unique area is now gaining increasing popularity. Its five quaint stone villages hugging the hillside sweeping down to the sea were, until recently, accessible only by boat or by foot and are a delight to explore. Just south of the area right on the Poet's Gulf is the adorable seaside town of Tellaro hugging the rock over the sea, where visitors make a point of stopping to have a memorable meal at the Miranda restaurant. Husband and wife team, Giovanna and Angelo, have their own inimitable and ever-varying style of cooking based on fresh seafood which is present in the inexhaustible series of antipasti plates. Angelo has received plenty of press and praise (Michelin star) for these extraordinary dishes. Meals are served in one of the newly renovated dining rooms, pleasantly appointed with scattered antiques. In the same vein are the bedrooms, most with gulf view, which Aunt Miranda used to rent out and are now in the capable hands of son, Alessandro. A cozy common living room with fireplace where guests can convene has just been added. *Directions*: Leave the A12 autostrada at Sarzana, following signs for Lerici on route 331. Tellaro is 4½ km down the coast—the Miranda is on the main road before town.

LOCANDA MIRANDA
Hosts: Angelo & Giovanna Cabani
Via Fiascherino 92
Tellaro (SP) 19030, Italy
Tel: (0187) 968130 or 964012, Fax: (0187) 964032
www.karenbrown.com\italy\locanamiranda.html
8 rooms with private bathrooms
Lire 150,000 double B&B
  140,000 per person half board
3-day minimum stay
All meals served
Closed February Credit cards: all major
English spoken well, Region: Liguria

The Residenza San Andrea al Farinaio is located so far off the beaten path that you must write or call ahead for detailed instructions if you ever hope to find it, but its location makes it quite convenient as a home base for exploring both Tuscany and Umbria. And for those looking for well-priced accommodation without sacrificing comfort, this bed and breakfast might be a perfect choice. The oldest part of the inn dates back to the 13th century when it was home to the priests tending a church across the road. The present owner, Patrizia Nappi, is a warm and gracious hostess, speaks excellent English, and has lovingly transformed the old stone house into a cozy inn, combining modern pictures, furniture, and knickknacks with lovely antiques. Of the five bedrooms, three have private baths. A personal favorite is the large guestroom at the top of the stairs. The most wonderful area in the house is the dining room with its massive darkened-wood beams, large open fireplace, beautiful antique trestle table, colorful plates adorning the walls, and lots of copper pots and pans. If you make arrangements in advance, you can dine here with other guests, sharing a simple, superb meal family-style at the long, handsome candlelit table in front of a crackling fire. *Directions*: Head southeast from Cortona to Terontola (approximately 10 km) and follow signs for Stadio. Continue until you see a sign on right for San Andrea.

RESIDENZA SAN ANDREA AL FARINAIO
Hostess: Patrizia Nappi
San Andrea al Farinaio, 118
Terontola di Cortona (AR) 52044, Italy
Tel & fax: (0575) 677736
5 rooms, 3 with private bathrooms
Lire 150,000 double B&B
Breakfast & dinner served
Open all year
Fluent English spoken, Region: Tuscany

Practically 70 percent of the families residing in the Alto Adige mountain region offer bed-and-breakfast accommodations so, unless it's Christmas or August, a bed is not hard to come by. This is a region with a distinct Austrian flavor where more German than Italian is spoken, and where more *wurstel* than pasta is likely to be served at the table. The warm Trompedeller family heartily welcome international travelers to their typical Tyrolean-style home. The six guestrooms each have a private bath and are modestly decorated with basic light-wood furniture and accented with orange and brown curtains and bedspreads—a decor common to the bed and breakfasts in this region. The cozy wood-paneled dining room boasts a splendid panoramic view over the mountain cliffs and green foothills. The house is located several kilometers outside the quaint town of Tiers on a road which comes to an end at a babbling brook surrounded by hushed woods with hiking trails. Depending on the season, guests can take advantage of the Val Gardena ski slopes or summer mountain climbing. *Directions*: From the Verona-Brennero autostrada, exit at Bolzano Nord and follow signs for Tiers. Go through the town and make a hairpin left turn at the chapel.

VERALTENHOF
Hosts: Josef Trompedeller family
Oberstrasse 61
Tiers (BZ) 39050, Italy
Tel: (0471) 642102, Fax: none
www.karenbrown.com\italy\varaltenhof.html
6 rooms with private bathrooms
Lire 60,000 per person half board
Breakfast & dinner served
Open all year
No English spoken, Region: Trentino-Alto Adige

Since 1830, the remote 12th-century castle and 4,000-acre farm of Titignano have belonged to the noble Corsini family who ten years ago decided to offer guests six rooms in the main house, later adding a swimming pool and three new apartments in what was originally the farmer's quarters. They are pleasantly decorated with scattered country antiques. Management is in the hands of Monica and Clara, delightful hostesses who take care of everything from looking after guests to cooking and serving. Meals are shared at a long table in one of the castle's graciously neglected rooms with an enormous gray stone fireplace sporting the family coat of arms, and lofty ceilings made of the stamped terra-cotta blocks typical of Umbria. Off the dining hall are the spacious bedrooms, each with modernized pink travertine bathrooms and decorated eclectically with unrefined antiques and wrought-iron beds. They have a worn charm about them. Common areas include a living room with bright floral sofas around a fireplace, a game and TV room for children, and a large terrace with a breathtaking, sweeping view covering three regions. Bikes are available for touring the regional park of the Tiber river (part of the property). *Directions*: Leave the Roma-Firenze A1 autostrada at Orvieto. Follow signs for Arezzo, turning on route 79 for Prodo. Follow the long winding road for 26 km past Prodo to Titignano. (30 km from Orvieto.)

FATTORIA TITIGNANO
Hosts: Monica Gori & Clara Cortesi
Localita: Titignano
Orvieto (TR) 05010, Italy
Tel: (0763) 308322 or (075) 8947678, Fax: (075) 8947679
www.karenbrown.com\italy\fattoriatitignano.html
6 rooms with private bathrooms, 3 apartments
Lire 120,000 double B&B
  80,000 per person half board
Breakfast & dinner served
Open all year
English & French spoken well, Region: Umbria

The Adriano is a small, family-run hotel with a long-standing tradition in hospitality and exceptionally good local cuisine. The operation has just recently been handed down to the third generation of the Cinelli family—siblings Umberto, Patrizia, and Gabriella. Gabriella works her magic in the kitchen creating innovative dishes which won her several European culinary awards. While congenial host, Umberto, deals directly with guests at reception and in the main dining room, sister Patrizia bakes cakes and creates marvelous pastries. She also finds time for watercolor painting, examples of which are found throughout the inn. Breakfast is served either out in the pretty garden seen from the large windows of the dining room, or in the intimate sitting room just left of reception with large gray-stone fireplace. Newly renovated rooms upstairs with all amenities are tastefully coordinated with elegant antiques and rich fabrics. The inn is uniquely situated right next door to the beautiful park and ruins of Emperor Hadrian's villa (circa 120 A.D.) which makes it a quiet spot at night. The park is literally all yours around closing time at sunset. Take a peek at the guest book where such illustrious guests as Queen Elizabeth and John F. Kennedy have signed. Altogether a delightful combination. *Directions*: From either the A24 from Rome, or A1 from Florence or Naples, exit at Tivoli, and follow signs for Villa Adriana, below the actual city of Tivoli.

HOTEL ADRIANO
Hosts: Cinelli family
Via di Villa Adriana 194
Tivoli (RM) 00010, Italy
Tel: (0774) 382235, Fax: (0774) 535122
7 rooms with private bathrooms, 3 suites
Lire 160,000–260,000 double B&B
All meals served
Open all year
Credit cards: MC, VS
Some English spoken, Region: Lazio

In the midst of the bucolic countryside surrounding Todi sits the refined bed and breakfast of Poggio d'Asproli. Bruno Pagliari, a sculptor with a long family history in the hotel business, transferred his family from Naples to this 16th-century stone farmhouse and ex-convent several years ago and has succeeded in his aim of creating elegant but comfortable surroundings to make guests feel at home. Each of the romantic guestrooms is unique in style and decor. Rich fabrics draped at bedheads give a canopy effect with matching bedspreads and nice big bathrooms have travertine marble sinks. To the back is a large two-bedroom suite with a separate entrance. The home is filled to the brim with antiques and lovely artwork (some by Bruno's sister, Lilli) which blend in well with the stone walls, worn brick floors, and beamed ceilings. Breakfast and candlelit dinners are served either on the outside terrace or in the elegant dining room. At one end is a cozy sitting area with white sofas around an enormous fireplace. A swimming pool among the trees is a cool spot for relaxing. Daughter, Claudia, is slowly taking over the general management of the bed and breakfast. *Directions*: From Todi, follow signs for Orvieto and take a left at the sign for Izzalini. Before town, take the turning for Asproli and follow signs to the bed and breakfast.

POGGIO D'ASPROLI
Hostess: Claudia Pagliari
Localita: Asproli
Todi (PG) 06059, Italy
Tel & fax: (075) 8853385
www.karenbrown.com\italy\poggiodasproli.html
8 rooms, 1 suite, all with private bathrooms
Lire 200,000–290,000 double B&B
2-day minimum stay
Breakfast & dinner served
Open all year Credit cards: MC, VS
English spoken wel, Region: Umbria

Fortunate travelers who book a room in 1998 at the fascinating Tenuta di Canonica will be the very first to experience what promises to be an unforgettable stay. Maria and Daniele searched far and wide before purchasing the massive stone tower with foundation dating to the ancient Roman period and adjoining turn-of-the-century house. They have transformed it into a bed and breakfast of dreams. Through the arched front doorway to the open ochre-colored entrance, the spacious living room with stone fireplace is reached down a few stairs and looks out over the stunning valley down to Lake Corbara. Outstanding medieval architectural features such as stone walls, brick floors, and high beamed ceilings have been enhanced by Provence-inspired colors. Stairs lead up to the library and bedrooms are divided between the three-story tower and house, respecting the epoch of each: bathrooms in the medieval quarters have gray stone tiles and travertine, while the other side has white tile alternating with terra-cotta pieces. Each tastefully decorated room has some attractive feature, whether it be the more suite-like arrangements with sitting area or the smaller corner rooms with head-spinning views over hills and up to Todi. Common areas include a dining room and large swimming pool taking advantage of the full 360-degree views. *Directions*: From Todi take the road for Prodo and turn left at Corvigliano. Pass Villa Bianchini and go to the end of the road.

TENUTA DI CANONICA   **New**
Hosts: Maria & Daniele Fano
Localita: Canonica
Todi (PG) 06059, Italy
Tel & fax: (075) 8947581, Cellphone: (0335) 369492
11 rooms with private bathrooms, 2 apartments
Lire 150,000–180,000 double B&B
2-day minimum stay (3 in low season)
Breakfast & dinner served upon request
Open all year
English & German spoken well, Region: Umbria

The countryside surrounding Rome has surprisingly few agritourism accommodations, even though attractions of cultural interest are many, so Il Leccio, which offers the peace and quiet of a country home an hour away from the city, is a real find. Cristina and Giuliano, from Rome, carry on their careers as journalist and lawyer besides offering accommodation for guests in one of the two stone houses on their countryside property. The identically sized apartments, one on each floor, include a living room (one with fireplace) with corner kitchen, double bedroom, and bathroom, pleasantly decorated in country style. Both have lovely views over the hilly countryside and although meals are not regularly offered, dinner can be arranged upon request and served under the 300-year-old holm oak which lends its name to the place. The gracious hosts are happy to suggest local itineraries and also to organize such artisan demonstrations as gilding of antique frames, sculpture in stone, embroidery, or cooking lessons with a wood-burning oven. This predominantly agricultural area bordering Umbria (famous for its quality olive oil) is dotted with off-the-beaten-track medieval hilltop villages. *Directions*: From the A1 autostrada exit at Magliano Sabina. Turn right and follow signs for Poggio Mirteto/Stimiglano (third left). Continue for 16 km and call from Torri.

IL LECCIO
Hosts: Maria Cristina & Giuliano Fleres
Via Pizzuti 56
Torri in Sabina (RI) 02049, Italy
Tel & fax: (06) 37353076 or (0765) 62412
2 apartments
Lire 150,000 per apartment daily for 2 persons
 800,000 weekly
2-night minimum stay
Dinner upon request
Open all year
English spoken very well, Region: Lazio

When the Marti family from Rome came across the abandoned castle of Montegualandro eleven years ago, it was love at first sight—only pure passion could have driven them to tackle such an overwhelming project as the entire restoration of the property following original plans. A winding dirt road (1½ kilometers) leads up to the gates of the walled 9th-century castle. As you enter into the open circular courtyard, the main building and family residence lies to the left and immediately to the right is the long stone house, originally farmer's quarters, with small tower, stable, pottery kiln, dove house, and private chapel. Four apartments have been fashioned for guests, cleverly incorporating all original architectural features. All different, each has a living area with fireplace, kitchen, and bathroom and is characteristically furnished with country-style antiques. A walk up in the turreted walls gives a glimpse of the spectacular view out over olive groves (the property produces its own olive oil) to the lake. The Martis' daughter, Cristiana, takes special interest in guests' needs, suggesting easy day trips from the castle and recommending favorite local restaurants. Lovely Cortona is just 10 kilometers away. *Directions*: Montegualandro is marked on most maps. Leave the Perugia highway 75bis at Tuoro towards Cortona and Castiglione. After 3 km, before a curve to the left, take a small unmarked road at S. Angelo up to the castle or call from town.

CASTELLO DI MONTEGUALANDRO
Hosts: Franca & Claudio Marti
Via di Montegualandro 1
Tuoro sul Trasimeno (PG) 06069, Italy
Tel & fax: (075) 8230267
www.karenbrown.com\italy\castellodimontegualandro.html
4 apartments for 2 to 4 persons
Lire 700,000–1,200,000 weekly
No meals served
Open all year
English spoken very well, Region: Umbria

La Dogana means customs house in Italian, and the fascinating history of this 16th-century building—which until 1870 served as the Papal customs house for travelers through the Grand Duchy of Tuscany—boasts visits from luminary artists such as Michelangelo, Goethe, Byron, and Stendhal. The 100-acre property belongs to young hosts Emanuele and Paola and, aside from the main villa, includes a stone farmhouse and a building near the stables across the street. In these two "extra" buildings 25 apartment-suites have been created. The guest quarters vary widely in condition, but all feature a living area, kitchen, bathroom, and sleeping accommodations for two to six people. Each apartment is unique in decor, containing mixed antiques, prints, old sofas, and wrought-iron beds. Up on a hillside, guests have a lovely view over Lake Trasimeno whose encircling highway is audible even from here. Although no meals are served, the Dogana is conveniently situated near Perugia, Cortona, and Montepulciano, where an excellent meal is a cinch to find. *Directions*: From Perugia, take N75 toward Firenze, exiting at Tuoro. Turn left at the first intersection, continuing 3 km to La Dogana on the right side of the road.

LA DOGANA
Host: Marchese Emanuele de Ferrari
Via Dogana 4
Tuoro sul Trasimeno (PG) 06069, Italy
Tel: (075) 8230158 or (0330) 280845
Fax: (075) 8230252
www.karenbrown.com\italy\ladogana.html
25 apartments
Lire 75,000–120,000 per apartment daily
  400,000–900,000 weekly
  (July & August)
No meals served, Open all year
English spoken very well, Region: Umbria

The area of Lazio north of Rome known as "Tuscia" is rich in Etruscan history, small medieval villages, nature reserves, and three picturesque lakes. It is the homeland of the illustrious and powerful Farnese family whose palazzos and fortresses still stand as monuments of their glorious past. In the heart of this fascinating area not far from the coast is the ancient walled town of Tuscania, completely restored after the dramatic earthquake in 1978. Perla and her Argentine husband José just recently brought back to life one of the buildings right in town and opened its doors as a cozy bed and breakfast and Michelin-star restaurant. A small reception area leads to a courtyard and the cheerful, luminous restaurant with large windows looking out over the tiled rooftops. The "gallo" (rooster) motif is carried out within the three rooms with its checked drapes and tablecloths, antique armoire, and still-life paintings. It is here where José works his magic, serving innovative creations using seasonal local produce. Upstairs the very comfortable and appealing carpeted bedrooms each has its own color theme in matching floral wallpaper, drapery, and bedspread. They have all amenities including air conditioning and are spacious, with high ceilings and marble bathrooms. Gracious hostess Perla guarantees guests' comfort and assists them in arranging local itineraries. *Directions*: In the center of Tuscania, well marked.

HOTEL AL GALLO   *New*
Hosts: Perla Blanzieri & José Pettiti
Via del Gallo 22
Tuscania (VT) 01017, Italy
Tel: (0761) 443388, Fax: (0761) 443628
12 rooms with private bathrooms
Lire 186,000 double B&B
All meals served Restaurant closed Mondays
Open all year, Credit cards: all major
English spoken well, Region: Lazio

Those who have fallen in love with the enchanting countryside of Tuscany, but found its roads too well traveled, should investigate the northern part of the Marches surrounding Urbino. The scenery is magnificent, the ancient towns perfectly preserved, and the ambiance authentic. The Blasi families, hard-working farmers, have dedicated themselves to balancing a productive farm with a bed and breakfast. The brother's side of the family tends to the fields, while Amadeo, his wife Maria, and their two sons see to the guests. Three simple terra-cotta-roofed houses make up the farm, and horses, cows, sheep, and even peacocks roam the grounds. The guestrooms, each with private bath, are spartan, and the decor uninspired, but the familial warmth of the hospitality, the excellent home cooking, and the value compensate. In the rustic dining room with red-checked tablecloths or on the windowed veranda overlooking the gently rolling, wooded countryside, guests indulge in Maria's spinach ravioli or hand-cut tagliatelle, fresh-baked bread, and local wine. *Directions*: From Urbino take the road to Urbania. Pass through town and follow signs for Acqualagna. After 9 km turn right where indicated and follow signs up to L'Orsaiola.

L'ORSAIOLA
Hosts: Blasi families
Localita: Orsaiola
Urbania (PS) 61049, Italy
Tel: (0722) 318988, Fax: none
9 rooms with private bathrooms
2 apartments
Lire 60,000 double
All meals served
Open March to Christmas
Very little English spoken, Region: Marches

The Aiola opened its doors to guests just last year when daughter Federica and her husband Enrico restored the farmers' houses on the wine estate's vast property in Chianti. The family's villa with its ancient origins sits across the street from the guest quarters almost completely hidden by enormous oak and cypress trees. The eight bedrooms, one of which sleeps four persons, are divided between two floors of a stone house, each having a separate outside entrance. Original architectural features have been preserved and rooms are decorated with wrought-iron beds and antique or reproduction armoires—although they still need to be "broken in" for extra coziness. The vineyards come right up to the house and a wide, open view of the hills is offered to the other side. The barn next door includes common areas such as the breakfast (buffet) room and a living room. With Federica's mother, Signora Malagodi, being the President of the Wine Tourism Association, visits to the cellar and wine tasting begin right here at the Aiola and are organized in many other wine areas of Tuscany. At 12 kilometers from Siena and an easy distance from the highlights of the region, the Aiola serves as an excellent touring base. Total silence reigns here, with only the buzz of cicadas breaking it. *Directions*: From Siena follow route 102 just past Vagliagli—the Aiola property (well marked) is on this same road.

CASALI DELLA AIOLA   New
Hosts: Federica & Enrico Campelli
Vagliagli (SI) 53010, Italy
Tel & fax: (0577) 322797
8 rooms with private bathrooms
Lire 140,000–200,000 double B&B
Breakfast only
Open all year
Credit cards: all major
English spoken well, Region: Tuscany

Varenna is a quaint little village sitting halfway up Lake Como's eastern edge. It is situated at the point where the car-ferryboats cross over to the other side of the lake to Menaggio. In the main piazza lakeside is the generations-old family-run Olivedo hotel with its pale yellow façade where Signora Laura welcomes her guests. Time seems to have stood still within its old-fashioned interior. The reception area and side bar are dressed with faded floral wallpaper, scattered antiques, and a large grandfather clock chiming the hour. Off to the other side of the reception area is a dining room/restaurant with its simple frescoes, serving all meals. A curved stairway takes guests up to the 19 rooms most with en-suite bathroom and lake views. These are decorated simply with grandmother's furniture and old prints. There is no need to worry about noise except for Saturday nights since traffic is not allowed in the piazza. Bathrooms are being progressively renewed and added. *Directions*: From the Como branch of the lake, head north on either side of lake and take the ferry over from either Bellagio or Menaggio.

OLIVEDO
Hosts: Colombo family
Piazza Martiri 4
Varenna (LE) 23829, Italy
Tel: (0341) 830115, Fax: none
www.karenbrown.com\italy\hotelsantostefano.html
19 rooms, 10 with private bathrooms
Lire 100,000–150,000 double B&B
All meals served
Open all year
English spoken well, Region: Lombardy

It is a pleasure to be able to include such a perfectly efficient, family-run hotel as the Due Fanali, located in a lovely square next to the 12th-century San Simeon church with its original Tintoretto painting. The hotel is also housed in a 12th-century palazzo, once part of the church complex. The Feron family had the building lovingly restored just two years ago to include the sixteen bedrooms (some with smaller "French" double) on the top three floors. A small elevator has just been added for the conveni·rce of guests. Extra care has been taken in the selection of appropriate antiques f·r the guestrooms, reception area, and breakfast room. The soft ambiance is that of an elegant yet warm home, accentuated by lovely Oriental carpets and rich-cream draperies. Breakfast is taken either out in the "garden" in front of the hotel or up in the delightful third-floor veranda, under the open terrace, with its superb view over the square to the Grand Canal. As an alternative to the hotel, there are four independent apartments near San Marco Square, divinely decorated and including bedroom, living room with view, kitchenette, and bathroom with hydromassage tub. Take all these esthetic elements accompanied by the exceptional hospitality offered by Signora Marina and her daughter, Stefania, and you have a true winner of a hotel. *Directions*: The hotel is a five-minute walk from the train station or you can take the No. 1 water bus to the Riva di Biasio stop.

HOTEL AI DUE FANALI
Hosts: Marina Feron family
Santa Croce 946
Venice 30135, Italy
Tel: (041) 718490, Fax: (041) 718344
16 rooms with private bathrooms
Lire 320,000 double B&B
Breakfast only
Open all year, Credit cards: all major
English spoken well, Region: Veneto

Around the corner from the Santa Maria del Giglio square, sitting on a small private canal's edge is the small and intimate San Moise hotel, named after the nearby church. Hospitality is a tradition in the Donzello family who owns three other hotels in Venice and hostess and owner Signora Irvin obviously takes pride in her work as seen in the attention to detail of her newly renovated accommodation. Upon entering the pale-yellow 15th-century building, one finds the reception desk and the stairway up to the guestrooms immediately on the right. To the left is the very small but cozy combination lounge/breakfast room decorated with elegant antiques, Murano glass chandeliers, and walls covered with soft-pink flocked fabric. Bedrooms on the second and third floors are in the same vein with variations in the color scheme, some having the advantage of a partial canal view without the usual noise. Rooms are fully equipped with all amenities including air conditioning and you can even leave your gondola at the private dock! *Directions*: Take the No. 1 water bus to stop 15, San Marco, walk straight up to Calle 22 Marzo and turn left. Pass the church on the left and turn right at the sign for the hotel.

HOTEL SAN MOISE
Hostess: Irvin Donzello
San Marco 2058
Venice 30124, Italy
Tel: (041)5203755, Fax: (041) 5210670
16 rooms with private bathrooms
Lire 344,000 double B&B
Breakfast only
Open all year
Credit cards: all major
English spoken well, Region: Veneto

With just eleven rooms paired up throughout the six-floor building (luckily with an elevator), the intimate Santo Stefano was actually the watch tower to an ancient convent. The compact hotel, most recently a private home, is right in the middle of one of Venice's largest squares, leading to St. Mark's on one side and to the bridge for the Accademia on the other. Although in close proximity to the busy center, here one can observe the Venetians going about their daily business. The hotel has just been taken over by Roberto and Marcello of the Hotel Celio in Rome (page 148), who have added fresh decorating touches to bedrooms and reception area. Just beyond is a miniature breakfast room, looking out to an ancient well, for days when the weather does not permit having it served out in the front piazza. Touches of elegance in Venetian style follow through in rooms appointed with Murano chandeliers, coordinated draperies and bedspreads, and painted antiques with floral motif. Many amenities are offered including air conditioning at an extra charge. The Quatrini brothers are experienced and amiable hosts with a definite aim to please their guests. *Directions*: Take water bus No. 1 or 82 to the San Samuele stop. Pass over the bridge and straight into Campo Santo Stefano.

HOTEL SANTO STEFANO
Hosts: Quatrini Family
San Marco 2957
Venice 30124, Italy
Tel: (041) 5200166, Fax: (041) 5224460
www.karenbrown.com\italy\hotelsantostefano.html
11 rooms with private bathrooms
Lire 250,000–310,000 double B&B
Breakfast only
Open all year
Credit cards: all major
English spoken well, Region: Veneto

With admirable determination and family pride, Alessandro and his darling wife, Debora, took on the task of renovating and running the hotel property which has been part of the family for three generations. They deserve great credit since they are more concerned with providing warm hospitality and attention to guests' needs than with keeping up with Venice's inflated hotel rates. Indeed, this is the only accommodation under 200,000 lire that met our standards. The spacious and luminous reception area with white travertine floors is a welcome oasis amid the city's more cramped hotels, bustling squares, and crowded narrow streets. Although only a three-minute walk from the Guggenheim collection and Accademia, it has the feeling of being away from the mainstream traffic. The front rooms have water views (higher rate) and all rooms maintain an original flavor of simplicity with parquet floors and matching wood furniture, velvet rose-colored chairs, new bathrooms, and air conditioning. Four bedrooms have private terraces and other guests will enjoy the newly opened rooftop terrace. A full buffet breakfast is served either in the breakfast room with country accents or out on the large front dock terrace where you can watch the boats going by. *Directions*: Take the No. 52 water bus to Zattere, then follow the quay to the right where you will see the hotel terrace.

PENSIONE LA CALCINA
Hosts: Alessandro & Debora Szemere
Dorsoduro 780
Venice 30123, Italy
Tel: (041) 5206466, Fax: (041) 5227045
www.karenbrown.com\italy\pensionelacalcina.html
40 rooms, 30 with private bathrooms
Lire 170,000–280,000 double B&B
Breakfast only
Open all year, Credit cards: all major
English spoken well, Region: Veneto

At first glance the exterior of the Pensione Seguso appears quite bland: a rather boxy affair with few of the elaborate architectural enhancements so frequently evident in Venice. Inside, however, the *pensione* radiates warmth and charm, with Oriental rugs setting off antique furniture and an heirloom silver service. The hotel is located on the "left bank" of Venice: across the Grand Canal from the heart of the tourist area, about a 15-minute walk to St. Mark's Square (or only a few minutes by ferry from the Accademia boat stop). For several generations the hotel has been in the Seguso family, which provides a homey ambiance for guests who do not demand luxury. In front there is a miniature terrace harboring a few umbrella-shaded tables. Several of the bedrooms have views of the canal (although these are the noisiest due to canal traffic). Being a simple *pensione*, most of the rooms share a bathroom, so if you are looking for hotel amenities, Seguso may not be your "cup of tea." The pleasant surprise is that the value-conscious tourist can stay here with breakfast and dinner included for the price of a room alone at most Venice hotels. *Directions*: The Seguso is a ten-minute walk from the Accademia boat stop.

PENSIONE SEGUSO
Hosts: Lorenzo Seguso family
Grand Canal Zattere 779
Venice 30123, Italy
Tel: (041) 5286858, Fax: (041) 5222340
www.karenbrown.com\italy\pensioneseguso.html
36 rooms, 19 with private bathrooms
Lire 190,000–210,000 double B&B
* 140,000–150,000 per person half board*
Breakfast & dinner served
Open March to November
Credit cards: all major
English spoken well, Region: Veneto

Just 20 kilometers from the Swiss border, halfway along the shore of Lake Maggiore, at the point where the road curves back down to Verbania, is a farmhouse situated high above the lake (700 meters). It commands a 360-degree view which includes the Alps and Lakes Mergozzo, Monate, Varese, and Maggiore with its miniature Borromeo islands (accessible by ferryboat). A long 5-kilometer road with hairpin turns winds its way up to the turn-of-the-century house with tower. Energetic and friendly hostess, Iside Minotti, and her family run the inn and rustic restaurant, which is busy spot in the summer when locals come up to dine and take advantage of the cooler air and the spectacular view. Menu ingredients come directly from the vegetable garden and orchards to the kitchen, where sumptuous local specialties are prepared. Even Papa Minotti gets involved and can be heard singing folk songs in front of the open grill. The 25-acre farm includes riding stables, and the bed and breakfast can also arrange for a helicopter from Fondotoce for a breathtakingly scenic ride over the lake. Nine basic and modern, though comfortable, double rooms with bath are available for overnight guests. *Directions*: Before Verbania, at Pallanza, take Via Azari to Monterosso (left turnoff) up 5 km of winding road that includes over 40 hairpin bends.

IL MONTEROSSO
Hostess: Iside Minotti
Cima Monterosso-C.P. 13
Verbania (NO) 28048, Italy
Tel: (0323) 556510 or 551578, Fax: (0323) 556718
www.karenbrown.com\italy\ilmonterosso.html
9 rooms with private bathrooms
Lire 80,000 double B&B
  70,000 per person half board
All meals served
Open all year
Some English spoken, Region: Piedmont

The San Zeno is a marvelous combination of comfortable accommodation in an ancient building right in the center of one of Veneto's most beautiful and historical cities: Verona. Signora Bottacini has cleverly transformed part of her family's many properties in the city into much-needed accommodation. The result is a wide mix of various rooms and apartment situations with one or two bedrooms, kitchenettes, and living rooms. Opposite the walls of the old city and bridge over the Adige river, the doors to the 15th-century complex open off the main street to a quiet, inner cobblestoned courtyard. Signora greets guests in her office and from there you go up to rooms each appointed with a mix of antiques and family possessions, giving you the definite feeling of being in someone's home. Original stone or wood floors, brick archways, and beamed ceilings have all been preserved and add much to the overall fascination of the place. A buffet breakfast is served to non-apartment guests in an enormous room with large windows and stone walls. Very unique. *Directions*: Consulting a city map, from Porta Pallio follow straight to the city gate "Castelvecchio" and turn left along the river on Regaste S. Zeno. Parking is available for guests.

RESIDENCE SAN ZENO   ***New***
Hosts: Bottacini family
Regaste S. Zeno 3
Verona 37123, Italy
Tel: (045) 597721, Fax: (045) 8002439
10 rooms with private bathrooms, 10 apartments
Lire 220,000–260,000 double B&B
  200,000–380,000 per apartment
2-day minimum stay
Breakfast only
Open all year
English spoken well, Region: Veneto

With great finesse, determined Viola and Paolo, an editor, managed to purchase this magnificent Renaissance villa—no easy feat, considering the 400-acre property had been in one family for 700 years. The pale-yellow villa with handsome lawns and surrounding cypress woods commands a spectacular view over the immense valley and Mugello mountain range. This is the area north of Florence known for its concentration of Medici villas. The guestrooms in the villa have been restored to their original splendor, with high Florentine woodworked ceilings, carefully selected antiques, and delightful blue-and-white-tiled bathrooms. The honeymoon suite features a grand gold-crowned red canopy bed. The entry leads to the frescoed dining rooms where original combinations of fresh local produce are served with great attention to detail, accompanied by an excellent selection of wines (meals are expensive). Recent additions include six apartments, each with two bedrooms, a lovely swimming pool, and horse stables. Villa Campestri offers refined and romantic accommodations in the vicinity of Florence. *Directions*: Exit at Barberino di Mugello from the A1 autostrada and follow signs for S. Pietro Asieve, then Cardetole, then Sagginale, and finally up the road on the right to Vicchio—35 km from Florence.

VILLA CAMPESTRI
Hosts: Viola & Paolo Pasquali
Localita: Campestri 19/22
Vicchio di Mugello (FI) 50039, Italy
Tel: (055) 8490107, Fax: (055) 8490108
17 rooms with private bathrooms
Lire 250,000 double B&B
Breakfast & dinner served
Open April to December
Credit cards: MC, VS
English spoken well, Region: Tuscany

A warm "welcome back" goes to Andrea and Silvia of La Volpaia, one of our readers' favorite spots in Tuscany, after having been out of operation for two years for personal reasons. The property is as lovely and the hospitality as warm as ever, with international guests gathering together in the evenings out on the patio or in the converted barn for one of Silvia's delightful meals based on fresh vegetables or Andrea's barbecued duck, pheasant, or lamb. Conversation is never lacking with meals accompanied by La Volpaia's own Chianti—Andrea, native Roman architect and sculptor, bought the wine estate with its 16th-century villa 12 years ago. The ten rooms appointed with antiques are divided between the main house and another farmhouse just down the road facing out to the spectacular swimming pool with its rose garden and heavenly views of what can only be described as a truly classic Tuscan landscape. Seven groomed horses, personally trained by the hosts, are available for excursions into the surrounding countryside. Guests are made to feel immediately right at home and so it is no wonder that many become "regulars" to this idyllic spot. *Directions*: From the town of Vico d'Elsa follow Via della Villa for 2 km, turning left at the wooden signpost for La Volpaia.

LA VOLPAIA   New
Hosts: Silvia & Andrea Taliaco
Strada di Vico 5–13
Vico d'Elsa (FI) 50050, Italy
Tel: (055) 8073063, Fax: (055) 8073170
Cellphone: (0368) 248287
10 rooms with private bathrooms
Lire 150,000 per person half board
2-day minimum stay
Breakfast & dinner served
Open all year
English spoken well, Region: Tuscany

On the northern outskirts of the beautiful city of Treviso is a busy farm which was once a convent. The long building has been made into several residences, one belonging to the two Milani brothers, where a restaurant and six bedrooms have been fashioned for guests. All of the bedrooms have private baths, and their decor is very much in keeping with the simple country style of the farm. Typical Venetian antiques enhance the rooms, which also feature homey touches such as white-lace curtains and soft floral armchairs. Guests can observe the wine production taking place on the farm and are also welcome to take horses out on excursions, or take riding lessons if desired. The popular restaurant prides itself on serving local specialties prepared with the farm's fresh produce and game. The restaurant with its large, open central hearth, is a welcoming gathering spot, decorated with lots of pictures, brass pots, pink tablecloths, and fresh flowers. Although the immediate surrounding flat countryside is the not most inspiring, this a great base for visiting Venice, Padova, Vianza, and Verona. *Directions*: From Venice (34 km away), take route N13 through Treviso, and on toward Villorba, turning left at the sign for the Podere. Or exit at Treviso Nord from the A27.

PODERE DEL CONVENTO
Host: Renzo Milani
Via IV Novembre 16
Villorba (TV) 31050, Italy
Tel & fax: (0422) 920044
6 rooms with private bathrooms
Lire 90,000 double B&B
  80,000 per person half board
All meals served Restaurant closed Tuesdays
Open all year
Credit cards: AX, VS
No English spoken, Region: Veneto

Ninni Bacchi has done wonders in transforming her family's 300-acre tobacco and grain farm (just 38 kilometers from Orvieto) into a very comfortable bed and breakfast in an area that was once the heart of the Etruscan civilization. Arriving guests are warmly received by manager, Monica, in the luminous, open living room furnished with antiques surrounding a grand fireplace. Downstairs is the large, arcaded restaurant dating back to the 15th century, where guests can enjoy the typical cuisine of the Lazio region or dine outdoors by the saltwater pool. The five bedrooms off the courtyard in the main house have the most character with architectural features intact, while the remaining 15 suites are lined up in two cottage-like wings, and are more spacious and modern in decor. A good job has been done with the landscaping, pleasingly distracting the eye from the rather bland and flat countryside hereabouts. Unfortunately, the commercial zone of Viterbo is slowly invading the area—don't be alarmed by the unattractive approach. Tennis, biking, and horseback riding, plus the nearby thermal spa are some of the activities available as well as visits to ancient Viterbo and the gardens of Villa Lanti. *Directions*: From Rome (120 km away) follow signs for Viterbo. Take the Cassia road north of Viterbo for 3 km toward Montefiascone, turning right at the Rinaldone sign.

RESIDENCE RINALDONE
Hostess: Ninni Bacchi
Strada Rinaldone, 9-S.S. Cassia km 86
Viterbo 01100, Italy
Tel: (0761) 352137, Fax: (0761) 353116
www.karenbrown.com\italy\residencerinaldone.html
5 rooms, 15 suites with private bathrooms
Lire 145,000 double B&B
2-day minimum stay
All meals served
Open April to November, Credit cards: all major
Some English spoken, Region: Lazio

Given the unbearable August heat in most parts of the country, and the inevitably overcrowded conditions at the seaside resorts during that month, it is small wonder that the cooler elevations of the Alps and Dolomites have become a favorite vacation destination for Italian families. In addition to offering the ideal atmosphere for relaxation and recharging, they offer invigorating fresh mountain air, numerous outdoor activities, spectacular scenery, and, best of all, the least expensive "getaway" available in the country. The darling Merlhof bed and breakfast is owned and operated by the Kompatschers, who have created seven guestrooms within their family home in the town of Fiè. The traditional, Tyrolean-style white-and-dark-wood dwelling has geraniums cascading brightly from each windowsill, and looks directly onto Sciliar mountain at the back. The guestrooms are simply furnished with light-pine wood beds and side tables, and only one has its own bathroom. The breakfast room overlooks the town and a small swimming pool, which is a welcome feature indeed on hot summer afternoons or after a day of hiking. *Directions*: Exit at Bolzano Nord from the Verona-Brennero autostrada. Follow signs for Siusi and Völs (also called Fiè) and, at the main intersection, turn right to Merlhof.

MERLHOF
Hosts: Maria Kompatscher family
Via Sciliar 14
Fiè allo Sciliar (Völs) (BZ) 39050, Italy
Tel: (0471) 725092, Fax: none
7 rooms, 1 with private bathroom
Lire 45,000 per person B&B
Breakfast only
Open all year
No English spoken (German)
Region: Trentino-Alto Adige

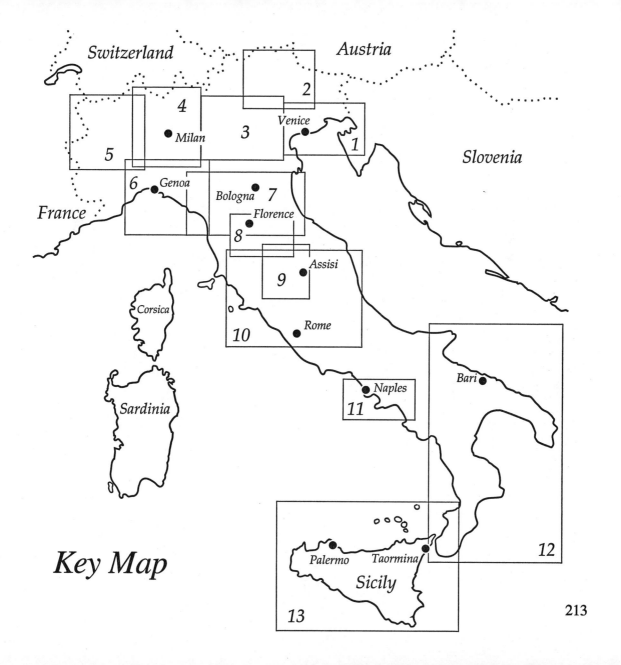

Switzerland

Austria

2

4

● *Milan*

3

Venice ●

1

Slovenia

5

6 *Genoa* ●

Bologna ● *7*

France

Florence ●

8

Assisi

9 ●

Corsica

Rome ●

10

Naples ●

11

Bari ●

Sardinia

12

Key Map

Palermo ●

Taormina ●

Sicily

13

213

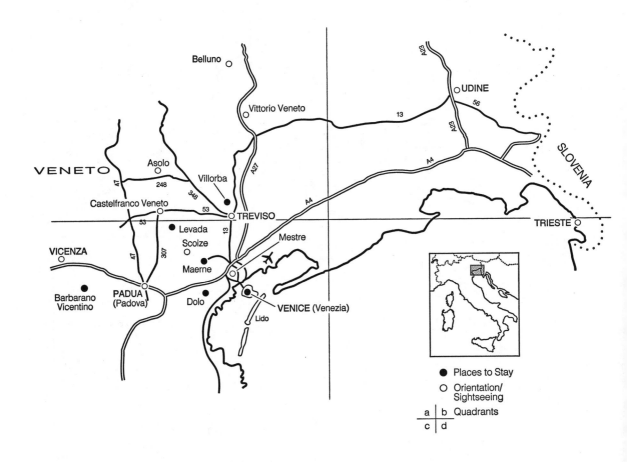

Map 1

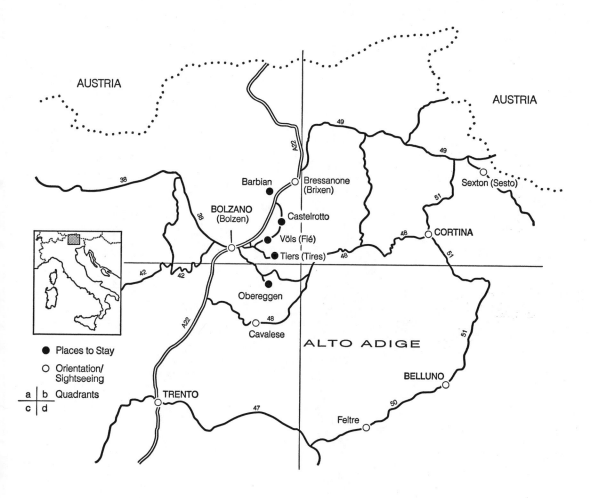

AUSTRIA

AUSTRIA

38

A22

Barbian

Bressanone
(Brixen)

49

49

Sexton (Sesto)

BOLZANO
(Bolzen)

38

Castelrotto

51

Völs (Fié)

48

CORTINA

Tiers (Tires)

48

51

42

A22

Obereggen

Cavalese

48

ALTO ADIGE

51

● Places to Stay

○ Orientation/
  Sightseeing

BELLUNO

a | b   Quadrants
c | d

TRENTO

47

50

Feltre

Map 2

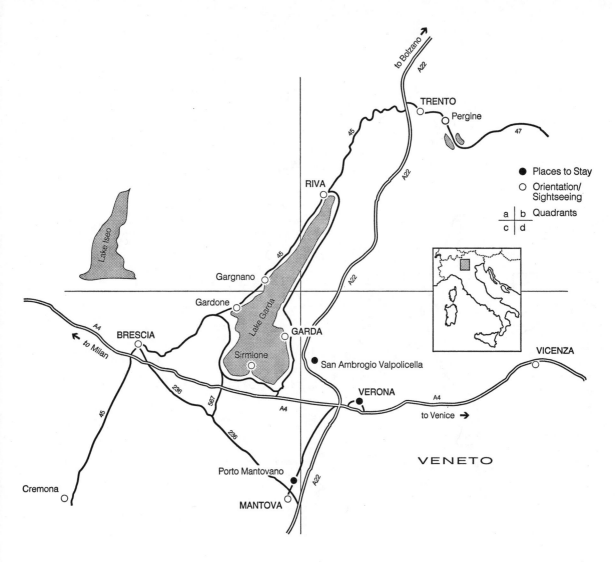

Places to Stay

Orientation/
Sightseeing

a	b	Quadrants
c	d

to Bolzano

A22

TRENTO

Pergine

47

45

A22

RIVA

Lake Iseo

45

Gargnano

Lake Garda

A22

Gardone

A4

GARDA

to Milan

BRESCIA

Sirmione

San Ambrogio Valpolicella

VICENZA

236

VERONA

A4

567

A4

to Venice →

236

A22

VENETO

Porto Mantovano

Cremona

MANTOVA

Map 3

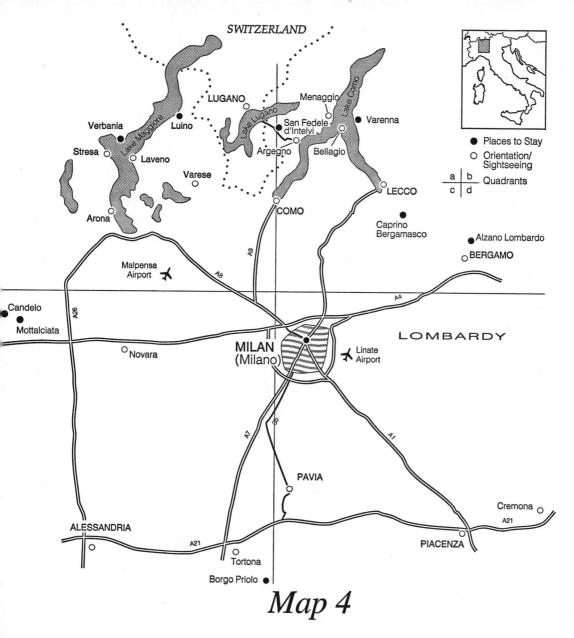

Map 4

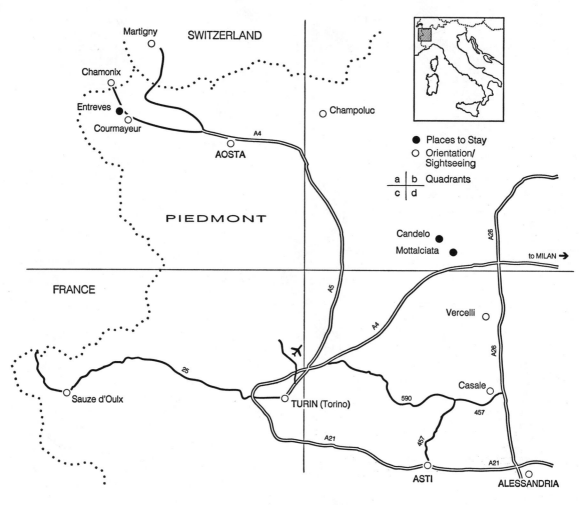

Martigny

SWITZERLAND

Chamonix

Entreves

Courmayeur

AOSTA

A4

Champoluc

● Places to Stay
○ Orientation/
    Sightseeing

| a | b | Quadrants |
| c | d | |

PIEDMONT

Candelo ●
Mottalciata ●

A26

to MILAN →

FRANCE

A5

Vercelli ○

A4

A26

Sauze d'Oulx

25

Casale ○

590

457

TURIN (Torino)

A21

457

ASTI

A21

ALESSANDRIA

Map 5

218

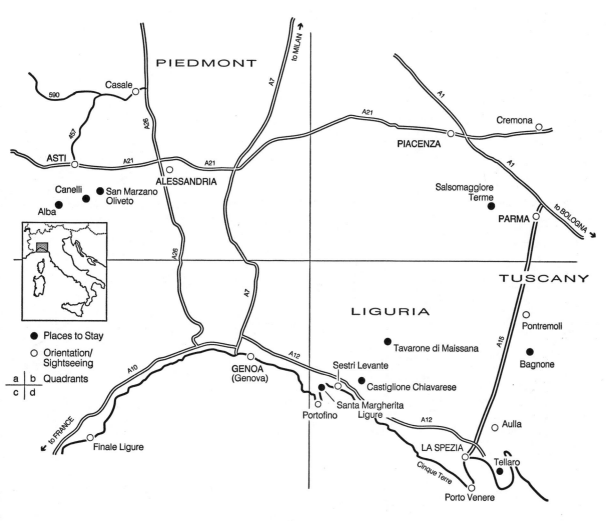

Map 6

219

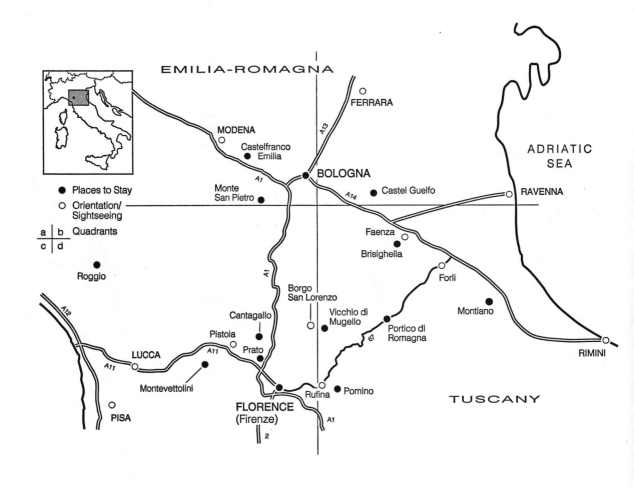

EMILIA-ROMAGNA

○ FERRARA

A13

MODENA ○

Castelfranco
● Emilia

A1

● BOLOGNA

A14

Monte
San Pietro ●

● Castel Guelfo

○ RAVENNA

ADRIATIC
SEA

● Places to Stay
○ Orientation/
   Sightseeing

| a | b | Quadrants |
| c | d | |

Faenza ○

● Brisighella

A1

● Forli ○

Borgo
San Lorenzo

Montiano ●

● Roggio

Cantagallo

Vicchio di
Mugello ○ ●

A12

Pistoia

Portico di
Romagna ●

67

LUCCA ○

A11

● Prato

A11

● Montevettolini

Rufina

● Pomino

TUSCANY

RIMINI ○

○ PISA

FLORENCE
(Firenze)

A1

2

Map 7

220

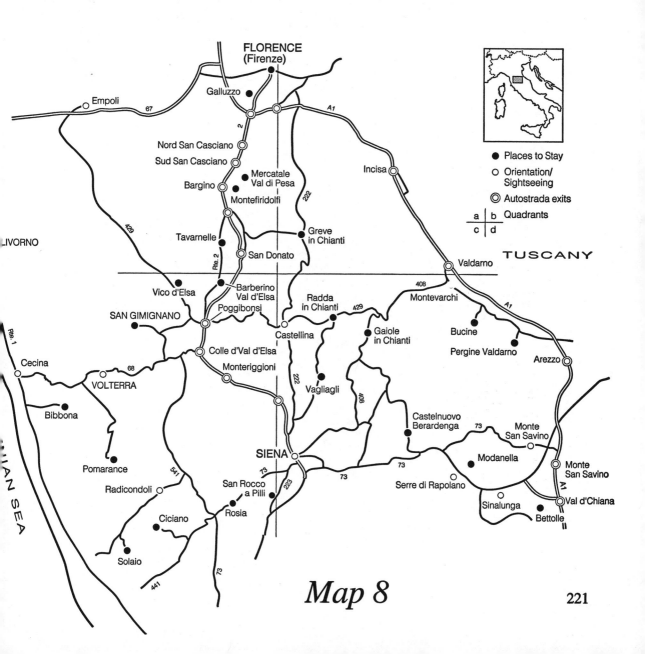

FLORENCE
(Firenze)

Empoli

Galluzzo

67

2

Nord San Casciano

Sud San Casciano

Bargino

Mercatale
Val di Pesa

Montefiridolfi

LIVORNO

429

Tavarnelle

Greve
in Chianti

San Donato

Incisa

222

A1

● Places to Stay

○ Orientation/
Sightseeing

◎ Autostrada exits

a | b
c | d Quadrants

TUSCANY

Rte. 2

Vico d'Elsa

Barberino
Val d'Elsa

Poggibonsi

Valdarno

Radda
in Chianti

429

408

Montevarchi

A1

Bucine

SAN GIMIGNANO

Castellina

Gaiole
in Chianti

Pergine Valdarno

Rte. 1

Colle d'Val d'Elsa

Cecina

Monteriggioni

68

VOLTERRA

222

Vagliagli

Arezzo

408

Bibbona

Castelnuovo
Berardenga

73

Monte
San Savino

Pomarance

SIENA

Modanella

Monte
San Savino

Radicondoli

541

San Rocco
a Pilli

73

223

73

73

Serre di Rapolano

A1

Val d'Chiana

Ciciano

Rosia

Sinalunga

Bettolle

Solaio

73

441

Map 8

TUSCANY

← to Florence
A1

Monte Savino
73

○ AREZZO

○ SIENA

326
A1

Val d'Chiana
● CORTONA
15

Montalcino
Pienza
● Montepulciano
—San Quirico
Chiusi
● Macciano
A1
Ripa d'Orcia ●
Sarteano ●
Radicofani ●
San Casciano
(dei Bagni)
Ficulle
220
A1

Panicale
● Paciano
Citta della
Pieve

2

Orvieto exit
ORVIETO ●
Baschi

Lake Boisena

● Places to Stay
○ Orientation/ Sightseeing
◎ Autostrada exits
a | b Quadrants
c | d

73

○ URBINO
Urbania ●
○ Fossombrone

3

Citta del Castello ○
GUBBIO ○
Ronti ● ● Umbertide
Lisciano Niccone ●
Mengara ●
3
UMBRIA
● Terontola
● Tuoro Sul Trasimeno

Lake Trasimeno

Ponte Pattoli ●
15
Pianello ○
PERUGIA ○
Colle San Paolo
Castel del Piano Umbro
3

Gaifana ●
ASSISI
Armenzano ○

● Deruta
Spello ○
Foligno ○

San Venanzo ○
Monte Castello di Vibio ●
Ospedaletto ○

Trevi ○
● Bovara di Trevi

TODI ●
Titignano ○
Lake Corbara
SPOLETO ○

to Rome →
A1

3
TERNI ○

Map 9

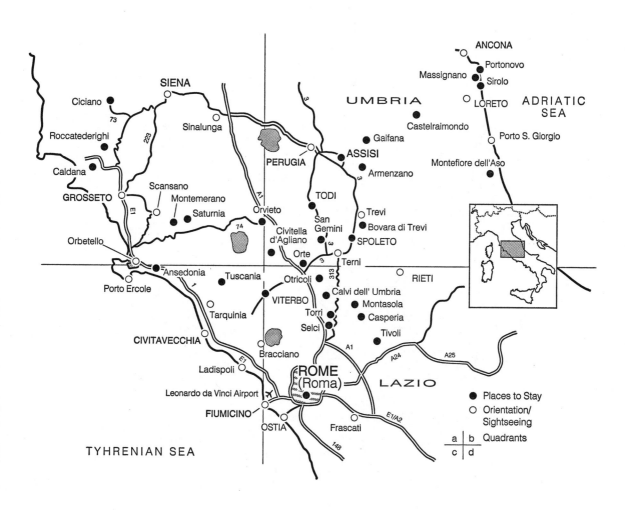

Map 10

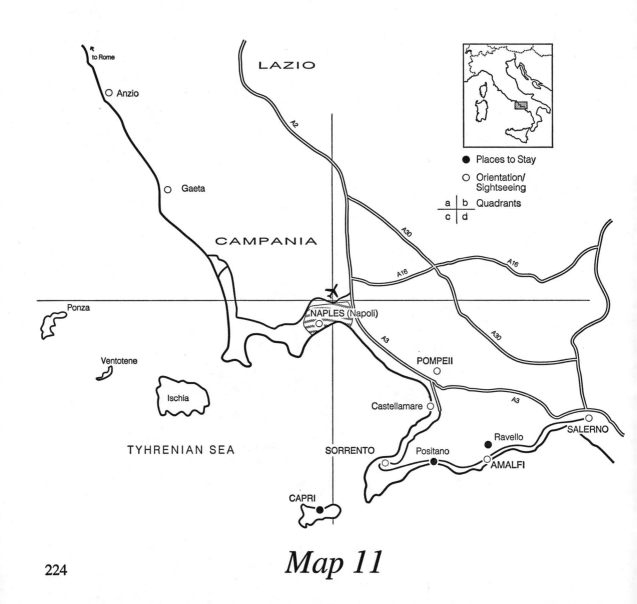

Map 11

224

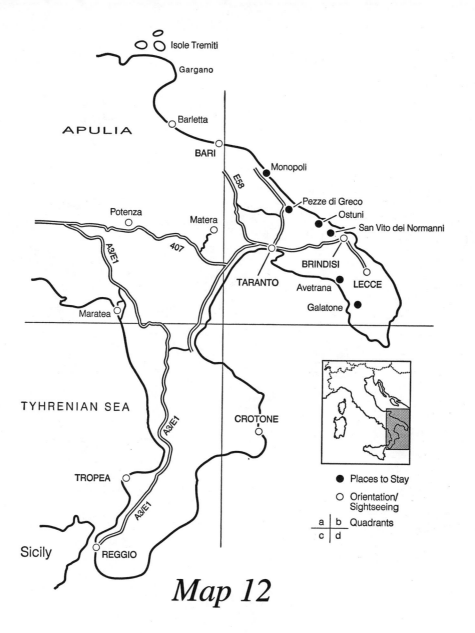

Isole Tremiti

Gargano

APULIA

Barletta

BARI

Monopoli

E58

Pezze di Greco

Ostuni

Potenza

San Vito dei Normanni

Matera

407

A3/E1

BRINDISI

TARANTO

Avetrana

LECCE

Maratea

Galatone

TYHRENIAN SEA

A3/E1

CROTONE

TROPEA

A3/E1

Sicily

REGGIO

Map 12

● Places to Stay

○ Orientation/
Sightseeing

| a | b | Quadrants |
| c | d | |

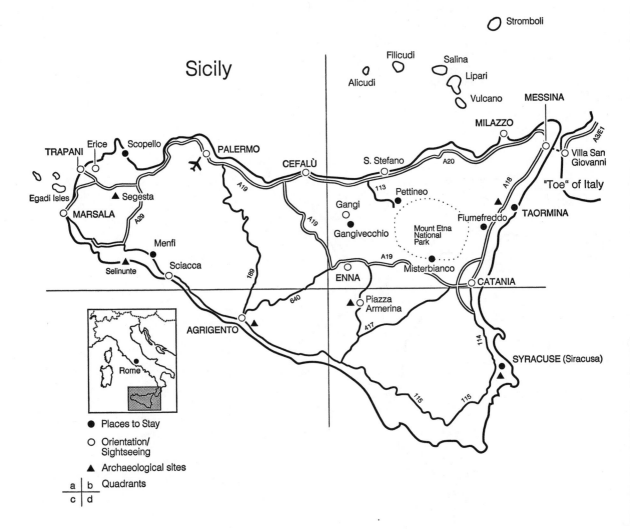

Sicily

Stromboli

Filicudi
Salina
Alicudi
Lipari
Vulcano

MESSINA

MILAZZO

TRAPANI
Erice
Scopello
PALERMO
CEFALÙ
S. Stefano
A20
Villa San Giovanni
"Toe" of Italy

Egadi Isles
A19
113
Pettineo
A18
TAORMINA

Segesta
A19
Gangi
Fiumefreddo

MARSALA
A29
Gangivecchio
Mount Etna National Park

Menfi
A19
Misterbianco

Selinunte
189
ENNA
CATANIA

Sciacca
840
Piazza Armerina

Rome
417
114

AGRIGENTO
115
SYRACUSE (Siracusa)
115

● Places to Stay

○ Orientation/ Sightseeing

▲ Archaeological sites

a	b
c	d

Quadrants

Map 13

Valle d'Aosta

Piedmont

Milan

Lombardy

Trentino-
Alto Adige

Friuli-
Venezia
Giulia

Veneto

Venice

Emila-Romagna

Liguria

Genoa

Florence

Tuscany

Marches

Umbria

CORSICA
(France)

Abruzzo

ROME

Lazio

Molise

Sardinia

Campania

Naples

Bari

Basilicata

Apulia

Calabria

Cagliari

Palermo

Sicily

Regions of Italy

227

Bed & Breakfasts by Region

Apulia

Avetrana, Bosco di Mudonato
Galatone, Masseria Lo Prieno
Monopoli, Masseria Curatori
Ostuni, Masseria Lo Spagnulo
Pezzi di Greco, Masseria Salamina
San Vito dei Normanni, Tenuta Deserto

Campania

Capri, La Minerva
    Villa Krupp
    Villa Vuotto
Positano, Casa Cosenza
    La Fenice
    Villa Rosa
Ravello, Villa Maria

Emilia-Romagna

Bologna, Hotel Orologio
Brisighella, Il Palazzo
Castel Guelfo, Locanda Solarola
Castelfranco Emilia, Villa Gaidello
Monte San Pietro, Tenuta Bonzara
Montiano, Le Radici
Portico di Romagna, Albergo al Vecchio Convento
Salsomaggiore Terme, Antica Torre

Lazio

Casperia, La Torretta
Civitella d'Agliano, L'Ombricolo
Montasola, Montepiano
Orte, La Chiocciola
    Torre Amena
Ponza, Isola di, Gennarino a Mare
Rome, Casa Stefazio
    Hotel Celio
    Hotel Due Torri
    Fontana Hotel
    Hotel Locarno
    Hotel Venezia
    Hotel Villa del Parco
Rome (Boccea), Tenuta Santa Rufina
Selci Sabino, Villa Vallerosa
Tivoli, Hotel Adriano
Torri in Sabina, Il Leccio
Tuscania, Al Gallo
Viterbo, Residence Rinaldone

Liguria

Castiglione Chiavarese, Monte Pu
Santa Margherita Ligure, Villa Gnocchi
Tavarone di Maissana, Giandriale
Tellaro, Locanda Miranda

Lombardy

Alzano Lombardo, Cascina Grumello
Borgo Priolo, Castello di Stefanago
Caprino Bergamasco, Ombria
Luino, Camin Hotel Colmegna
        Camin Hotel Luino
Milan, Hotel Regina
Porto Mantovano, Villa Schiarino Lena
San Fedele d'Intelvi, Villa Simplicitas
Varenna, Olivedo

Marches

Castelraimondo, Il Giardino degli Ulivi
Massignano, La Biancarda
Montefiore dell'Aso, La Campana
Portonovo, Hotel Emilia
      Fortino Napoleonico
Sirolo, Locanda Rocco
Urbania, L'Orsaiola

Piedmont

Alba, Cascina Reine
Candelo, La Mandria
Canelli, La Luna e i Falo
Mottalciata, Il Mompolino
San Marzano Oliveto, La Viranda
Verbania, Il Monterosso

Sicily

Fiumefreddo, Borgo Valerio
Gangivecchio, Tenuta Gangivecchio
Menfi, Ravida

Misterbianco, Alcala
Pettineo, Casa Migliaca
Scopello, Pensione Tranchina
Siracusa, Limoneto
Taormina, Villa Schuler

Trentino-Alto Adige

Barbian, Bad Dreikirchen
Castelrotto, Marmsolerhof
Castelrotto (Osvaldo), Tschotscherhof
Obereggen, Gasthof Obereggen
Tiers (Tires), Veraltenhof
Völs (Fiè), Merlhof

Tuscany

Ansedonia, Grazia
Bagnone, Villa Mimosa
Barberino Val d'Elsa, Fattoria Casa Sola
    Il Paretaio
    La Chiara di Prumiano
    La Spinosa
Bettolle, Locanda la Bandita
Bibbona, Podere Le Mezzelune
Bucine, Iesolana
Caldana, Montebelli
Cantagallo, Ponte Alla Villa
Castelnuovo Berardenga, Borga Villa a Sesta
Chiusi, La Querce
Ciciano, Casa Italia
Cortona, Stoppiacce
Florence, Hotel Aprile
    Hotel Ariele

Tuscany (cont.)
Florence, Hotel Hermitage
    La Residenza
    Hotel Silla
    Hotel Splendor
Gaiole in Chianti, Castello di Tornano
Galluzzo (Florence), La Fattoressa
    Fattoria Il Milione
Greve in Chianti, Casa Nova
Macciano (Chiusi), Macciangrosso
Mercatale Val di Pesa, Salvadonica
Modanella (Serre di Rapolano), Godiolo
    Castello di Modanella
Montefiridolfi, Fattoria La Loggia
Montemerano, Villa Acquaviva
Montemerano (Poderi di), Le Fontanelle
Montevettolini, Villa Lucia
Pergine Valdarno, Fattoria Montelucci
Pienza, Santo Pietro
Pienza (Montichiello di), L'Olmo
Pomarance, Casa Zito
Pomino, Fattoria di Petrognano
Prato, Villa Rucellai di Canneto
Radda in Chianti, Azienda Agricola Vergelli
    Le Selve II
    Podere Terreno
    Podere Val delle Corti
    Torre Canvalle
Radicofani, La Palazzina
Ripa d'Orcia, Castello di Ripa d'Orcia
Roccatederighi, Fattoria di Caminino
Roggio, La Fontanella

Rosia, Montestigliano
San Casciano dei Bagni, La Crocetta
    Podere le Radici
San Gimignano, Il Casale del Cotone
    Casanova di Pescille
    Casolare di Libbiano
    Podere Villuzza
San Rocco a Pilli, Fattoria di Cavaglioni
Sarteano, La Sovana
Saturnia, Villa Clodia
Solaio (Radicondoli), Fattoria Solaio
Tavarnelle Val di Pesa, Podere Sovigliano
Terontola, Residenza San Andrea al Farinaio
Vagliagli, Casali della Aiola
Vicchio di Mugello, Villa Campestri
Vico d'Elsa, La Volpaia

Umbria
Armenzano (Assisi), Le Silve di Armenzano
Assisi (Capodacqua), Malvarina
Assisi (Tordibetto di), Podere la Fornace
Baschi, Pomurlo Vecchio
Bovara di Trevi, Casa Giulia
Calvi dell'Umbria, Casale San Martino
Castel del Piano Umbro, Villa Aureli
Citta della Pieve, Madonna delle Grazie
Colle San Paolo (Panicale), Villa di Montesolare
Deruta, Antica Fattoria del Colle
Ficulle, La Casella
Gaifana, Villa della Cupa
Lisciano Niccone, Casa San Martino
Mengara (Gubbio), Oasi Verde

Umbria (cont.)
Montecastello di Vibio, Fattoria di Vibio
Niccone (Umbertide), La Maridiana
Orvieto, Fattoria la Cacciata
    Locanda Rosati
    Villa Ciconia
Ospedaletto (San Venanzo), Borgo Spante
Otricoli, Casa Spence
Paciano, Locanda della Rocca
Ponte Pattoli, Il Covone
Ronti (Citta di Castello), Palazzo Terranova
San Gemini, Palazzo Canova
Spoleto, La Terrazza del Duomo
Titignano, Fattoria Titignano
Todi, Poggio d'Asproli
    Tenuta di Canonica
Tuoro sul Trasimeno, Castello di Montegualandro
    La Dogana

Valle d'Aosta

Entreves (Courmayeur), La Grange

Veneto

Barbarano Vicentino, Il Castello
Dolo, Villa Goetzen
Levada di Piombino Dese, Gargan
Maerne, Ca'delle Rondini
San Ambrogio Valpolicella, Ca'Verde
Venice, Hotel Ai Due Fanali
    Hotel San Moise
    Hotel Santo Stefano
    Pensione La Calcina

Venice, Pensione Seguso
Verona, Residence San Zeno
Villorba, Podere del Convento

Index

Luino
    Camin Hotel Luino, 91
Luna e i Falo, La, Canelli, 51

M

Macciangrosso, Macciano–Chiusi, 92
Macciano–Chiusi
    Macciangrosso, 92
Madonna Delle Grazie, Citta della Pieve, 68
Maerne
    Ca'delle Rondini, 93
Malvarina, Assisi (Capodacqua), 30
Mandria, La, Candelo, 50
Map—Key Map for B&B Locations, 213
Map—Regions of Italy, 227
Maps Showing B&B locations, 214, 215, 216, 217, 218, 219, 220, 221, 222, 223, 224, 225, 226
Marches Bed and Breakfasts, 229
Maria, Villa, Ravello, 143
Marmsolerhof, Castelrotto, 63
Masseria Curatori, Monopoli, 100
Masseria lo Prieno, Galatone, 84
Masseria lo Spagnulo, Ostuni, 118
Masseria Salamina, Pezze di Greco, 122
Massignano
    La Biancarda, 94
Menfi, Sicily
    Ravida, 176
Mengara (Gubbio)
    Oasi Verde, 95
Mercatale Val di Pesa
    Salvadonica, 96
Merlhof, Völs (Fiè allo Sciliar), 212
Mezzelune, Le, Podere, Bibbona, 42
Migliaca, Casa, Sicily-Pettineo, 178
Milan
    Hotel Regina, 97
Milione, Il, Fattoria, Galluzzo (Florence), 86
Mimosa, Villa, Bagnone, 33
Minerva, La, Capri, 53
Miranda, Locanda, Tellaro, 187

Misterbianco, Sicily
    Alcala, 177
Modanella (Serre di Rapolano)
    Castello di Modanella, 99
    Godiolo, 98
Modanella, Castello di, Modanella (Serre di Rapolano), 99
Mompolino, Il, Mottalciata, 110
Monopoli
    Masseria Curatori, 100
Monte Pu, Castiglione Chiavarese, 65
Monte San Pietro
    Tenuta Bonzara, 102
Montebelli, Caldana, 48
Montecastello di Vibio
    Fattoria di Vibio, 103
Montefiore dell'Aso
    La Campana, 104
Montefiridolfi in Chianti
    Fattoria la Loggia, 105
Montegualandro, Castello di, Tuoro sul Trasimeno, 195
Montelucci, Fattoria, Pergine Valdarno, 121
Montemerano
    Villa Acquaviva, 106
Montemerano (Poderi di)
    Le Fontanelle, 107
Montepiano, Casperia, 101
Monterosso, Il, Verbania, 206
Montesolare di, Villa, Colle San Paolo (Panicale), 70
Montestigliano, Rosia, 156
Montevettolini
    Villa Lucia, 108
Montiano
    Le Radici, 109
Mottalciata
    Il Mompolino, 110
Mudonato, Bosco di, Avetrana, 32

N

Napoleonico, Fortino, Portonovo, 132

Hidden Treasures of Italy

Hotel/Bed & Breakfast Travel Service

Reserve any of the bed and breakfasts in this guide through author Nicole Franchini's travel service, **Hidden Treasures of Italy**.

Available services include car rentals, wedding/honeymoon planning, villa and city apartment rentals, special interest tours (cooking classes, wine and garden tours, horseback riding), and personalized planning of individual itineraries.

CONTACT US!
Tel: (847) 853-1312 Fax: (847) 853-1340 E-mail: htreasures@compuserve.com

A two-night minimum stay is required per hotel/bed and breakfast
$35 booking fee per reservation (non refundable)
Full prepayment by check or credit card (MasterCard or Visa)

We will do our best to accommodate changes in dates or hotel/bed and breakfast choice; however, this can never be guaranteed. Each additional request will require a supplemental booking fee.

Cancellation insurance is strongly recommended

Hidden Treasures of Italy, Inc, 934 Elmwood Avenue, Wilmette, IL 60091, USA
Tel: (847) 853-1312   Fax: (847) 853-1340 E-mail: htreasures@compuserve.com
Italy Office: Tel & fax: 39-6-3052537

Hidden Treasures of Italy

Travel Service Reservation Request Form

If you wish to forward your reservation by fax, you may use the following form as a guideline.

Name(s) of traveler(s):_____

Total number in party: _____ Number of children: _____ Ages: _____

Address: _____

_____

Tel: _____ Fax: _____

B&B name and location: _____

Second choice: _____

Type of accommodation: Single _____ Double reg _____ Double twin _____

    Double used as single _____ Triple _____ Apartment _____

Date of arrival: _____ Date of departure: _____

Total numbers of nights: _____ Total number of rooms: _____

Meal plan: B&B _____ Half board _____ Full board _____

Special Requests:

Hidden Treasures of Italy, Inc, 934 Elmwood Avenue, Wilmette, IL 60091, USA
Tel: (847) 853-1312   Fax: (847) 853-1340 E-mail: htreasures@compuserve.com
Italy Office: Tel & fax: 39-6-3052537

SHARE YOUR REVIEWS WITH US

We greatly appreciate first-hand evaluations of places in our guides. Your critiques are invaluable to us. To keep current on the properties in our guides, we keep a database of readers' comments.

Please list your comments about properties you have visited. We welcome accolades, as well as criticisms.

Name of hotel or b&b _____ Town _____ Country _____
Comments:

Name of hotel or b&b _____ Town _____ Country _____
Comments:

Your name _____ Street _____ Town _____ State _____
Zip _____ Country _____ Tel _____ e-mail _____ date _____

Please send report to: Karen Brown's Guides, Post Office Box 70, San Mateo, California 94401, USA
tel: (650) 342-9117, fax: (650) 342-9153, e-mail: karen@karenbrown.com, www.karenbrown.com

SHARE YOUR REVIEWS WITH US

We greatly appreciate first-hand evaluations of places in our guides. Your critiques are invaluable to us. To keep current on the properties in our guides, we keep a database of readers' comments.

Please list your comments about properties you have visited. We welcome accolades, as well as criticisms.

Name of hotel or b&b _____ Town _____ Country _____
Comments:

Name of hotel or b&b _____ Town _____ Country _____
Comments:

Your name _____ Street _____ Town _____ State _____
Zip _____ Country _____ Tel _____ e-mail _____ date _____

Please send report to: Karen Brown's Guides, Post Office Box 70, San Mateo, California 94401, USA
tel: (650) 342-9117, fax: (650) 342-9153, e-mail: karen@karenbrown.com, www.karenbrown.com

SHARE YOUR DISCOVERIES WITH US

Outstanding properties often come from readers' discoveries. We would love to hear from you.

Please list below any hotel or bed & breakfast you discover. Tell us what you liked about the property and, if possible, please include a brochure or photographs so we can share your enthusiasm. We keep a permanent database of all of your recommendations for future use. Note: we regret we cannot return photos.

Owner _____ Hotel or B&B _____ Street _____

Town _____ Zip _____ State or Region _____ Country _____

Comments:

Your name _____ Street _____ Town _____ State _____

Zip _____ Country _____ Tel _____ e-mail _____ date _____

Please send report to: Karen Brown's Guides, Post Office Box 70, San Mateo, California 94401, USA
tel: (650) 342-9117, fax: (650) 342-9153, e-mail: karen@karenbrown.com, www.karenbrown.com

SHARE YOUR DISCOVERIES WITH US

Outstanding properties often come from readers' discoveries. We would love to hear from you.

Please list below any hotel or bed & breakfast you discover. Tell us what you liked about the property and, if possible, please include a brochure or photographs so we can share your enthusiasm. We keep a permanent database of all of your recommendations for future use. Note: we regret we cannot return photos.

Owner _____ Hotel or B&B _____ Street _____

Town _____ Zip _____ State or Region _____ Country _____

Comments:

Your name _____ Street _____ Town _____ State _____

Zip _____ Country _____ Tel _____ e-mail _____ date _____

Please send report to: Karen Brown's Guides, Post Office Box 70, San Mateo, California 94401, USA
tel: (650) 342-9117, fax: (650) 342-9153, e-mail: karen@karenbrown.com, www.karenbrown.com

KB Travel Service

Quality * Personal Service * Great Values

- Staff trained by Karen Brown to help you plan your holiday
- Special offerings on airfares to major cities in Europe
- Special prices on car rentals with free upgrades
- Countryside mini-itineraries based on Karen Brown's Guides
- Reservations for hotels, inns, and B&Bs in Karen Brown's Guides

For assistance and information on service fees contact:

KB Travel Service

16 East Third Avenue
San Mateo, California, 94401, USA
tel: 800-782-2128, fax: 650-342-2519, email: kbtravel@aol.com

---

For additional information on places in the Karen Brown's Guides, visit the following websites:
www.karenbrown.com and www.innsandouts.com

✈ UNITED AIRLINES

is the

Preferred Airline

of

Karen Brown's Guides

and

Karen Brown Travel Services

Seal Cove Inn

Located in the San Francisco Bay Area

Karen Brown Herbert (best known as author of the Karen Brown's guides) and her husband, Rick, have put 20 years of experience into reality and opened their own superb hideaway, Seal Cove Inn. Spectacularly set amongst wild flowers and bordered by towering cypress trees, Seal Cove Inn looks out to the distant ocean over acres of county park: an oasis where you can enjoy secluded beaches, explore tidepools, watch frolicking seals, and follow the tree-lined path that traces the windswept ocean bluffs. Country antiques, original watercolors, flower-laden cradles, rich fabrics, and the gentle ticking of grandfather clocks create the perfect ambiance for a foggy day in front of the crackling log fire. Each bedroom is its own haven with a cozy sitting area before a wood-burning fireplace and doors opening onto a private balcony or patio with views to the park and ocean. Moss Beach is a 35-minute drive south of San Francisco, 6 miles north of the picturesque town of Half Moon Bay, and a few minutes from Princeton harbor with its colorful fishing boats and restaurants. Seal Cove Inn makes a perfect base for whale-watching, salmon-fishing excursions, day trips to San Francisco, exploring the coast, or, best of all, just a romantic interlude by the sea, time to relax and be pampered. Karen and Rick look forward to the pleasure of welcoming you to their coastal hideaway.

Seal Cove Inn • 221 Cypress Avenue • Moss Beach • California • 94038 • USA
tel: (650) 728-4114, fax: (650) 728-4116, e-mail: sealcove@coastside.net, website: sealcoveinn.com

NICOLE FRANCHINI, author of *Italy: Charming Bed & Breakfasts,* was born in Chicago and raised in a bilingual family, her father being Italian. She received a B.A. degree in languages from William Smith College and the Sorbonne, Paris, and has been residing in Italy for the past 14 years. Currently living outside Rome with husband, Carlo, and daughters, Livia and Sabina, she runs her own travel consulting business, Hidden Treasures of Italy, which organizes specialized group and individual itineraries. Nicole also represents several hotels and bed and breakfasts.

ELISABETTA FRANCHINI, the talented artist responsible for the illustrations in *Italy: Charming Bed & Breakfasts*, lives in her hometown of Chicago where she paints predominantly European landscapes and architectural scenes. On her annual trip to Italy she enjoys accompanying her sister, Nicole, on her travel research. A Smith College graduate in Art History and French Literature, Elisabetta has exhibited extensively in the Chicago area for the past 14 years, and has had extremely well-received shows in Miami, New York, and San Francisco.

JANN POLLARD, the artist responsible for the beautiful painting on the cover of this guide, has studied art since childhood, and is well-known for her outstanding impressionistic-style watercolors which she has exhibited in numerous juried shows, winning many awards. Jann travels frequently to Europe (using Karen Brown's guides) where she loves to paint historical buildings. Jann lives in Burlingame, California, with her husband, Gene.

Travel Your Dreams • Order your Karen Brown Guides Today

Please ask in your local bookstore for Karen Brown's Guides. If the books you want are unavailable, you may order directly from the publisher. Books will be shipped immediately.

_____ *Austria: Charming Inns & Itineraries* $17.95

_____ *California: Charming Inns & Itineraries* $17.95

_____ *England: Charming Bed & Breakfasts* $16.95

_____ *England, Wales & Scotland: Charming Hotels & Itineraries* $17.95

_____ *France: Charming Bed & Breakfasts* $16.95

_____ *France: Charming Inns & Itineraries* $17.95

_____ *Germany: Charming Inns & Itineraries* $17.95

_____ *Ireland: Charming Inns & Itineraries* $17.95

_____ *Italy: Charming Bed & Breakfasts* $16.95

_____ *Italy: Charming Inns & Itineraries* $17.95

_____ *Portugal: Charming Inns & Itineraries* $17.95

_____ *Spain: Charming Inns & Itineraries* $17.95

_____ *Switzerland: Charming Inns & Itineraries* $17.95

Name _____ Street _____

Town _____ State _____ Zip _____ Tel _____ email _____

Credit Card (MasterCard or Visa) _____ Expires: _____

For orders in the USA, add $4 for the first book and $1 for each additional book for shipment. California residents add 8.25% sales tax. Overseas orders add $10 per book for airmail shipment. Indicate number of copies of each title; fax or mail form with check or credit card information to:

KAREN BROWN'S GUIDES
Post Office Box 70 • San Mateo • California • 94401 • USA
tel: (650) 342-9117, fax: (650) 342-9153, e-mail: karen@karenbrown.com

For additional information about Karen Brown's Guides, visit our website at www.karenbrown.com